Selected Studies on Social Sciences

Edited by

Ahmet Kirkkilic, Enes Emre Başar
and Yusuf Soylemez

Cambridge
Scholars
Publishing

Selected Studies on Social Sciences

Edited by Ahmet Kirkkilic, Enes Emre Başar and Yusuf Soylemez

This book first published 2018

Cambridge Scholars Publishing

Lady Stephenson Library, Newcastle upon Tyne, NE6 2PA, UK

British Library Cataloguing in Publication Data
A catalogue record for this book is available from the British Library

ISBN (10): 1-5275-1619-9
ISBN (13): 978-1-5275-1619-9

TABLE OF CONTENTS

Chapter Two
Linguistics and Literature

Chapter Three
Education

Chapter Four
History and Geography

LIST OF TABLES

LIST OF ILLUSTRATIONS

FOREWORD

The book is a collection of essays concerned with society and the relationships among individuals within the society. The essays are circumscribed to fields of business, economics, linguistic, literature, education, history and geography. The essays are grouped into four sections. The first, "Business Economics and Management", discusses issues such as contemporary urban theories, multiculturalism and the informal economy. The second section, "Linguistics and Literature", encompasses topics such as Russian-Chinese bilingualism and training of Russian phraseology by foreigners. The third, "Education" discusses issues such as language teaching and use of the learning cycle model and the Socratic Seminar Technique while the fourth, "History and Geography", looks at history education, historical consciousness, and cultural geography. The book will appeal to educators, researchers, and students involved in social sciences.

Editors

CHAPTER ONE

BUSINESS ECONOMICS AND MANAGEMENT

Contemporary Urban Theories and the Importance of Urban Space

Hayriye Şengün and Seçil Gül Meydan Yildiz

Introduction

Urban theories illuminate the formation of public spaces and the century when the theory was born. Indeed, sociologists have addressed the city in many ways. In line with the versatility of the city, the theorists have assessed the changes in the behaviours of individuals living in the city in the light of social problems or social movements where the class struggle emerged. Throughout the 19th century, the city was interpreted by considering urban lifestyle as the ideal lifestyle. The theorists, who reveal their ideas about urban science, develop functionalist or structuralist approaches about the urban space as a reflection of systemic criticism and the search for the ideal.

The development of the theoretical approaches about the space

Functionalism is an approach that acknowledges that no element alone has a determinant feature, since the elements that make up society have a unique function, and these elements function in an interdependent relationship. It is defined as a situation in which every part of the same body is maintained as an organic ensemble, as each part of the same body can function as a whole and the body as a whole, and all parts of the whole ensure the continuation of each other. The interdependence of human communities and their differentiated lifestyle constitute the foundation of the urban space, according to the functionalist approach. In addition, functionalism is based on two basic assumptions, differentiation and integration.

The critique of functionalism, made by the Marxist point of view, focuses on ignoring the conflict between the units forming the whole, which is considered the reason for changing the system. It was a point of a defence that the incidents related to urban spaces were more stable than those related to the function. Structural analysis has developed very rapidly in the last two decades and reinterpreted Marx's theory. The concepts of the social structure under the influence of Marxist perspective, moreover, the structure of capitalist society, have been updated.

The approach that Castells uses to describe the capitalist city and define the class of cities is another approach that emphasizes the importance of inter-constitutional relations. Structuralism is used in sociology to describe approaches that prioritize the social structure against the social action at the most general and flexible level. Structuralism is based on the idea implying that the basic structure underlying the generally fluctuating and changing appearances of the social reality may be observed. The social system is dominated by a determinant structure. While this structure describes an integrity, which may be explained in its own subjectivity, the space differs from the individuals and relations that form it. According to structuralism, the relations between the individuals are important, not the individual himself/herself. Despite the fact that Marx and Engels did not directly provide a regular theoretical approach about urban life, Engels' study on urban observations in England is considered the most comprehensive work of urban space in terms of political strategies. Urban space is both modernizing and far from rural influences and values. Theoretical explanations of the main concepts such as labour, private property, mode of production, social forms and stages of development, social classes and class struggle are redefined by the climate change in the 21st century, and after the processes of liberal transformation of capital and globalization.

The cities losing the rural characteristics after industrialization became important again in the 21st century, by the principles of conservation, equality and sustainability focused on the participation. Ebenezer Howard signifies the idealism created by the structuralist approach to urban theory by the idea of a socially fair city, as a response to the conditions of the urban community, the use of space, the physical structure and the structure of the industrial city in the early 1900s. Howard's Garden City model intends to integrate the positive features of the city with the positive features of the rural area, which will stop the differentiation between the rural and urban spaces of the industrial city and prevent people from becoming distant from nature (Meydan Yıldız, 2016).

The consideration of the city as a whole, the arrangement of housing according to appropriate health and climate conditions, the creation of recreational areas for leisure activities, the creation of green spaces, the construction of buildings for common use of the community, and the fact that they are easily accessible from the residences of the people are included in the discipline of urban planning and became official with the Athens Charter. The reduction of the distance between the working area and housing, the placement of the industrial areas outside the city, the separation of the industrial area from the city with the green belt and the protection of historical sites have become the protection policies which are applied in 21st-century urban planning. As it is comprehended by these principles, urban space is defined as an area that should be addressed in a relational structure. It is because an appropriate and healthy social life may be provided by the alteration of the urban space. Le Corbusier, a prominent contributor to the preparation of the Athens Charter and the writer of the preface of the Charter, like Howard, strove to create an ideal city for the resolution of the problems that industrialization caused in cities. Le Corbusier, who is not an ideologist, has idealized his work under the influence of modernization and rationalization. He wants to show that his beloved city incorporates the social ideals, in addition to being a rational and beautiful space. For Le Corbusier, industrialization meant "great cities where large bureaucracies could coordinate production." In place of the old buildings that we can entitle the vertical structure, he dreamed about geometrically arrayed skyscrapers of glass and steel that would rise out of parks, gardens, and superhighways, since the cities were not intense at the beginning of the 20th century. Le Corbusier planned to demolish and rebuild urban centres and planned to place technocratic elites consisting of planners, engineers, intellectuals in the city centres while placing their subordinates into satellite cities. Le Corbusier called his plan "the Radiant City" 20th century technology is the utmost prominent tool that situates at the centre of Le Corbusier's work as well as Horward's. In this era, when the search for an ideal way of life was the pioneering idea to solve every problem through planning, it was widely accepted that if cities changed physically and technologically, urban life would also change. It is stated that space involves social struggle and that every social group that aims to protect or change the relations of power creates a certain level of control over the space.

Theoretical perspective of 20th century urban life: The Chicago School

Industrialization has produced similar results in Europe as well as in the United States. At the beginning of the 20th century, immigration from industrial cities, from Europe and South America, and from rural areas, caused the emergence of significant social problems. Regarding these issues, Robert E. Park, a young, journalist-social scientist of the period, started working with Ernest W. Burgess and Louis Wirth in the years 1915-1925 following World War I. These studies, which are called the Chicago School because they are conducted in the surroundings of the University of Chicago, can be considered the first systematic urban studies in the modern sense. These studies had a considerable impact on urban studies from the early 20th century until today. This approach, called the Ecological Approach, argues that the people living in the city should be in contact with each other, cooperating with each other or maintaining a struggle with each other in order to maintain their lives and to determine the structure of the city to a great extent (Güllüpınar, 2013). The natural space incorporates a certain part of the population; it is possible to observe different areas of a city that have different traditions, different patterns of behaviour, and different levels of life, different ages and genders. The Chicago School called the "ecological school" is also called the "culturalist school" since it is interested in the diversities of the sources. Another research subject of the Chicago School was urban life. In Louis Wirth's article "Urbanism as a Way of Life," the city is interpreted as a place not only offering more jobs and housing to people, but also a centre, attracting people from far away, organizing the regions, people and activities in a certain order, as a pioneer and auditor of the economic, political and cultural life. According to Wirth, another function of the city is the historical melting pot function, which melts the races, people, and cultures in the same pot, thus creating a development area for new biological and cultural combinations. Population size, population density, and heterogeneity in urban areas were investigated in a planned way by researchers of the Chicago School for the first time as characteristics specific to urban life. According to this school's perspective, a) cities have a unique way of life unlike rural communities; b) cities consist of natural regions with special functions in the economy, as they exist in rural communities; c) these regions have their own personality, institutions, and groups. The studies of the Chicago School on urban life have focused on two issues in particular. These are as follows: 1) the effect of spatial arrangements of cities on social relations and 2) the cultural life of urban people and their traditions.

The first studies, which signify the foundation of an ecological approach, argue that not only the natural environment but also the environment created by the humans in the local community should be examined. It seems that the Chicago School adopts a functionalist approach in its studies. Each of the elements that form the city has its own unique function. Consequently, the relationship between the structures is not enough to determine the whole according to the theoretical point of view of the Chicago School. In the strict sense, according to the functionalist perspective, the choice of the independent variable to explain the problem is entirely subjective. Researchers at the Chicago School have perceived the city as a laboratory and have benefited from the diversity that the city of Chicago offers as a "laboratory" to conduct empirical research on various structures (Pınarcıoğlu et al., 2013).

The article "Urbanism as a Way of Life," written by Luis Wirth and published in 1938 in the "American Journal of Sociology", which is considered a classic treatise on urban studies, describes the effects of rural and urban life on human life, the definition of the city in terms of sociology, the distinction between urbanization and living in the city, the urban lifestyle, the impact of city size on individual behaviour, the relationship between urbanization theory and urbanization as a social organization as well as urban personality. Wirth has addressed urban problems as a problem of personality and understanding. Urbanization is related to a change in the way of life, according to Wirth, and this change occurs in various forms. Wirth classifies these changes according to the three elements used while describing the city, which are size or number of population, density, and degree of heterogeneity. Wirth strove to demonstrate individually the changes of these three elements on the lifestyle and personality. By taking the city as the object to review, Wirth considers urbanization an equivalent of modernity. Wirth's definition of urbanization is still valid for today's developing cities.

Another researcher at the Chicago School, Burgess, based on a study of the city of Chicago, has argued that the city has expanded in circles from the common centre to the periphery. According to Burgess, these circles represent both the expansion of the city over the space and its development in time. The inner circle consists of trade and industry centres. The second circle, called the transition zone, signifies the expansion area for business and small industry. The third circle consists of working class residential homes while the fourth circle signifies middle-class homes (self-employed, small business owners and civil servants) and the outer circle indicates the commuter's zone (satellite towns). Burgess suggests that these circles are divided into economically and culturally segregated spaces within themselves and that all divisions gave the city a certain shape. McKenzie, who defines concentration, centralization, segregation and invasion as the main processes that guide the development in the city, emphasizes in his urban studies that these are the essential ecological processes, but that intermediate processes take place within the essential processes.

The Chicago School was largely criticized in terms of empirical studies and theoretical approaches. The researchers defending that the cities do not develop in regular lines and emphasizing the oversimplifying features of the theory criticize the approach. Since the consequences of the results of studies conducted for the city of Chicago have lost their validity in a short period, the critics were amplified even among the researchers of the School. The influence of positivism is evident in the theoretical framework of the Chicago School. Therefore, critics are predominantly focused on positivism. Here are the essential assumptions of positivism as a scientific perspective: distinction between subject and object, the ability to know the world by using appropriate methods, the selection of society as an examination object in nature, the implementation of observation and experiment which dominate the natural sciences, from society and achievement to the generally accepted rules. In this context, the Chicago School has been criticized by explaining the society by natural processes in a competitive environment of the city, according to which the strong will survive while the weak will be destroyed, within the framework of "Social Darwinism." It is stated that the outside world does not operate regularly as positivism predicts. On the other hand, positivism is criticized for concentrating on the existing structure while striving to explain what is scientific and prioritizing the information over ideology, doctrine or philosophy. Particularly, positivism has a strong relationship between the social-political organizations; it is accepted that positivism legitimizes the current order in this way.

Urban approach of contemporary urban theorists

Contemporary urban theorists have concentrated on finding the effects of state involvement on the market mechanism. They are separated from the traditional approach of not assessing the location of the cities as data and have strived to establish a link between the theory and real life since these effects are reflected in the structure of urban space. While the city has been established, the concept of a desire line has established an approach that takes account of the relationship between the housing and workplaces.

After World War II, the new political winds in the world have led to the development of different urban life approaches and different efforts of urban perspective. The perspectives on direct analysis of urban issues in terms of space, production, and consumption have emerged. These approaches, based on the economic and political meaning of social movements and focused on working life, are now exploring the city differently. The city, which is considered the centre of production, surplus value, and the reproduction of labour, has become the essential point for the relationship between production and social reproduction. Henri Lefebvre explains that spatial features are shaped based on the changing and varying social systems. Lefebvre, who classifies space as the perceived, designed, and experienced space, defines the space providing profit by investment activities as the abstract space and space which reflects the daily life as the concrete space. Henri Lefebvre explains that spatial features have changed according to changing and diversifying social systems. Lefebvre emphasizes the results of production analysis, which reveal the significant differences of Marxists' view of urban space and the transition from the production of the commodities in space for the production of the space itself. The use of space in capitalism here signifies the use of an abstract space. Since capitalism is concerned with exchange value, not concrete value, thus is the use of the space. The historical production and use of place and the social values that it represents become meaningful if they contribute to the exchange value of the space. For Lefebvre, space is a social subject that depends on social values and meanings (Güllüpınar, 2013). Lefebvre eliminates the rural-urban contradiction in this context, revealing a new social space, the urban revolution, dependent on the city but away from what is traditional.

In Lefebvre's analysis, space occupies an essential place. In the face of an understanding of space prioritizing the abstract space and the exchange value imposed by the capitalism (capital and state), he advocates a sense of space emphasizing the concrete place and use value of daily life. Lefebvre argues that space is not objective and passive, but that it becomes meaningful by being reproduced with various practices. These practices are first concretized in a form of artificial environment, and then become meaningful by the mobility of property and capital (Meydan, 2012: p.628).

Manuel Castells, as an urban theorist and a structuralist Marxist, argues that the approach to the urban problem is based on the reproduction of the labour and class differences and struggles. The basic approach of space is structural, according to Castells. In his observations, which are considered structuralist in approach, Castell stated that to consider the space as an expression of social structure would signify examining the structure of the space by the influence of the economic and political elements as well as the social practices that derive from these elements. Castells refers to the function of "consumption" in defining urban space because it is organized at higher levels of production. It considers the consumption function to be specific to the city level. In his book "City Class and Power" he emphasizes that urban problems become increasingly a political problem, caused by the combination of the consumption means with the socialization of the production means. Thus, urban problems play a strategic role in the course of everyday life. Castells (1997) based this on the two main reasons for the development of urban contradictions in the developed capitalist societies and their placement at the very centre of the social and political sphere. The first is the essential role played by the consumption process in developed capitalism and the second is the expansion of the ideology of the city in a form specific to the dominant classes. State intervention for increased socialization of consumption and its management situates at the core of the urban problem and Castells emphasizes that these are the key elements in the organization of consumption. Because, according to Castells, the contradictions are intensifying while they get politicized. He acknowledges the expansion specific to the dominant class of the urban ideology as an urban form of class contradictions and naturalizes this process. Castells explains that the relationship between the structures, which are the essential features of structuralism, is due to the close relationship and dependence of the different elements of the basic urban system with each other. Thus, he argues that the process of the collective consumption is not only commodity related but also related to the process as a whole; hence it wouldn't be possible to regulate housing by intervening in transportation or vice versa. In addition, he stresses that the definition of "urban problems" is insufficient and that the crises and contradictions of the urban system exist.

Castells notes that the structure and processes of the urban system are determined by the logic of the direct capital, in the forms specific to the capitalist system. With his criticism of "functionalism," Castells denominates the Chicago School as a great intellectual adventure. He suggests that the theoretical orientation of the Chicago School is not meaningful in terms of demographic and geographical empirical-theoretical categories and social issues, and it is based on data aggregating spatial distributions of activities using complex statistical techniques. Among the critics of the Chicago School, the criticism of modernity, particularly in the context of Wirth's approach, attracts attention. According to these criticisms expressed by Castells, a direct connection is established between urban culture and western culture and a myth of urban culture is created. Castells also criticizes the evolutionist approach of culturalist theory, which considers modernization to be the equivalent of urbanization. Thus, it is expressed that the dichotomies predicted by the Chicago School in relation to the city, such as rural-urban, society-community, does not reflect reality (Pınarcıoğlu et al., 2013).

According to geographer David Harvey (2002), adopting the Marxist perspective that space is constantly reproduced for continuity of capitalism, the spatial transformation is an ideological process that has a significative position in production and reproduction. Harvey indicates that giving structural and authentic characteristics to the city, independent of capital accumulation would be faulty, and the urban space is directed towards the investment in order to maximize the profits of the capital entrepreneur, and the urban space become meaningful through capital accumulation processes (Harvey, 2002). Hence, new investments and spatial changes in the city change the values of use of the space. This is not realized according to urban internal dynamics (Alkan & Duru, 2002: p.1) but to the ideology of the dominant class. Urbanization process is the spatial organization style of industrial society (Harvey, 2001). Harvey describes the structuring of the artificial environment in the organization of the individual and social relationship as a method for capitalism to be established and sustained. In addition, he considers the production of unequal and segregationist spaces as a reflection of the capitalist capital accumulation process. Harvey advocates the neo-Marxist structure of post-modernism. The production assumptions standardized by the Fordist production system during the rise of the industrial city have begun to control the space through a new flexible production system, which is developed in parallel with the economic crises (Harvey, 2001). Thus, space has transformed into a tool that supports the processes of consumption.

In lieu of conclusion

The choice of location of the capital on urban space and the consumption-oriented decisions ensure that space is renewed, and gain value and capitalism defeat their own internal contradictions. The integration of safe luxury residential areas and shopping centres, residences and skyscrapers are the reflection of the reproduction of the environment, built by investments, through the exchange of urban space. Henri Lefebvre, Manuel Castells and David Harvey are contemporary urban theoreticians who contribute greatly to finding a solution of today's urban problems. The tools used by these three theoreticians to explain the city are shaped according to the structuralist approaches. It is observed that the three theoreticians regard the processes of capital accumulation, class struggle, and collective consumption as the main starting points to develop an urban approach. Structuralist approaches require in-depth observation and analysis. The theorists concentrate on collective unity rather than individual activity in the light of neutrality and scientific observation. Hence, there is a neo-Marxist perspective when defining the space. According to Harvey, cities that have become part of the capital accumulation process constantly renew themselves as industrial products for urban production, consumption, and change. The way to ensure the economic stability is to direct the capital into the built environment and solve the problem of excessive accumulation (Harvey, 2003). The policy of creating urban rents, which is the solution of the economic crises experienced by the capitalist system, is supported by the urban transformation projects and functionalist decisions applied today. Castells, Lefebvre, and Harvey explain the politicization of urban services and the social movements that are formed in accordance with this politicization and which are developed with a focus on rent, consumption, and capital (Keleş, 1972). Therefore, the concepts of collective consumption, alienation, freedom, and rights are integrated into the space. In the capitalist system of production, the theoreticians state that space is a dominant ideology on the social constructions and define the city as a web of relations consisting of political and ideological perspectives. Theorists argue that the urban space, which is selected according to vital needs, shall be designed free, fair and equitable rather than being designed based on the ideology and perceptions of relationships; hence, consider urban rights as a problem of the modern urbanization process.

References

Alkan, A. & Duru, B. (2002). *20. Yüzyıl Kenti*, İmge Kitabevi, Ankara.

Castells, M. (2005). *Ağ Toplumunun Yükselişi*, İstanbul Bilgi Üniversitesi Yayınları, İstanbul.

Castells, M. (1997). *Kent Sınıf İktidar*, Çev. Asuman Erendil, Bilim ve Sanat Yayınları, Ankara.

Güllüpınar, F. (2013). Kent Kuramları, Ed. Prof. Dr. Fatime Güneş, *Kent Sosyolojisi*, Anadolu Üniversitesi Yayınları, Yayını No: 1932, Eskişehir.

Harvey, D. (2008). *Umut Mekânları*, Metis Yayınları, İstanbul.

Harvey, D. (2003). *Şehir ve Sosyal Adalet*, Metis Yayınları, İstanbul.

Harvey, D. (2002). "Sınıfsal Yapı ve Mekânsal Farklılaşma Kuramı", Der. Ayten Alkan, Bülent Duru, *20. Yüzyıl Kenti*, İmge Kitabevi, Ankara.

Harvey, D. (2001). *Postmodernliğin Durumu*, Metis Yayınları, İstanbul.

Holton, R. J. (1999). *Kentler Kapitalizm ve Uygarlık*, Çev. Ruşen Keleş, İmge Kitabevi, Ankara.

Keleş, R. (1972). *Şehirciliğin Kuramsal Temelleri*, Ankara Üniversitesi Siyasal Bilgiler Fakültesi Yayınları, No: 332, Ankara.

Lefebvre, H. (2014). *Mekanın Üretimi*, Sel Yayıncılık, İstanbul.

Lefebvre, H. (2011). *Kentsel Devrim*, Sel Yayıncılık, İstanbul.

Marx, K. & Engels, F. (1987). *Alman İdeolojisi*, Çev. Şevim Belli, Sol Yayınları, Ankara.

Meydan Yıldız, G. S. (2016). Çevre Bilinci ve Eko-Kent Planlaması: Gölbaşı Özel Çevre Koruma Bölgesi Örneği, Ankara Üniversitesi Sosyal Bilimler Enstitüsü Yayınlanmamış Doktora Tezi, Ankara.

Meydan, S. G. (2013). "Kent Planlama Sürecinde Çevre Bilinci ve Kentsel Rant İlişkisi" Türk *Bilimsel Derlemeler Dergisi*, 6 (1): 175-179.

Meydan, S. G. (2012). "Kapitalizmin Gölgesinde Kır-Kent Çelişkisi: Kırsal Dönüşüm ve Etkileri", *Mekansal Değişim & Dönüşüm*, 8 Kasım Dünya Şehircilik Günü 36. Colloquium, Ankara, pp. 621-634.

Pınarcıoğlu, N. Ş., Kanbak, A & Şiriner, M. (2013). Kent Kuramları, Der. Örgen Uğurlu, Nihal Şirin Pınarcıoğlu, Ayşegül Kanbak, Makbule Şiriner, *Türkiye Prespektifinden Kent Sosyolojisi Çalışmaları*, Örgün Yayınları, İstanbul.

Şengül, T. (2001). *Kentsel Çelişki ve Siyaset*, Demokrasi Kitaplığı, İstanbul.

Urry, J. (1999). *Mekanları Tüketmek*, Ayrıntı Yayınları, İstanbul.

Yörükhan, A. (1968). *Şehir Sosyolojisinin Teorik Temelleri*, İ.İ.B. Mesken Genel Müdürlüğü, Ankara.

EFFECTS OF RIO HABITAT CONFERENCES ON TURKEY'S SETTLEMENT, CITY AND ENVIRONMENT POLITICS

ESMERAY ALACADAĞLI

Introduction

Topics like protection of the environment, control of population movements, and resolution of the problems created by immigration in cities, occupy a constant place in the agenda of states and are the subjects of various sections. These issues are frequently discussed in international platforms, and they also constitute the main theme of the regulations made by international organizations. One of these organizations is the United Nations (UN) with 193 state members, which was established with the aim of "protecting world peace and security and creating an economic, social and cultural cooperation". The UN has been closely interested in development, environment, settlement and growth problems and has been working on these issues since its establishment in accordance with its mission to provide peace and the principles of the Universal Declaration of Human Rights (Keleş, 1996).

"The UN Human Environment Conference", held on June 5, 1972 in Stockholm by the UN, was the first meeting where environmental problems were evaluated on an international level and "environmentally compatible economic development" was discussed by world leaders. At the end of this conference, June 5th was set as the World Environment Day. One of the most concrete consequences of this conference, which presented a Declaration with 26 articles and an Action Plan with 109 articles, was the establishment of the UN Environment Program (UNEP). In accordance with a decision taken at this conference and with the contributions of the Housing, Building and Planning Centre (Keles, 1996), the Conference of Human Settlements (HABITAT) was held in Vancouver in May 1976. In this conference, with the participation of 131 countries, an action plan with 64 proposals was approved. The Vancouver Declaration, the basic vision of which is that "the situation of human settlements determines the quality of life in that country to a great extent," approaches the settlement problem as a human rights problem on this basis. The HABITAT Centre, established after the meeting, started to work in Nairobi in 1978. The Human Settlement Fund, which is expected to provide incentives for settlement problems in underdeveloped countries, has been linked to this centre (Keleş, 1996).

In 1987, the Report of the UN Commission on Environment and Development, known as "Our Common Future," was published. Our Common Future defines "Sustainable Development" as "meeting the needs of this day without compromising the ability of future generations to meet their own needs".

In June 1992, the UN Conference on Environment and Development was held in Rio. At the end of this meeting, in which 179 countries participated, five key documents emerged, including two declarations, two contracts and one main action plan. These are the Rio Declaration, Agenda 21, Forest Principles, the Convention on Climate Change, and Biological Diversity, respectively. The Rio Declaration, which confirms the Stockholm Declaration, defines the human right to use the environment and the responsibility for the protection of the environment. The action plan called Agenda 21 and the documents called Forest Principles, which define the activities required to adopt the principles defined in the Rio Declaration, were approved by the heads of states and governments of the participating countries and the Conventions on Climate Change and Biodiversity was opened for signature. Turkey approved the Rio Declaration, Agenda 21 and Forest Principles and signed the Convention on Biological Diversity. The Convention on Climate Change, the ultimate aim of which is defined as "stopping the accumulation of greenhouse gases in the atmosphere at a level that would prevent dangerous effects on the climate system", was signed in May 2014, and Turkey became a party of the Kyoto Protocol in 2009 (Ministry of Environment and Urban Planning, 2012).

The second of the UN Human Settlements Conferences was held in Istanbul in 1996. HABITAT II states its objective as "affordable housing for everyone and the development of sustainable human settlements in an urbanized world" (New Turkey, 1996). The main message of the Istanbul Conference is "a new ethic of settlement." The published declaration also emphasizes the importance of compromise, partnership and participation to fulfil the responsibilities and it is foreseen that the main actors are local governments in the implementation of the principles.

In 2002, in Johannesburg on the 10th anniversary Rio Summit, and again in Rio on the 20th anniversary, meetings were held on a continuous and balanced development. In the Johannesburg Declaration; it is emphasized that sustainable development, global prosperity, stability and security depend on the elimination of differences and distinctions between the rich and the poor, the developed and the developing. In the third meeting, also known as Rio+20, the document, on which a consensus is achieved, is titled "The Future We Want." One of the most important innovations adopted in Rio+20 is the adoption of the "Green Economy" approach, involving the concept of "Degrowth" to achieve the goal of sustainable development (Keleş, 2013).

HABITAT III was held in Prague, the Czech Republic, in 2016. The Prague Declaration declared after the meeting, the main theme, which was assigned as "Housing in Living Cities", proposing to promote green, environmentally-sensitive and productive cities, as well as sustainable, participatory, governance-based, integrated urban planning and management. The main features of this framework are: creative and productive cities; green, compact, resource-efficient and durable cities; inclusive and safe cities; and good city governance (Ministry of Environment and Urban Planning, 2017).

As a member, meeting participant, and contributor, the UN documents that have been approved as generally in compliance with internal laws and that have become a part of the national legislation; impose obligations and responsibilities on our country on both a national and international platform. The aim of this study is to reveal the effects of the United Nations, in particular its work on environment, on policies and practices in our country at the national level. In this context; Stockholm, Rio and HABİTAT conference results and the produced documents that have been carried out by the UN and have an important effect on environmental and urban development processes are examined.

The situation of Turkey in terms of settlement, urbanization, and environment: 1970-2000

After the 1970s, Turkey experienced an accumulation of population and capital in the Marmara and Aegean regions and the Mediterranean coast. In this process, after 1980, factors such as export-oriented industrialization, new world order, the beginning of the determination of the distribution of resources with market processes, changes in life patterns, speculative construction of second homes and encouraging tourism investments played a role (National Report and Action Plan, 1996). From 1960 to 1990, urban population quadrupled by increasing from 6.9 million to 31.4 million. The number of cities in our country is also in a continuous increase; the number of cities increased from 66 in 1927 to 424 in 1990 (when a place with more than 10,000 people is called a city). Big cities have increased their share of the urban population; a vast majority of the growing population settled in these cities between the years of 1960-1990 (Khan, 1997). Our country has been experiencing an ongoing internal migration since the 1950s. Research reveals that the cause of the migration is economic, but deterioration of the safe living conditions in the Eastern and South Eastern Anatolia is also a factor (Khan, 1998). The cities that attract migration the most are also the cities that experience environmental problems the most. In these provinces, one of the biggest problems created by migration and unhealthy urbanization is the housing presentation format particular to us: squatting. The number of squatters increased from 80 thousand in 1950 to 1.5 million in 1983. According to 1995 data, the number of squatters is 2 million and 35% of our urban population is living in slums (Khan, 1997). Based on the spatial layout and production activities of industrialization, our land, water and air are polluted. According to an inventory drawn up by the Ministry of Environment and Urban Development; the prior environmental problem is water pollution in 32 provinces, air pollution in 27 provinces, and waste in 19 cities. During this period, some regulations were executed even though they were holistic. The Undersecretary of the Environment was established in 1978, environmental law was enforced in 1983, the organizational structure changed to the Ministry in 1991, and the environment was defined as a right in the Constitution.

The effects of Rio Habitat and studies conducted in our country

Development plans

Development plans are documents determining basic policies in all sectors, and they are obligatory documents for all public institutions. The posterior plans such as regional plans and city plans have their own characteristics, but they have an approach in accordance with the basic principles defined in development plans (Keleş, 1997). In this respect, the development plans should be assessed first to evaluate the effects of HABITAT and Rio.

When the developments are evaluated in parallel with the historical process, in the Fourth Plan (1979-1983), corresponding with the principles of the HABITAT I, the size of the venue is introduced for planning decisions, ensuring balance in the distribution of the services mentioned.

The weight is given to regions with a priority in development; mid-sized cities are promoted to prevent the accumulation in big cities with intimidating measures.

The Fifth Plan (1985-1989) adopts the principles of conservation and development of resources for the benefit of future generations while it is emphasized that the municipalities are responsible for the provision of urban services. The plan proposes the planning of housing, land, and infrastructure production problems ahead of the growth rate of the cities; the specialization of the cities; the disallowance of dispersed housing; and the establishment of transportation of organized industrial zones in settlement centres with industrial potential and transport facilities. These predictions align with recommendations in the Vancouver Action Plan and Our Common Future. The transfer of the construction authorization to local administrations, with the introduction of the Construction Law in 1985, is an approach compatible with the principle of localization of services.

The basic principle of The Sixth Plan (1990-1994) is to ensure the management of natural resources by protecting human health and the natural balance, allowing continuous economic development, and to leave a natural, physical and social environment suitable for humans for future generations. The principles of the plan (preventing construction accumulation on coasts, increasing field production, taking the use of land under control, developing a new model for the city management, and making necessary changes in the organizational structure in this framework of policies) are similar to the principles and approaches of the Rio Declaration and Agenda 21.

In the Seventh Plan (1996-2000), implementation of policies to prevent the migration to large cities is mentioned, and the specialization of cities is valued. Making at least one city an international autonomous centre is a goal at the end of the plan. The Seventh Plan proposes necessary adjustments to the Constitution and laws for an effective environmental management and reorganization of the authority and responsibilities of Ministry of Environment and other relevant ministries and local governments (Alacadağlı, 1997).

In the Eighth Plan, the next five-year development plan, solutions are proposed by giving weight to the issues of the scale problem in the settlement structure: the local government finance, control systems, participation methods, the needs of democratization, disadvantaged social categories, and the detection of problems of natural environment protection. In addition, it is stated that urbanization is a process developed by the migration of those who prefer urban poverty to rural poverty. The basic characteristics of the cities in Turkey are specified as poverty, squalidity, violation of laws, disorder in everyday life, transportation and infrastructure inadequacies, pollution, uncontrolled growth, and city parts consisting of illegal structures.

The Ninth Development Plan (2007-2013), was prepared in accordance with the concept of strategic planning. Its vision is determined as, "stability in growth, a fair revenue sharing, competitiveness on a global scale, transition to an information society in Turkey." According to the plan, "conservation of the environment and development of urban infrastructure" is the most important factor to increase competitiveness. Sustainability in transportation and the sustainable use of natural resources is pointed out; it is stated that, "rapid population growth and industrialization process continue to be a significant pressure on the sustainable use of natural resources."

The Tenth Plan, prepared as a five-year plan again and still in effect, aims at four targets: "qualified person-strong community, innovative production, stable high growth, liveable spaces, [and] international cooperation for sustainable environment and development." The plan highlights the importance of investment in human resources and emphasizes that stable high growth rates cannot be reached with the perception of classical production, a living space is only possible with the concept of sustainability and nothing can be achieved alone in a global world. The plan has adopted its sub-goals to reach each target in line with these concepts.

The national environmental strategy and action plan

In the Rio Declaration, it is emphasized that each nation should have a "National Environmental Strategy and Action Plan" (NESAP). In this context, Turkey's NESAP is prepared with the participation of over 800 experts and an advisory team of 38 people. In NESAP, it is stated that the environmental management system of Turkey and its organizational basis was prepared before the 1992 Rio Declaration and Agenda 21, and national environmental policies should be harmonized with such international documents. The contributions of Non-Governmental Organizations (NGOs) on this subject are specified, underlying the importance of participation. Privatization is supported in NESAP, indicating that "government enterprises are a burden for the economy."

National and Local Agenda 21

The most important of the documents approved in Rio is Agenda 21, which serves as an implementation plan and defines the necessary activities of governments and all related organizations, sectors in all areas that affect the environment and development. Agenda 21, each word of which is developed and adopted by governments, is the most comprehensive international program (Algan, 1995). Agenda 21, which gives responsibility to every person and organization that has an effect on nature or is affected, is not state-oriented but community-oriented unlike Vancouver, and a multi-actor/participatory management approach is put forward (Kate, 1998). Turkey's National Agenda 21, prepared by the Ministry of the Environment (MoE), is an action plan focusing on two basic points: bringing the processes of social development and environmental protection together and removing obstacles for the management of environmental protection with participation and collaboration. One of the most important recommendations of Agenda 21 is the preparation of local action plans (ÇB, 1993). Local Agenda 21 (LA 21), defined as the decisive word of the works in terms of preparation for the 21st century, is the effort for a successive, joint solution of the "local" and "common" issues, and in this context, for making existing resources sustainable. In Turkey, LA 21 studies started in the context of a project. When the number of the project-partner local authorities exceeded 50 in 1997, the Project was converted into "Turkey LA 21 Program." The work of Turkey LA 21 Program is supported by the decisions of the Council of Ministers.

Turkey LA 21 Program is coordinated by International Union of Local Authorities, Section for the Eastern Mediterranean and Middle East Region (IULA-EMME) at the national level. Coordination of LA 21 processes in program-partner cities is realized by the General Secretary of LA 21, established in each city. LA 21, as an important local democratization program, aims for the participation of the civil society in decision-making and their effect on local investments. The local decision and implementation mechanisms of the program are the local stakeholders organized under the umbrella of City Council. City Councils are supported by special interest groups such as Women and Youth Councils, Working Groups, Children, the Handicapped, and Elders Platform.

Turkey National Report and Action Plan

The National Report of Turkey is prepared by the Housing Development Administration (TOKİ) in a participatory process with the establishment of a National Committee representing the relevant groups of the society. The report is aimed at bringing awareness to the society and the relevant actors on the issues of sustainable settlements and adequate housing for everyone, the main themes of the HABİTAT II. In the report, the settlement system in our country and developments about housing are evaluated in three periods, including 1945-60, 1960-80 and 1980 to the present. Urban Indicators, one of the indicators prepared in accordance with the criteria determined by the HABITAT, are created under six modules specified as Poverty, Employment and Productivity; Social Development; Infrastructure; Transportation; Environmental Management; and Local Administrations. Housing Indicators are prepared under the two modules "Affordability and Competence of Housing" and "Housing Presentation." Economic, social, demographic and political processes are also ranked in the report, in addition to a National Action Plan. 28 priority topics defined in the Action Plan are classified under three separate titles, and the importance of each priority topic and strategy, the proposed solution, work to do, monitoring method, and responsible actors are determined. The report has determined the basic principles of the National Action Plan as: goal-oriented quality; sustainability, liveability, fair share and instrumental quality; city dependence, accessibility and multi-actor governance (HABITAT II Turkey National Report and Action Plan, 1996).

Other Works

Besides these three reports prepared in the context of HABITAT and the Rio Declaration, some changes are made in the constitution and law in regard to city, environment, region and housing; new applications are applied in parallel with new regulations. The 1982 Constitution gives the duty of protecting and developing to the state and citizens by defining the environment as a right in Article 56. Article 57 defines responsibilities of the state for housing. In 2006, Environmental Law, and in 2011 Environmental Organization Law were revised in accordance with the basic principles of the Rio Declaration and HABITAT II. With the restructured Environmental Organization Law, broad authority is given to the Ministry on construction plans of cities and urban renewal applications. In 2012, with the "Law on Transformation of Areas under Disaster Risk," broad authority on planning, design, and conversion in cities is given to the Ministry and Housing Development Administration (TOKI).

Our Common Future, the UN Environmental Program, and the Rio Declaration left their mark on Environment Councils, organized by the Ministry of Environment in the period from 1991 to 1997. This aspect is expressed clearly in council reports. Expertise commissions created for the preparation of development plans, such as the Environmental Expertise Commission, gave wide coverage to resulting documents and decisions of these conferences in their work.

The 1972 Human Environment Conference and HABITAT I had effect on the creation of specially protected environmental areas in Development Law and the involvement of a regulation for the foundation of "Special Environmental Law." The Council of Ministers has been given the authority to create protected areas, and with this authority, Köyceğiz, Fethiye, Göçek, Gökova were declared specially protected environmental areas in 1988. Regional development projects (e.g. Eastern Anatolia Project, the Black Sea Development Project) have been prepared in compliance with the philosophy of elimination of inequalities in living conditions, one of the basic principles of the HABITAT I and also mentioned in Rio. Mediterranean Environmental Technical Assistance Programme (METAP) participated in Mediterranean Action Plan, the Black Sea Environmental Programme, and Regional Agenda 21. Our country monitors the quality of sea water in compliance with the requirements of MEDPOL III phase, and contributes to Mediterranean Agenda 2 (MoE, 1999).

Within the framework of the decisions, suggestions and commitments in the aftermath of the HABITAT I and II, Housing Law was enforced in 1981 and the production of mass housing began. During this period, municipalities increased their activities related to housing. Ankara-Batıkent and İzmir-Egekent (two international prize winners on this topic) are the most well-known examples.

Within the context of the work carried on for reorganization and transformation of urban areas, urban development projects such as "Portakal Çiçeği Valley, Dikmen Valley, and Hacıbayram Square Environmental Plans" were introduced (Keles & Geray, 1999). The first legal regulation to form the basis of these activities was established in 2004 for the urban transformation of Ankara. In 2005, with the law on "Protection and Renovation of Historical and Cultural Assets" a regulation was made for this issue. Today, starting from Ankara and İstanbul, urban transformation projects continue with the support of TOKİ to prevent unplanned urbanization in all our cities and to ensure sustainable urban development. The authority of municipalities on this subject has increased with Municipality Law no. 5393 and Metropolitan Municipality Law no.

5216. Mechanisms of the municipalities for cooperation with private sector and privatizing the service have increased. "City Councils", one of the primary participants of the Local Agenda 21 process in Turkey at the city scale, have found a strong legal foundation along with Youth Councils and the other participators in July 2005 with the Article 76 of the Municipal Law no. 5393. Turkey Local Agenda 21 Program has been an initiative that aroused wide interest in various platforms in terms of meeting international commitments to solve the problems of the youth.

Conclusion

Even though it is considered negative by some groups of people suggesting that it threatens the nation states, today, we live in an era where the wheels of change and transformation are spun by multi-actor organizations in the international arena. Transnational approaches and regulations put forward by these actors both shape national policies and constitute the base of the new legislations made by the states. Today, organizations, especially those whose members are the states, play a decisive role in the creation of policies of the country in areas such as environment, trade, human rights and immigration across the world. The goal is to create a more liveable world together. However, despite all the studies carried out on the national and international level, and the universal and regional contracts signed by states to prevent pollution, protect the environment, ensure peace, and improve the living environment of the people, the problems still continue to exist. Still, the pollution caused by settlement problems and the increase in the number of homeless people continue, and the environment is being polluted despite all the work. According to the statements made by the authorities of the UN; "the number of the people who left their countries and those who became homeless has exceeded the 60 million limits; more than a billion people are deprived of adequate housing conditions; 100 million people are homeless."

In our country, as stated in the official report of the State; the urbanization experiment and housing presentation formats experienced by Turkey have not enabled the separation of public space and the protection of green areas in cities for the public use or restrained the building of green systems in urban spaces. In addition, migration from rural to urban areas constitutes the basis of various economic and social problems and risks for those living there. In the 1980s, various laws were enacted in order to bring solutions to settlement problems. On the other hand, illegal housing has been supported by "amnesty laws," and the formation of slums has been allowed by the law. With the urban transformation initiated by laws, the owner of the illegal structure who seized the public land became a partner of urban income, and urban resources have not been used for public welfare (Keles, 2016).

The data of this study, in which the effects and the applications of UN regulations in our country have been examined, show that what is reached does not comply with the purpose, and legal regulations and contracts don't work when the practice and the expression don't match in general. On the other hand, documents prepared by HABİTAT and the Rio conferences include the universal principles such as sustainability, localization, equitable life, housing, improving the participation and the notice of goodwill, along with some regulations increasing the pollution of transportation and exploitation in the disadvantage of developing countries. Flexibility mechanisms in the Convention on Climate Change indicated that emissions will remain stable across the world, and the developed countries will have more right to pollute by this means. These and similar arrangements show us that the rules established by the leadership of international organizations, in the context of factors constituting the background of the principles, include the demand for new markets and new market share for capitalist crises.

It is a mistaken approach to think that the imbalances between cities and regions can be eliminated without the state's supervision or control. Because, the private sector will not invest in any area that does not seem profitable and these differences will grow even larger due to its nature. The Civil Society can neither be successful in encouraging participation nor defining and applying a policy for development without the power of the state. Thus, we have to realize our transformation as a country, suitable for the realities of the country, to settlement systems that are open for the participation of different masses living in every settlement and are respectful of the right to live of future generations and environmental ethics. From this point of view, it will be useful not to ignore the fact that the policies applied in the first years of the Republic for the development of society consist of a specific and usable model that is unique to us, including participation, localisation and of course natural democratization, and they can be enhanced and reused.

References

Alacadağlı, E. (1997). *Industrialized Turkey and Environmental Pollution,* Unpublished Master Thesis, Public Administration Institute for Turkey and Middle East

Algan, N. (1995). *Model Search in Regional Environmental Management,* Ankara, Turkey: Publications of the Ministry of Environment (MoE).

Alkan, A. (1998). *Housing Problem of Low Income Citizens and Housing Cooperatives in Turkey after 1980,* Ankara, Turkey: İmaj Publishing.

Anayasa (1982). *The New Constitution 1982,* İstanbul, Turkey: Yasa Publishing.

Aytaç, F. (1996). Thoughts on the Habitat City Summit, *Provinces and Municipalities Magazine,* 51 (604), 80-82.

Bostanoğlu, Ö. (1995). Habitat Close to 2000s, *Public Administration Magazine,* 28(12), 84-93.

Habitat III National Report, Retrieved from http://www.csb.gov.tr/db/mpgm/ editordosya /file/HABITAT/ HABITATIII ULUSAL RAPOR_TURKCE.pdf

Hamamcı, C., Keleş, R., Çoban, A. (2009). Environment Policy, Ankara, Turkey: İmaj Publishing

Geray, C., Keleş, R. & the others (1999). *Acquisition of Urban Land Rent to the Public,* Ankara, Turkey: Öteki Publishing.

Geray, C. (1996). Habitat II Urban Peak and After, *TÜRKKENT City Cooperatives Monthly Bulletin,* (74-75-76).

Geray, C. (1996). Adequate Housing for Everyone and Politics of Collective Housing in Our Country, *New Turkey Habitat II Special Edition,* (8), 7-9

Karaman, Z. T. (1998). Habitat II ve Local Agenda 21 Responsibility, *Turkish Administration Magazine,* Year 70, (421), 348-350.

Keating, M. (1993). *Agenda of the Change,* Ankara, Turkey: Publishing of UNEP Turkey Commitee

Keleş, R. (1997&2016). *Urbanization Policy,* 4th Print &15th Print, Ankara, Turkey: İmge Bookstore.

Keleş, R. (1996). Habitat II Approaching, *New Turkey Habitat II Special Edition,* (8), 3-4.

Keleş, R. (1996). Importance of Habitat II for Our Country, *TÜRKKENT City Cooperative System Bulletin,* (July-Agust-September 1996), 3-4

Ministry of Environment (1997). *Turkey Agenda 21,* Ankara, Turkey: Publications of the Ministry of Environment (MoE)

Ministry of Environment (1993). *United Nation Environment and Development Conference (UNCED),* Ankara, Turkey: MoE Publishing.

Niksarlı, M. (1996). Habitat II and Looking into Future, Our Political Parties and Cooperative System, *City Cooperatives 11th Technical Congress, 7-11 October*, Antalya, Türkler Publishing

State Plannig Organization, (SPO). (1999). *Various Indicators of Provinces and Regions*, Ankara: SPO Publishing

SPO (1999). *National Environment Activity Plan*, Ankara: SPO Publishing

Şahin, Y. (2015). *Urbanization Policy*, 5th Edition, Bursa, Turkey:Ekin Publishing

Tekeli, İ. (1996). *Conference Notes on Habitat II*, Ankara, Turkey: TOKİ Publishing,

The Habitat Agenda (1996). *United Nations Conferance on Habitat II*, 3-14 June 1996, İstanbul, Turkey

Turkey Statistical Institute (2013). Population and Housing Research 2011, Issue 15843, 31 Ocak 2013,. Retrieved from http://habitatdernegi.org/projeler/ yg-21/

REMIGRATION TENDENCY

SİNAN YAZICI

Introduction

Migration is one of the most prominent problems in our country that must be resolved. The problem persists today. Just as in the other countries in the process of industrialization, the migration from the countryside to the city began in Turkey in 1945 and continued until 1975. Since 1975, due to the inequality in the distribution of economic opportunities according to the locations, people started to migrate from cities to cities (Tekeli, 2008: p.50-62).

Migration between the cities, which started to become popular in 1975, causes an extreme growth in the cities, thus creating social, economic and environmental problems in urban areas. In this context, cities face essential problems both in the production and supply of basic urban services such as housing, water, electricity, sewage and environmental planning (Keleş, 2008: p.48-50). Emigrant locations are also experiencing significant problems. The first of these problems is the loss of population of emigrant locations. Since the population is lost, the accommodation units are minimized. The minimization of the accommodation units causes significant loss of function and brings the danger of identity loss at the same time. Some living problems are related to this development, such as lack of infrastructure, the inadequacy of social opportunities, and the inability to meet energy needs (Bayramoglu & Durmaz, 2017: p.81). Within this scope, it is significant that 283 municipality legal entities have been abolished since the population fell below 2,000 people; this proves the loss of identity and function in the accommodation units[1].

The loss of the population living in emigrant accommodations and the dysfunctional situation afterward also impedes the possible contribution of these accommodations to the economy of the country, particularly to

---

[1] http://www.resmigazete.gov.tr/eskiler/2008/03/20080322M1-1.htm (Accessed on 25.04.2017)

agriculture and animal husbandry. The dysfunctional status of emigrant centres and the problems emanating from the overpopulation in the cities should be solved. Hence, the idea of remigration is an essential alternative for solving these problems.

Unlike the abundance of work on migration in the literature, there are few studies about remigration. In this context, Guresci (2011) examined the remigration to Ispir Kirik, a town in Erzurum, from the Kemalpasa district of İzmir. Guresci strived to conduct a survey researching 48 households migrating to Kemalpasa. The households were selected randomly. The rate of those who would like to remigrate was found to be 14.63% according to the study of Guresci. The essential deficiency of the mentioned study is that in the survey research, the opinions of women, the most prominent members of the family, are not included.

Sunata (2014) has studied brain drain from Germany to Turkey. Sunata's study discussed the role of social networks both in migration and remigration. The study is remarkable since it discusses the remigration of highly educated people to our country and examines only the migration of a highly qualified labour force.

Tutar and Ozyakıshır (2013) investigated the causes of migration movements from the TRA 2 region to Istanbul. This study aimed to reveal the causes of migration. This research strived to measure indirectly the remigration tendency. The study revealed that 82.6% of migrants from Agrı, 66.3% of migrants from Kars, 44.5% of migrants from Igdir and 55.5% of migrants from Ardahan do not consider the possibility of remigration. However, this study for the TRA 2 region, which does not distinguish the village, has examined immigration to Istanbul for the whole region.

Gumuş and Gulersoy (2013) investigated the migrations from the city to the villages in their study. The study is remarkable since the remigration is through the village, the vast majority of the migrants are retired and the age average is high.

This study examined the remigration tendencies of Aydintepe district of Bayburt, one of the most emigrant cities of our country, to the centre of Bayburt, İstanbul, and Kocaeli. The study aimed to solve the problems derived from overpopulation in the immigrant accommodation units and lack of population in emigrant accommodation units and thus to contribute to the literature since there are few studies on this subject.

After giving the overview of this study in the introduction, the method of the research is explained. Then, the findings are introduced, and the effects of the remigration on the region are discussed in the conclusion.

Methodology

Primary and secondary data are used in the study. The secondary data of the study are the data obtained from the websites of the accommodation units, the TUIK (Turkish Statistical Institute) and the literature survey. The primary data are the data obtained from the survey research using direct sampling.

This study was carried out by the means of the Aydintepeliler Association, located in the Kaynarca quarter of the Pendik district of İstanbul. Membership records of the association have been examined in line with the information obtained from the association management. According to the examination results and the recommendations of the association, a survey was implemented on 93 subjects. The survey is implemented to 110 persons including the subject located in the centre of Bayburt. 5 were discarded due to the inconsistency of the information in the survey.

The questions of the survey were asked to 17 subjects in the center of Bayburt, which is chosen as the pilot area. All the subjects are members of the Aydintepeliler Association and selected randomly. The troubles observed in this implementation have been eliminated. In addition, a similar study was carried out in İstanbul-Kocaeli by estimating that there might be some problems. The survey was implemented to 10 subjects for the Istanbul-Kocaeli section of the study, field study and in-depth interview techniques were used. Survey questions were reviewed according to these studies. The necessary adjustments were made taking into consideration the opinions of the subjects. Thanks to the in-depth interview conducted with 10 people, it was also possible to better analyze the immigrant-receiving region. The survey consists of questions about personal information, occupational status, the level of interest in the place of residence, economic situation, and the thoughts about remigration.

The questions were closed-ended questions; open-ended questions were also used when deemed necessary. The Aydintepeliler Association provided the addresses and telephone numbers of the subjects within the scope of the sampling. Two female and two male high school graduates volunteered to help us get in contact with the subjects. The data obtained are registered in the SPSS program.

In addition, since migration is a decision taken by family members, it has been emphasized that not only men but also women are included in the survey. In this context, we have reached 40 women in order to achieve this objective.

The Findings

The findings obtained with the survey are presented below. In this section, the findings are divided into the subheadings as follows: the demographic information, the awareness of problems about the environment where the subjects live in, the economic conditions, the findings of the migration and the tendency for remigration. Descriptions of the data are given below the tables.

Findings about demographic information,
education and occupation

The information on the personal and occupational status of the subjects is presented in Tables 1-1, 1-2, 1-3 and 1-4. Table 1-1 displays the places where subjects live after the migration, Table 1-2 exhibits the education details, Table 1-3 shows the occupational status and finally, Table 1-4 presents the information about the migration date.

Table 1-1. Places Where Subjects Live

District	Frequency	%
Pendik-Kaynarca	35	33.3
Bayburt-Merkez	17	16.2
Kocaeli-Çayırova	13	12.4
Istanbul-Esenyurt	11	10.5
Istanbul-Ümraniye	9	8.6
Istanbul-Sultanbeyli	6	5.7
Other Districts of Istanbul	14	13.4

Out of 105 subjects, 62% are male and 38% are female. 3.8% of the women were 15-19 years old, 3.8% were 20-29 years old, 15.23% were 30-39 years old, 11.42% were 40-49 years old, 2.85% were 50-59 years old and 0.95% were over 60 years old. 24.76% of the men were 30-39 years old, 22.85% were 40-49 years old, 13.33% were 50-59 years old and 09.5% were 60 years old and over.

According to Table 1-1, the places where the subjects live are as follows: 33.3% in Pendik-Kaynarca, 16.2% in Bayburt Center, 12.4% in Kocaeli-Çayırova, 10.5% in İstanbul Esenyurt, 8.6% in Istanbul Ümraniye, 5.7% in Sultanbeyli and 13.4% in other districts of Istanbul.

Table 1-2. Education of Subjects

	Women Frequency	%	Men Frequency	%
Illiterate	5	4.76	0	0
Primary School Graduate	16	15.24	3	2.86
Secondary School Graduate	7	6.67	14	13.33
High School Graduate	9	8.57	21	20
Vocational High School Graduate	0	0	1	0.95
College Graduate	2	1.9	9	8.57
University graduate	1	0.95	17	16.19
Total	**40**	**38.1**	**65**	**61.9**

According to Table 1-2, the rate of illiteracy among females is 4.76%, the ratio of primary school graduates is 15.24%, the ratio of secondary school graduates is 6.67%, the ratio of high school graduates is 8.57%, the ratio of college graduates is 1.90% and the ratio of university graduates is 0.95%. The education details of male subjects are as follows: The ratio of primary school graduates is 2.86%, the ratio of secondary school graduates is 13.33%, the ratio of high school graduates is 20%, the ratio of vocational high school graduates is 0.95%, the ratio of college graduates is 8.57% and the ratio of university graduates is 16.19%. Thus, it is easy to observe that the educational status of female subjects is lower than that of men. Illiterate subjects are 50 years old and older. It has been observed that younger subjects tend to study high school, college, and university.

Table 1-3. Occupational Status of Subjects

Occupation at the District			Occupation at the place of living		
Occupation	Fr.	%	Occupation	Fr.	%
Unemployed	21	20	Housewife	22	21
Farmer	18	17.1	Officer	18	17.1
Housewife	16	15.2	Private Security Guard	15	14.3
Officer	12	11.4	Worker	14	13.3
Worker (construction etc.)	11	10.5	Retired	9	8.6
Artisan-Craftsman	9	8.6	Driver	5	4.8
Student	6	5.7	Artisan-Craftsman	7	6.7
Retired	5	4.8	Subcontracted Worker	4	3.8
Private Security Guard	2	1.9	Sales clerk	2	1.9
Not specified	5	4.8	Other (9 different occupations)	9	8.6
Total	105	100	Total	105	100

According to Table 1-3 in which the occupation at the district is compared to the occupation at the place of residence, the occupational status of the subjects is as follows: 20% unemployed, 17.1% farmers, 15.2% housewives, 11.4% officers, 10.5% workers in various sectors, 8.6% artisans and craftsman, 5.7% students, and 1.9% private security guards. 4.8% of the subjects did not specify any occupation.

When monitoring the occupational status after migration, the first point of note is the housewives with 21%. It is observed that women who declared their occupation as farmer and artisan-craftsman did not continue to do these jobs after migration. Retired persons constitute 8.6% of the subjects, and the drivers 4.8%, the artisans-craftsman 6.7%, subcontracted workers 3.8%, and 1.9% of the subjects are working as sales clerks. 8.6% are working in 9 different professions.

When Table 1-3 is generally evaluated, unemployment which constitutes the largest group before migration has completely disappeared after migration. The farming occupation, which constituted the second place before migration, became one of the other 9 professions with 0.95% after migration. In addition, those who declared themselves as students in the districts have chosen to work in various professions after migration. The housewife category increased from 15.2% to 21.0%. The reason why women choose to stay at home is influenced by the income of the family being sufficient and the professional life being unsuitable for women. As shown in Table 1-4, the economic situation of the family has improved according to the situation before the migration. The subjects were categorized themselves in nine different categories before the migration, but this number increased to 18 after migration.

Table 1-4. Migration Date of the Subjects

Years	Frequency	Percent
Between 0-5 Years	10.00	9.52
Between 5-10 Years	25.00	23.81
Between 10-15 Years	28.00	26.67
Between 15-20 Years	14.00	13.33
More than 20 Years	28.00	26.67
Total	**105.00**	**100.00**

It is expected to have a direct proportion between the year when the person migrated and the adaption to the new place. According to Table 4, the rate of those who declared that their migration dates between 0-5 years is 9.52%, between 5-10 years 23.81%, between 10-15 years 28%, between 15-20 years 13.33% and more than 20 years 28%. Hence, according to the table, it might be expected that 28% of the subjects are adapted to the place where they live in and their ties with the Aydıntepe district are weakened.

Recognition of the accommodation unit in which s/he lives and awareness of problems

It is anticipated that the people recognize the administrators of the settlements where they live, and they are aware of the local problems. Thus, the subjects were asked to answer some questions, aiming to measure the awareness of the people about the local problems and their knowledge about the administrators before and after the migration.

Table 1-5. Awareness of the Problems in the District and the Place Where They Live

	Before Migration		After Migration	
	Frequency	%	Frequency	%
I have no idea	20.00	19.05	17	16.19
Infrastructure Development Issues	15.00	14.29	13	12.38
Lack of Social Activity	7.00	6.67	20	19.05
Transportation	10.00	9.52	45	42.86
Unemployment	80.00	76.19	2	1.90
There is no issue	0.00	0.00	6	5.71
Other	5.00	4.76	16	15.23
Total	105.00	100.00	105	100.00

According to Table 1-5, 76.19% of the subjects mentioned the unemployment as the most prominent problem of the district. 19.05% of the subjects chose the "I have no idea" option while 14.29% of the subjects talked about the infrastructure and development problems, and 9.52% of them selected transportation. 6.67% of the subjects chose the lack of social activity, and 4.76% selected the "other" option.

While we examine the answers of the subjects after the migration, we observe that the leading problem is the transportation with 42.86% followed by lack of social activity with 19.05%. While 16.19% chose the "I have no idea" option, 15.23% selected the "other" option. The ones who selected "other" emphasized the security issue. The ratio of those who considered the infrastructure development problem as a problem in the settlement where they live in is 12.38%. 5.71% of the subjects stated they are satisfied with the settlement since they did not encounter any problem that would draw their attention. Only 1.90% of them considered unemployment to be a problem.

Table 1-6. Recognition of the Administrator in Aydıntepe and at the Place Where They Live

Recognition of the Administrator in Aydintepe		Recognition of the Administrator in the Place where they live		
	Frequency	%		Frequency	%
No	24.00	22.86	No	20.00	19.23
Partially	47.00	44.76	Partially	40.00	38.46
Yes	34.00	32.38	Yes	44.00	42.31
Total	105.00	100	Total	104.00	100

According to Table 1-6, 44.76% of the subjects partially recognize the administrators in the district. This option is followed by "Yes" with 32.38% and by "No" with 22.9%. After the migration, the subjects replied to the recognition question as follows, 41.9% replied "Yes," while 38.1% gave "Partially" as an answer and 19.23% of the subjects replied "No."

According to Table 1-5 and Table 1-6, it is possible to conclude that the subjects are maintaining their relationships with the districts as well as the settlements they migrated to.

The economic conditions

The economic conditions of the subjects before and after the migration are presented in Table 7. In order to determine the income levels of the subjects, specific questions were asked. According to the Statistical Package for Social Sciences, the monthly average income level of the subjects was calculated as 3,850 Turkish Liras. In 2010 and 2017 in Aydıntepe, the migration trend survey, which will be published soon, reveals this average income as TL 1,500 in 2010 and TL 2,200 in 2017. The minimum was TL 599 in 2010 in Turkey during the period of the research, while it is TL 1,405 in 2017. Hence, it is observed that there is a monthly difference of approximately TL 1,650 between the income in the district and the place where the subjects live.

Table 1-7. Economic Conditions Before and After Migration

	Economic Conditions Before Migration		Economic Conditions After Migration	
	Frequency	%	Frequency	%
Poor	37	35.2	10	9.5
Middle Class	65	61.9	89	84.8
Rich	3	2.9	6	5.7
Total	105	100.0	105	100.0

According to Table 1-7, 35.2% of the subjects considered themselves poor before the migration; this rate dropped to 9.5% after the migration. The ratio of those who declared themselves as middle class increased from 61.9% before the migration to 84.8% after the migration. The proportion of those who declared themselves as "rich" has increased from 2.9% to 5.7%. Thus, we may conclude that the economic situations of the subjects improved significantly after the migration.

Findings related to migration

Table 1-8. The Reason for Migration

Reason	Frequency	%
Unemployment, financial difficulty	53	50.5
Challenging climate conditions	2	1.9
The idea that I can do my job better in the new place where I migrate	10	9.5
For the future of my children	9	8.6
To be able to pay my loan or the loan for which I am a guarantor	3	2.9
Economic crisis	3	2.9
My relatives have migrated, to be close to them	5	4.8
Due to marriage	6	5.7
Due to civil service	2	1.9
I migrate with my family	1	1.0
Not specified	11	10.5
Total	105	100.0

When the reasons for migration in Table 1.8 were evaluated, 50.5% of the subjects cited unemployment and financial difficulty as the main reason. The idea that subject could do their jobs better in the new place where they migrated comes second with 9.5%. In third place, 8.6% of the subjects cited "for the future of their children." The proportion of those who mentioned marriage as the reason for migration is 5.7%, the proportion of those who want to be with the relatives who have already migrated is 4.8%, and the percentage of those who did not mark any option was 10.5%. When Table 1.8 is evaluated, it is perceived that economic problems and financial difficulties are the leading reasons for the migration.

Table 1-9. Satisfaction about the Migration

	Frequency	%
Yes	54	51.4
Partially	36	34.3
No	15	14.3
Total	105	100

According to Table 9, 51.4% of the subjects are satisfied to be migrated. The proportion of those who are partially satisfied is 34.3% and the proportion of those who are not satisfied is 14.3%. They are satisfied with the fact that the subjects have been able to work and they are able to make the living for their families. However, they stated that they are experiencing various problems of adaptation on the social and cultural level.

Table 1-10. The Idea of Remigration

	Frequency	Percentage
Yes	35	33.3
Partially	22	21
No	48	45.7
Total	105	100.0

According to Table 1-10, 45% of the subjects do not consider remigration as an option. 33.3% of the subjects responded "Yes." 21% of them answered "Partially". Table 9 and 10 show the justification for the idea of remigration, if answered "Yes" and "Partially" or "No."

Table 1-11. If Your Answer is "Yes" and "Partially"

	Frequency	%
My homeland should offer me job opportunities after being developed	30	28.6
There should be more social and cultural opportunities	1	1.0
Insufficiency of land must be removed	1	1.0
When I am retired, I would spend my vacation at my homeland	18	17.1
Other	2	1.9
Total	52	49.5

According to Table 1-11 in which the results of 52 subjects are included, 28.6% of the subjects (if we evaluate only the results of 52, the number represents 57% of the subjects) stated that they would consider the idea of remigration, if the homeland offers job opportunities after being developed. Secondly, the ratio of those wishing to spend the vacation at the homeland after retirement is 17.1%. The rate of those who want to improve the socio-cultural opportunities and improve the conditions of land disability is 2%.

Table 1-12. If Your Answer is "No"

	Frequency	Percentage
My family is peaceful here	17	16.2
I have favourable economic conditions	6	5.7
Negative thoughts about me	1	1.0
I am desperate about the future of my homeland	22	21
Other	5	4.8
Total	51	48.6

According to Table 1-12, to which a total of 51 subjects responded, 43% of the subjects (representing 21% of the total subjects) were considered desperate for the future of the homeland, 16.2% of the subjects are happy since their families are satisfied in the place where they migrated, and 6% of the subjects do not consider the remigration option since they have favourable economic conditions.

Evaluation and Conclusion

The population is a prominent element for cities both economically and socially. The cities, which showed rapid development with the industrial revolution, faced an intense migration wave and eventually faced accumulated population in the cities. On the other hand, the villages and the towns have lost their population and have become dysfunctional. This process started in Turkey in 1945 and accelerated. Migration from villages to the cities, due to unemployment as the main reason, has become a source of trouble for both sides. Hence, Bayburt, one of the most emigrant cities, shares the same destiny. It is expected that immigration, which is a case for our country, will be reversed due to the fulfilment of the transport capacities in the immigrant cities, problems created for the current population and at least some migrants being unable to find the opportunities that they are looking for. In this context, we desire to make some statements by using statistics about the research and using quantitative findings. The research was carried out in the Aydintepe district of Bayburt province on migration and remigration data.

At the end of this survey, it was understood that the subjects continued their relations with their hometown in large scale. The economic situation of the subjects is better in the new place where they migrated to in comparison with their hometown.. When the idea of remigration is asked, 45% of the subjects answered "No," 33% answered "Yes" and 22% "Partially." When the reasons for their responses are taken into account, it is understood that 28% of those who chose "Yes" and "Partially" would go back to their homeland if the homeland offered them job opportunities. It is also learned that 17% of the subjects are able to return to their homeland in retirement, while those who say "No" are desperate for the future of their homeland. This result corresponds to the meaningful relationship between job opportunities and the rate of migration (Doh, 1984: 57-60).

In short, we can summarize that remigration is a prominent alternative for the resolution of the problems experienced in the cities of our country and the tendency of remigration will be increased if the differences of development between the cities and villages are reduced and if the non-governmental and official organizations show more interest in this issue. Regional development agencies, universities, and local governments need to focus on this subject and raise awareness by supporting these studies.

References

Bayramoglu, T. & Durmaz, A. (2017). Sustainability in Economics, in E. E. Basar, & T. Bayramoglu, *Studies on Sustainability Research* (s. 75-86). Saarbrücken, Germany: Lambert Academic Publishing.

Doh, R. (1984). Inter-Provincial Migration in Turkey and its Socio-Economic Background: A Correlation Analysis". *Journal of Population Sciences*, 49-61.

Gumus, N., Ilhan, A., & Gulersor, A. (2013). An Example of Reverse Mıgratıon: Koprucuk Village (Varto-Mus / East Anatolıa). *Turkish Studies, 8*(6), 233-261.

Guresci, E. (2011). A Survey Over Emigrant to Urban from Rural: An Example, Kemalpasa-Ispir. Journal of *Adıyaman University Social Sciences Institute, 4*(7), 107-123.

Kaygalak, S. (2009). *Urban Refugees (Forced Migration and Urbanization in Neoliberalism).* Ankara: Dipnot Publishing.

Keles, R. (2008). *Urbanization Policy.* Ankara: Imge Bookstore.

Commission. (2012). *Statistical İndicators 1923-2011.* Turkish Statistical Institute (TUİK) Ankara:

Neuman, W. L. (2014). *Social Research Methods Qualitative and Quantitative Approaches* (Vol I). (S. Özge, Trans.) Ankara: Yayınodası Publishing.

Polat, T. (Winter 2016). Sustainable Urbanization Policies and Turkey. *Electronic Turkish Studies, 11*(2), 1267-1300.

Sunata, U. (2014). The Role of Social Networks on Reverse Brain Migration: Migration Experience and Perceptions of Turkish Engineer Returnees from Germany. *Turkish Psychological Articles 17*(34), 85-96.

Tekeli, I. (2008). Different Categorizations in the History of Migration in Turkey. in I. Tekeli, *Migration and Beyond* (p. 42-67). Istanbul: History Foundation and Home Publishing.

Tekeli, I. (2008). Establishing the Concept of Modernist Legitimacy in the Center of the Fast Urbanization Lived in Turkey. in I. Tekeli, *Migration and Beyond* (p. 240). Ankara: History Foundation and Home Publishing.

Tutar, H. & Ozyakısır, D. (2013). A Research on the Reasons for Migration Movements to Istanbul from TRA 2 Region. *Sociology Conferenes, 31*(58), 31-58.

THE INFORMAL ECONOMY

KÜBRA KARAKUŞ

Introduction

The concept of informal economy started to be investigated by economists and became a subject of economic studies in the 1970s. A few articles published towards the end of the 1970s attracted the attention of economists to the informal economy. The term is named as informal, underground, shadow, unrecorded, and back economy in the literature, but back economy is used most often. The first study related to informal economy was carried out by Cagan on prediction of the undeclared incomes in the United States in the years of the Second World War through monetary methods. In 1977, Guatmann applied this method to the USA economy and predicted informal national income of the USA (Ilgin, 1999).

The informal economy is a universal phenomenon in both developed and developing countries. It is known that the rate of the informal economy is around 10% in developed countries, 20-50% in developing countries and much higher in some countries, although there are different opinions about the extent of the informal economy (Aslanoglu, 2008). Taxpayers are considered as the most important actors of these activities. Therefore, the study conducted on taxpayers focuses on the reasons and the results of the activities. The increasing rates of informal economy lead to an unfair competition against formal economy while adversely affecting the tax system and leading to the reduction of sources of finance that need to be met through taxes with the purpose of financing public expenditures (Burgess & Stern, 1993).

Countries implement punishment, training, economic measures and legal proceedings to control these activities. The most important challenge in this regard is to detect who participates in these activities and how often these activities occur. Such information facilitates making effective decisions to prevent these activities (Yurdakul, 2008).

Informal economy and its components

Informal economy refers to the lack of registration of actual economic activities (Çetintaş, 2003). The definition of the informal economy varies in the literature. In general terms, "it refers to the whole income-generating economic activities which cannot be estimated by the known statistical methods used to calculate Gross National Income" (Derdiyok, 1993). Akbulak and Tahtakılıç (2003) define the informal economy as "unregistered, immeasurable, non-taxable, either legal or illegal income-generating economic activity". A variety of terms are used interchangeably with informal economy in the literature. These terms are legal-illegal, registered-unregistered, observed-non-observed, official-dark, official underground, official-secret, official-parallel, hidden-open, regular-irregular and so on (Halıcıoğlu, 1999). If the confidentiality of the activities is emphasized, the concept is referred to as the underground economy, the hidden economy, the black economy, the shadow economy, the dark economy, the gray economy and so on. If the emphasis is on the fact that the activities are carried out without the permission of the state, it is referred to as the informal economy, the unofficial economy and so on (Us, 2004).

Although it is known that the informal economy has been on the agenda since the 1970s, the first studies on this issue started in the 1940s. In 1977, Gutmann caught the attention of the scientific world with an article published on the informal economy. This concept, which was not considered an international phenomenon until the 1980s, came to the forefront at the first international conference on the informal economy in the city of Bielefeld, Germany, in 1983. The components of the informal economy can be examined under three titles:

- The semi-formal economy
- The underground economy (illegal activities)
- The unregistered economy

The semi-formal economy

This term includes activities carried out by people, the majority of whose income is unregistered although it is obtained through legal activities. People engaged in this activity are taxpayers whose income is legally unregistered and taken out of the scope of registration illegally. A taxpayer whose income is legally unregistered income was taxed in accordance with lump-sum procedure until 1999 and their income was excluded from registration. It is not possible to document the income and expenses of the taxpayers who are taxed according to the lump-sum procedure. In addition, the taxpayers, who are subject to this procedure, do not pay the tax that they have to pay and it causes the actual taxpayer to pay less by preventing the correct declaration of their income. In short, taxing according to the lump-sum procedure leads to unregistered incomes obtained from taxpayers' activities and causes disorder for the taxpayers engaged in economic activities by leaving these activities out of the scope of registration.

Due to these disruptions, taxation by the simple procedure replaced the lump-sum procedure. Taxpayers, who take their income out of the scope of registration illegally, keep their economic activities unregistered to pay less or no taxes. Although these activities can be found in every sector, the extent of such unregistered activities varies by sector. For example, doctors, lawyers, real estate agents, auto galleries, jewellery stores, hotel restaurants, buyers and sellers of agricultural products, foreign exchange bureaus, contractors, real estate leasers, project bureaus, auto spare parts sellers (Sarılı, 2002).

The underground economy (illegal activities)

Activities defined as underground or illegal activities are considered harmful or immoral by the society. These activities, which are prohibited to be conducted as registered economic activities, fall within the scope of informal activities. Moving economic activity underground implies taxable activities have moved underground which results in tax loss (Yılmaz, 1998). When these activities are detected, imprisonment and fines in the law are applied differently from the usual tax penalties. These activities can be exemplified as follows; arms, drugs, fake passports, smuggling of historical monuments, usury, human trafficking, bribery, organ trade and so on (Aydemir, 1994).

Causes of the informal economy

Causes of informal economy vary by development of countries. In developed countries, the reason for informal economy is generally considered to be taxation factors and regulations on the labour market. In developing countries, demographic factors such as population growth and urban migration, in addition to factors such as the tax and labour market, cause the unregistered economy (Aslanoglu, 2008). The most important cause of the informal economy is the increased tax burden and social security premium, increasing regulations, especially in the labour market, reducing weekly working hours and retirement at an early age. Increasing the tax burden and social security premium are the most important factors of the informal economy. As is known, taxes affect the employment of economic units and promote informal economy. Variations in labour cost in an economy lead employers to tend towards the informal economy (Öğünç & Yılmaz, 2000). Other contributing factors are financial and economic, social and political causes.

Financial and economic causes

Financial and economic factors are the basis of the agents affecting informal economy. Taxpayers conceal some of their income in order to not pay taxes, due to the erosion in purchasing power caused by inflation related to taxation of fictitious profits obtained particularly during the period of high inflation, the appearance of income high in inflation periods and extended tax bracket (Aslanoğlu & Yildiz, 2007). Agricultural and service sectors are the sectors in which unregistered activities are widespread due to the challenges in auditing. Inequality in income distribution, a large low-income group and a small middle-income group, constitutes rational for the informal economy. Economic crises and recession periods lay the ground for unregistered activities. Informal activities of workers due to the decrease in employment in times of economic recession or crisis cause informal economy as well (Isik & Acar, 2003). One of the reasons for the proliferation of unregistered economic activities is that the enterprises are composed of small and medium enterprises (SME's). In Turkey, SME's constitute 45% of the total employment and 27% of the total investments while using only 3-4% of total loans (Aydemir, 1995).

Legal Causes

The factors triggering informal economy can be exemplified as follows: frequent changes in laws; simple and descriptive legislations; punishments as ineffective deterrents; legal deficiencies; exceptions and exemptions; lack of confidence in law, technical aspects, personnel structure; and finally, insufficient auditing mechanisms (Altuğ, 2002). On the other hand, since it is not possible to detect the holder and/or bearer of payment instruments such as bearer checks, assets/bonds, notes, etc., the income obtained after the above-mentioned transactions may remain unregistered. The financial burdens imposed by legal regulations along with taxes also lead to informal activities. Legal arrangements related to labour and worker health, social security premiums and measures taken to protect the environment are cost-enhancing factors for employers and lead to the use of cheaper workforce (Us, 2004).

Social and Structural Causes

Social reasons leading taxpayers to informal activities can be cited as lack of tax morality, social value judgments, taxpayer psychology and historical reasons. The value judgments of the community are important to prevent and combat the informal economy. The most important factor preventing these activities is "Peer Pressure". To exclude unregistered income requires a normalized societal moral value which activates peer pressure against unregistered income. In this way, these activities will decrease with the impact of peer pressure. However, in places where there is no social norm to this end, the contrary effect will arise (Ülgen & Öztürk, 2007).

Positive and negative aspects of informal economy

There are positive and negative aspects of informal economy for countries. Negative aspects of informal economy are:

- Economic activities are not actually putting into practice; the tax is not paid, which consequently leads to budget deficit
- There are very few taxes paid due to the informal economy, yet the actual taxpaying moves towards the field which does not make much contribution to economic growth
- The tax burden is undertaken by the registered taxpayers solely, while those engaged in unregistered activities do not pay taxes which establishes tax injustice
- Informal economy leads to an increase in inflation and unemployment, which in turn reduces investment and production
- Unregistered activities do not take place in the calculation of national income and other statistical information, thus esteem is removed from existing economic indicators
- Informal economy reduces business scale, the number of employee's decreases, and the bargaining share of the unions is eliminated

Positive aspects of informal economy are:

- Shareholders engaging in informal economy do not pay taxes, insurance premiums, etc., thus production costs fall, leading to relatively lower selling prices. In this way, both the national and international markets are of great importance in improving the competitive power
- The informal economy contributes to increased employment
- The informal economy allows savings to turn into investments and moves growth rates upwards
- Unpaid taxes are distributed, thus production increases
- Unregistered economic activities increase employment, welfare level and income distribution.
- The income provided after the informal activities offer a fund source to the formal economy (Aslanoglu, 2008).

Measurement methods of the informal economy

It is difficult to measure growth since informal economic activities are carried out in secret. However, there are two methods to measure the extent of informal economic activities. These methods are direct (micro) and indirect (macro) methods. In indirect measurement methods, survey applications are used to estimate informal economy. These surveys include tax surveys, workplace surveys, household surveys and time-use surveys. Indirect measurement methods, on the other hand, consist of employment approach, detection of informal economy through tax audit and a monetarist approach (Us, 2004).

1. Direct (micro) methods

This method is used to measure the extent of informal economy through surveys on workplace, tax, households and so on. The information can be obtained through the most common and the most understandable method used by national statistical units. There are some disadvantages and advantages to this method. One advantage is that the most reliable information can be obtained regarding the extent of informal economy by means of the right analysis. A marked disadvantage is that individuals may not give correct answers to the questions in the survey (Sarıkaya, 2007).

2. Indirect (macro) methods

These are the most frequently used methods to measure informal economy. Indirect methods consist of measurement approach through Tax Audit, Gross National Product (GNP) Approach, Employment Approach, and Monetarist Approach.

2.1 GNP approach

The income used in the measurement of GNP refers to the uniformity of all outcomes regardless of the use of any income, production or expenditure methods. The difference between the methods used in this measurement is valuable to measure the extent of the informal economy. However, the presence of informal economy leads to systematic differences in the results obtained through different methods. Because of the challenges in obtaining relevant data regarding the income in Turkey, the GNP method which is measured by expenditures and which is measured by production is used in comparisons rather than the income method (Isik & Acar, 2003).

2.2 Measurement though tax audit

Taxpayers who are obliged to pay taxes need to declare their income to the tax office. Tax audits attempt to detect the extent of informal economy by determining the undeclared income of taxpayers. Taxpayers may show their income differently either willingly or unknowingly. In this case, if there is a deficiency in the declared income, the tax assessment differences are found. This estimation of the extent of informal economy occurs in consideration of these differences. However, the most important disadvantage of this approach is in determining the extent of untaxed economy rather than informal economy (Sarılı, 2002). It is assumed that all activities included in GNP measurements are taxed in the estimation of informal economy in the method of a tax audit. However, even if some activities are not taxed, they might still be included in national income. Although taxation is compulsory, there might be transactions excluded from tax. Therefore, there are two types of informality that cause tax loss and evasion. The first one is the tax losses which result from activities permitted to be kept unregistered with the law: in other words, tax losses related to exceptions and exemptions. The second is the informal economy created through tax loss and evasion which result from voluntary informal activities although the registration is necessary: in other words, in this case, the informal economy is created to pay no more or less tax.

2.3 The employment approaches

This approach is based on the estimation of the extent of informal economy depending on the changes in population, supply of civilian labour, and employment by time. To this end, it is assumed that informal activities are not carried out in the economy and the same developments are expected in the ratio of civilian labour force supply to total population and of employment to total population over time. Otherwise, in the case of unregistered employment, the ratio of civilian labour force to total population remains at a certain level while the ratio of employment to the total population decreases. In this approach, when informal activities are examined, unregistered activities are classified as totally unregistered and partially registered activities.

Totally unregistered

These activities are divided into two; being legal and illegal. Illegal economic activities take place within the scope of a crime, so it is considered that these activities should not be taken into consideration while detecting the value of the prohibited economic activity with the purpose of measuring the extent of unregistered activities. Legal Economic Activities are the activities that are hidden from official authorities and cause unregistered employment, as well as those activities that are taken out of the registry in the case where compulsory legal requirements related to business life are not fulfilled, despite being legal. In unregistered employment, regulations regarding aids such as annual leave, minimum wage, working hours, old age, death pension, disability etc., and labour safety and health, working conditions and age are not followed. There can also be activities aiming to create employment and obtain income which arise as a result of unemployment and economic inadequacies despite being in compliance with the legislation in question.

Partially registered

These activities are unregistered activities conducted during the establishment of the business or during the operation of the business. From the perspective of employees, there are two forms of informality in terms of either premiums or incomes. Underreporting regarding premiums is the fact that the actual number of days paid to the institution is not real, despite the social security of workers or employers. The informal economy which occurs as a result of the incomplete reporting related to income and wages refers to the fact that the obtained income is not fully reflected in official records. Therefore, tax, social cuts and the main premium that should be taken based on the difference between the realized income and recorded income indicate the loss of the state (Us, 2004).

2.4 Monetarist approach

It is the approach that measures the extent of informal economy through monetary data. The monetarist method is divided into three categories being: processor method, fixed rate and econometric methods.

2.4.1 Fixed rate method

This method, also called emission volume approach, refers to the fact payments to be made for hidden economic activities will mostly be made in cash. When the amount of money used in registered and unregistered economic activities is equal to the emission volume, which is the volume of money in circulation; and the ratio of the emission volume of total deposits increases on condition that the circulation rate of the money is constant; it means that informal economic activities will also increase (Cagan, 1958). In this method, one year is basically considered as the year when no informal economic activities have been carried out. However, there is no other objective option, the method is to select the year when the rate of current deposit (C / D) of the circulating money is the smallest in order to reach meaningful results. In summary, a period is selected assuming that there has been no unregistered activity in the economy and it is estimated that the deposit rate of money in circulation is constant over time (Isik & Acar, 2003).

2.4.2 Processor method

This approach is explained taking stand from Fisher's Quantity Theory. To this end, the following abbreviations are used: M for money supply, V for circulation rate of money, P for the general level of prices and T for transaction volume.

$$MV=PT$$

According to the above-mentioned equation, the value of total goods and services produced in a country is equal to multiplication of the money supply with circulation rate. Since V and T are fixed in the short-term, a change in the money supply is equal to the general level of prices (Feige, 1979).

2.4.3 The econometric approach

Cash demand is estimated by econometric methods according to some determinative factors. Assumptions are made taking stand from the results obtained and these assumptions are used in the estimation of the informal economy. In unregistered economic activities, it is assumed that payment instrument is cash money and that the rate of money circulation is the same both in the formal and informal economies. In this method, high tax rates are the most important reason for informal economy while cash demand is measured separately when the tax is applied and not applied. The difference between the figures obtained indicates the cash level of the informal economy (Akbulak & Tahtakılıç, 2003).

Recommendations to prevent informal economy

The first precautions to be taken combating the informal economy should be determined and put into practice. The fundamental precautions to be taken in preventing the informal economy are as follows: policies to combat the informal economy must be defined as state policies; they should be long-term and effective policies. A wide range of actions to prevent these activities is given under the following headings.

Economic precautions

Improving tax compliance of taxpayers is the initial financial precaution to be taken. Therefore, regulations must be made on tax policies. The following regulations must be made regarding taxes:

Reconsideration of tax policies

As a principle, taxation must be impartial. The tax structure must include changes. Intervention to economy through tax should be minimized. Instead of increasing the tax burden of taxpayers, the option of optimal tax burden should be included. Taxation should be carried out in accordance with both the principle of tax justice and impartiality (Gökbunar, 1997).

Fair distribution of tax and reduction of tax burden

At the beginning, tax rates and social security cuts should be reduced to a great extent while some taxes and fees that cause unregistered taxes (such as stamp tax and title/deed fees) should be removed altogether. Although the public revenues are believed to be reduced with these practices, income item will increase in the case that the tax spreads to the ground in the medium term. Since, these policies must be included to prevent unregistered activities which result from the current conditions (Ekesan, 2006). The tax burden injustice among some sections should be removed without causing unregistered activities and the tax burden of the employees should be reduced to decrease the tax cut on employment (Ilgın, 2002).

Changing the normality of tax amnesty

Tax amnesty, which damages the principle of certainty and justice and is carried out by state, adversely affects taxpayer's tax consciousness. Constant repetition of this amnesty practice puts taxpayers in the expectation of amnesty and increases their tendencies to take risks. On the other hand, it adversely affects the tax consciousness of taxpayers who pay tax regularly. Not only do taxpayers suffer from this situation, but also tax offices make great efforts to investigate, identify and collect unpaid taxes. More rigorous precautions should be taken on tax amnesty in order to prevent unregistered activities (Karatay, 2009).

Precautions regarding tax legislation

Tax legislation should be amendable when there is a problem about taxation. During the amendment, the following issues should not generally be taken into consideration: whether there are provisions in the existing law related the amendment in question or not; whether or not there are regulations to solve the problem in different branches of law as a whole and within a system without paying much attention to theoretical parts such as public law / private law or individual law branches; whether the existing laws in various branches of law, that can systematically solve the problem are used effectively or not. It is thought that these deficiencies will be remedied with the new legal regulations (Doğrusöz, 2004).

Taking control of tax exceptions, exemptions and incentives

Exceptions and exemptions in the taxation system have very different structures. These cases cause bureaucratic procedures and lead enterprises which cannot benefit from these means to get into unregistered activities. Enterprises that cannot benefit from exceptions and exemptions are at a disadvantaged position compared to others. In this case, tax evasion occurs for businesses and taxpayers. The businesses that will get tax discounts have to pass a certain amount of investment. This will result in higher tax burdens for businesses that cannot reach the certain amount. As incentives, exceptions and exemptions increase the imbalance between businesses in the market, and they will also cause holdings which have a wide activity area in the market to emerge. For this reason, these applications should be excluded from tax laws since they have a negative effect (Karatay, 2009).

Regulation of tax audits

The main cause of the rise and enlargement of informal economy is the audit of the tax authorities. In addition to insufficiency of tax audits, these audits are conducted on registered taxpayers while unregistered taxpayers are excluded from the audits. Coordination should be ensured between institutions in taxation with tax audit, regulations should be made regarding electronic commerce and document management should be done in compliance with the commercial law (Sugözü, 2008).

The agricultural sector must be taxed in the real sense

Agricultural as a sector is difficult to control due to its structural characteristics. Therefore, it is the sector with the highest number of unregistered activities. Taxation should be implemented to prevent these unregistered activities (Bicer, 2006).

Legal and administrative precautions

One of the things that must be done at the beginning in combating with informal economy is to solve the problem of legislation. Legal deficiencies leading to informal economy need to be carefully resolved. Unregistered activities should be clearly defined in terms of legislation and criminal sanctions to be applied should be detected. Legal and administrative precautions to be taken are as follows: efficiency should be ensured in the implementation of tax identification number, inter-agency coordination should be ensured, revenue administration should be reconstructed, powers and responsibilities of public accountants and certified public accountants should be increased, legal arrangements should be made related to electronic commerce, strategies of transition to formal economy should be prepared and applied in a dynamic framework (Tunç, 2015).

Conclusion

The most general definition of informal economy is the economic activities which are not included in GDP. It is one of the most important problems of developed and developing countries. The causes of informal economy are economic, social and legal. Additional reasons include crises, instability in the economy, inflation, excessive tax burden, and immigration. There is no consensus that informal economy has a positive or negative effect on a country's economy. It can be said that it has positive and negative effects on countries based on the developed or developing country status of the given country. There are indirect and direct methods to measure informal economy. Countries aim to minimize the negative effects of informal economy by implementing policies towards preventing unregistered activities.

References

Akbulak, Y. & Tahtakılıc, A. K. (2003). Thoughts on the Unregistered Economy, Journal of *Bank-Fiscal and Economic Comment, 468,* 17-41

Altuğ, O. (2012). Unregistered Economic Development Model and Fiscal B.C. Application, Retrieved from
www.aso.org.tr/asomedya/mart2002-ft.html#forum.

Aslanoğlu, S. & Yıldız, S. (2007). Shadow Economy and a Suggestion to Reduce the Shadow Economy in Turkey; Making an Efficient Auditing System by Using Ratio Analysis, Journal of *Socio-Economics,* 6(6),128- 146

Aslanoğlu, S. (2008). Unregistered Economy and Recommendations to Reduce the Unregistered Economy in Turkey, Journal of Accounting and Finance, 39, 199- 211

Aydemir, Ş. (1994). KOBİ'ler ve Kayıt Dışı Ekonomi, Türkiye Orta ölçekli işletmeler, Serbest Meslek Mensupları ve Yöneticiler Vakfı, Ankara.

Aydemir, Ş. (1995a). On the Unregistered Economy(I), Journal of Tax World, 161,72-86.

Biçer, Y. (2006). In Turkey Oriented to Prevent the Black Economy Tax Policies and Evaluation, Süleyman Demirel University, Master Thesis for the Department of Public Finance

Burgess, R. & S. Nicholas (1993). Taxation and Development, *Journal of Economic Literature*, 31, 762-830

Cagan, P. (1958). The Demand for Currency Relative to the Total Money Supply, *Journal of Political Economy,* vol 66, 303-328

Çetintaş, H. & H. Vergil (2003). Estimation of Underground Economy in Turkey, Journal of *Doğuş Üniversity*, 4(l), 15-30

Derdiyok, T. (1993). Estimation of Turkey's Informal Economy, *Journal's Economic of Turkey*, 5(14), 54–63

Doğrusöz, A. B. (2004). Kayıt Dışı Ekonomi ile Mücadele Açısından Vergi Hukuku Özel Hukuk İlişkilerine Bakış, *19. Türkiye Maliye Sempozyumu*, Antalya, 10-14 Mayıs, 158-176

Ekesan, N. (2006). *Kayıtdışı ekonomi, nereye kadar? Dış Ticarette Durum*, T.C Başbakanlık Devlet Arşivleri Genel Müdürlüğü Dökümantasyon Daire Başkanlığı Enformasyon Bülteni, Sayı:103, 70-73

Feige, E. L. (1979). *How Big is the Irregular Economy?* Journal Cahllenge, 22, 5-13

Gökbunar, A. R. (1997). Turkish Tax System Reform Reguirement, Prof. Dr. Nazif SÖNMEZ'e Armağan, Journal of Dokuz *Eylül University Faculty of Economics and Administrative Sciences*, 301-324.

Halicioglu, F. (1999). The Black Economy in Turkey: An Empirical Investigation, *The Review of Political Sciences of Ankara University,* Vol 53, 175-191

Işık, A. & Acar, M. (2001). Unregistered Economy: An Assessment on Measurement Methods, Dimension Benefits and Losses, Journal of Erciyes *University Faculty of Economics and Administrative Sciences*, 21, 117-136

Karatay, Ö. (2009). Unregistered Economy in The Country Economic Impacts and Social Cost Cumhuriyet of University Social Sciences Institute Master's Thesis.

Öğünç, F. & Yılmaz, G. (2000). Estimating the underground Economy ın Turkey, *The Central Bank of The Republıc of Turkey, Research Department Discussion Paper.*

Sarıkaya, H. E. (2007). Influence of Underground Economic Growth Example of Turkey (1980-2005). Selçuk of University Social Sciences Institute Master's Thesis

Sarılı, M. A. (2002). Dimensions of Unregistered Economy in Turkey, Causes, Effects and Measures to be Taken. Journal of Bankers, 41, 32–50

Sugözü, G. H. (2008). Taxation Policies in Struggling with the Underground Economy (1980-2004 Turkish Case). Selçuk of University Social Sciences Institute Doctorate thesis

Tunç, E. (2015). Combanting Informal Economy and The Case of Turkey, Adnan Menderes of University Social Sciences Institute Master's Thesis.

Us, V. (2004). Unregistered Economy Estimation Method Suggestion: Turkey Example, Discussion Paper, Turkish Economic Association, No. 2004/17

Ülgen, S. & Öztürk, U. (2007), Unofficial Economy, Turkey Adventure, Deloitte Publication.

Yılmaz, G. (1998). Approaches to Tax Loss Account Created by Underground Economy and Tax Loss Created by Underground Economy in Turkey, Journal of Marmara *University Faculty of Economics and Administrative Sciences Special Issue*, Prof. Dr. Halil Nadaroğlu'na Armağan, XIV,1, 483-500.

Yılmaz, I. (2002). Unregistered Economic Forecasting Methods and Situation İn Turkey, *Journal of Planning, 42 Special Issue*, DPT Publication.

Yurdakul, F. (2008). Unregistered Economy in Turkey: Formulating a Model, Journal of Ankara *University* Social Science Faculty, 6(34), 205-221

ENTREPRENEUR LEADERSHIP AND NEW PRODUCT DEVELOPMENT SUCCESS

ZELİHA TEKİN

Introduction

The innovative products that are submitted to market for the first time and the ones that change the existing products in certain ways count as new products. The process of developing new products requires people, who are ready to take risks, run and evaluate the development process, and act like a product manager. This is why an entrepreneur is a person who can expand the existing markets for a company and enter new ones through new products. Entrepreneurs with a leading spirit play important roles in the success of companies through making innovations, both in terms of products and ideas, to find gaps in the markets. The leading behaviour of an entrepreneur shapes his/her effectiveness as a leader and the success of the company. The innovative and entrepreneurial leader is the one who submits new products to the markets, utilizes new production techniques, discovers new markets as well as raw materials (Gerber, 1996) and takes initiative with creative ideas and a visionary spirit rather than following the competitors (İraz, 2010).

Entrepreneurship

One of the most commonly accepted definitions of "entrepreneurship" was proposed by Richard Cantillon in 1755 which links the concept to risk-taking. In this definition, an entrepreneur is the one who organizes the business for profit and takes risk to this end. Entrepreneurship is the process of creating unlimited assets in order to utilize opportunities (Morris et al., 1994). In the process of creating assets new information is generated and new opportunities are discovered or crafted from the very beginning (Hisrich & Peters, 2002). Entrepreneurship is creating access to new resources and combinations under the conditions of uncertainty and risk in order to actualize the targets of the businesses and exploit the opportunities in a proactive manner (Gupta et al., 2004). In brief, an entrepreneur is the person who establishes a new business or company to make profit in the existence of risk and uncertainty and combines resources to put together the necessary capital (Zimmerer & Scarborough, 1998).

Entrepreneurial personality traits and entrepreneurial leadership

What differentiate entrepreneurs from other people is certain personality traits. A research has been conducted in this field to bring some of these traits to the foreground (Kara, 2017). Entrepreneurial personalities do not back down from failures and have self-confidence; these personality types care about their freedom. They are also innovative, creative, risk-takers who are self-motivated and make fast decisions (Akpınar, 2009). Some personality traits underlined by different writers in different articles have been pointed out in the following table:

Table 1-13. Key Features of Entrepreneurs

Date	Author	Features
1725	Cantillon	Risk taking
1848	Mill	Risk taking
1917	Weber	Being a source of formal authority
1934	Schumpeter	Innovative, initiative, accomplishment, invent new rules
1954	Sutton	Take responsibility
1959	Hartman	Being a source of formal authority
1961	McClelland	Risk taking, need for success, need for power
1963	Davids	Ambitious, desire independence, take responsibility, self-confidence
1964	Pickle	Human relationship, communication skill, having technical knowledge
1965	Litzinger	Risk taking, desire independence, recognition request, fatherly, leadership
1965	Schrage	Correct detection, power motivation
1971	Palmer	Risk measurement
1971	Hornadey ve Aboud	Need for success, autonomy, need for power, recognition

1973	*Winter*	Need for power
1973	*Hisrich ve Peters*	Leadership and management skill, creativity, being a team player, communication ability Passion for work, forward-minded, recognizing opportunities, visionary
1974	*Borland*	Internal power focus
1974	*Liles*	Need for success
1977	*Gasse*	Turning to personal values
1978	*Timmons*	Motivation / self-confidence, purposefulness, moderate risk taking, locus of control, creativity, innovative
1980	*Brockhaus*	Risk taking
1980	*Sexton*	Energetic, ambitious
1981	*Mescon-Montanari*	Need for success, desire to establish dominance, desire independence, stamina, need for control
1981	*Welsh-White*	Locus of control, take responsibility, self-confidence, risk taking
1982	*Dunkelberg-Cooper*	Prospect for growth and craftsmanship
1982	*Wesls-Young*	Locus of control, self-confidence, innovative
1990	*Gartner*	Need for success, locus of control, risk taking, tolerance for ambiguity, Type a behaviour
1992	*Herron*	Innovative
1993	*Geisler*	Innovative, risk taking
1996	*Koh*	Need for success, risk taking, tolerance for ambiguity, innovative, self-confidence, locus of control
2000	*Lambing ve Kuehl*	Be enthusiastic about setting up a business, contentious, creativity, change orientated, need for success, perfectionism
2001	*Johnson*	Visionary, risk taking, responsibility taking, recognizing opportunities, innovative, tolerance for ambiguity, leadership
2003	*Henry vd.*	Visionary leader, risk taking, communication skill

2005	*Hisrich vd.*	Creating positive value, risk taking, change orientated
2005	*Hitt vd.*	Innovative, change orientated, creativitiy, communication skill, tenacity
2008	*Linan*	Recognizing opportunities, innovative, leadership, communication skill, problem solving, new product development skill
2009	*Hebert ve Link*	Innovative, risk taking, leadership skill
2010	*Zakarevičius ve Župerka*	High emotional intelligence

Source: Compiled from Güney, S. (2015); Bozkurt et al., (2012); Crant, M. (1996); Schumpeter (1934).

A leader is a person who is primarily responsible in a company to promote a culture of entrepreneurship. In this regard, the leader must set an example and have this culture him/herself (İraz, 2010). In entrepreneurial leadership, different models like democratic, visionary, autocratic, centrist, mission oriented, charismatic, full autonomist and paternalistic might be adopted. If an entrepreneurial leader is good at creating teams, identifying opportunities in order to mobilize a company's capabilities, overcoming difficulties, and can tolerate uncertainties, build confidence in his/her followers, and create new products through an energetic attitude, he/she can rebuild the company. Such a leader would have a lot in common with team-oriented, value-oriented and transitional leaders (Gupta et al., 2004). Entrepreneurial leadership is about influencing others to utilize company's capabilities strategically in order to use the opportunities and advantages of the business, knowing that things can be done in different ways and pursuing these ways (Stolper, 1994). In entrepreneurial leadership, there is always an element of economic risk taking. While the entrepreneurial leader channels the means of production into new avenues the others follow suit and try to do the same. Three basic elements play important roles in the motivation of an entrepreneurial leader: a desire to establish his/her own realm, presence of an urge and need for war stemming from a perception of superiority, and an instinct to create something (Schumpeter, 1934).

Entrepreneurial leaders also have to be good managers. As the owner and manager of an entrepreneurial business, they carry out duties like identifying the strategies for the business, creating new products and services, as well as new means of production and distribution (Dinçer & Fidan, 2011). They must also utilize their managerial skills effectively for planning, making decisions for the company and controlling the processes of the work in order to be successful. This is why the entrepreneurial leaders must have skills in creating effective managing models, communicating, reconciling, making decisions and bearing responsibility for them, motivating and coordinating people and the organization (İnce et al., 2015).

The personal traits that any entrepreneurial leader must have are as follows (İraz, 2010):

- Supporting the entrepreneurial personalities in the team: Entrepreneurial leader should work on the skills of creativity and swiftness of human capital and managing the strategic employment of company's resources.
- Making innovations and sharing the know-how with the staff to protect the innovations: Sometimes, the staff sees the innovations that change the status quo radically as threats for themselves and the business. An effective entrepreneurial leader convinces the staff that innovations are not threats and they bring utility.
- Detecting the opportunities: An effective entrepreneurial leader must identify the benefits that the existing opportunities promise for individuals as well as the organization and share this information with the staff.
- Questioning the dominant mentality: An entrepreneurial leader has to question his/her methods of utilizing the resources of the company in order to create advantage and challenge the basic assumptions pertaining to market and industry.
- Asking the basic questions: An entrepreneurial leader must review the survival capacity, targets and successes of the business as well its relations with partners.
- Creating a link between strategic management and entrepreneurship: Effective entrepreneurial leaders believe that their companies must be "strategic entrepreneurs" in order to create more value.

New product development success

Cooper is the first researcher who conducted studies on the reasons of success and failure for new products. According to Cooper, creating a unique and high-quality product, being well-informed about the market and technical and productive competency play important roles in the success of the new product (Cooper, 1979). In the age of heavy competition, success depends on providing high quality products and services for an adequate number of customers (Bradley, 2002). Furthermore, the product must have a consistency in terms of its usefulness, physical appearance, package and name. It must have properties that would differentiate it from its competitors. A greater positive difference means better success. Because the customer compares many options and chooses the product with a distinction rather than the most fitting one for him/her-self (Yıldırım, 1998). From this perspective, the entrepreneurial leader is the one who comes up with a new product or an innovation for an existing one.

Successful entrepreneurs have developed skills on three issues: identifying the opportunities, developing them, and creating an organizational structure in order to make these opportunities into successful enterprise. The common trait for all three skills is innovation and "the ideas for a new business". The process of innovation is sometimes shaped by utilizing the existing trends and sometimes by focusing on a specific product (Büyükbalcı, 2016). Through providing different products in the new and existing markets a competitive advantage and success is attained (Leenders et al., 2003).

The Concept of new product

The name "product" has connotations in terms of physical and chemical specifications, ingredients, mechanical structure, shape, package, reliability etc. The new product, as a means of long term growth opportunity, differentiation from competitors, removal of the inability to sell and competitive advantage for the companies come about in four different ways (Dinçer & Fidan: 2011):

- Unique and pioneering products (cell phone, microwave oven etc.),
- Products that replace the existing ones in the market with better features (fax machine replacing telex and e-mail replacing fax machine),
- Replacing the existing models with new models of the same product (cars etc.),
- Products that are known in the market but are new to producing companies. (Cola Turka entering the market as an alternative for Coca Cola)

New products do not only bring an advantage of distinction to the producing company but also provide sustainable growth and bigger profit margins. Furthermore, removing the dependency on a single product reduces the risk of failure. They also increase the efficiency of the distribution channels and bring competitive advantage using new technologies (Evans & Berman, 1992).

The process of developing new products

Kotler and Armstrong (2012) define the development of new products in 8 phases.

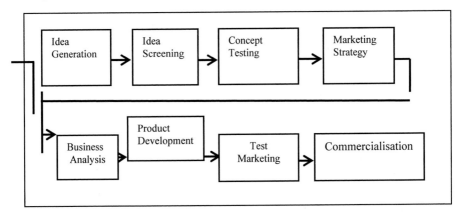

Figure 1-1. New Product Development Steps
Source: Kotler, P., Armstrong, G. (2012) Principles of Marketing, England: Pearson Education Limited, p. 285

At the end of a lengthy process, an entrepreneurial project leader can make sure that the process is run well at the final step which is commercialization. The leader must make careful planning, utilize skills and resources efficiently and make the right decision about the timing of entering the market for the process to be successful (Kılıç, 2016).

Management and success of developing new products

There are five criteria for success with new products: they must create utility, be unique, timely, and sustainable in the market, and reach customers easily, that is to say be marketable (Doyle, 2008). Businesses can implement the right models that would bring success, make the right decisions and decrease the risk that is brought on by uncertainty in the market. Rosenau and Moran (1993), proposed that implementation of methods like, quality management, market change rate, and cross-functional teamwork would bring success for a new product. Companies utilize cross-functional teams mostly because of their intellectual capital which brings advantage in terms of decision making and problem solving. These teams also perform well in executing multidimensional complex tasks (Reus & Liu, 2004). Bowen et al., (1994) mention seven factors which shape the success of the new product: the vision of the company shared by the team members, evaluating the project in systemic approaches, the pace of learning for the company, the capacity to correct mistakes, team spirit stemming from an existing feeling of belonging and responsibility, utilization of the skills and capacities of the company, the capacity to take the next steps, and the character of the organization and entrepreneurial project leader. The entrepreneurial project leader must employ the resources of the company in efficient and effective ways. Efficiency and effectiveness are the golden keys for success in developing the new product. Effectiveness is about responding to the demands of the customers in proper ways (actualizing the ideal capacity) while the efficiency is about creating the new product with minimal costs through wise decisions (Baker and Sinkula, 2005). An effective manager must be able to increase the quality of the input to get the desired output. In short, the support and sensitivity of the management is a common factor in the success of a product (Chorda et al. (2002); Varela and Benito (2004); Perreault (2013)). According to Freeman and Soete (2003), what singlehandedly determines the success of a new product understands the needs of the customer. Designing new products and their process of development well enough to respond to special demands of the future customers depend on understanding the markets today. The role of the entrepreneur here is bringing together technology with the market. In other words, his/her role is to understand the needs of the customers better than the competitors and finding resources to enter the market. New ideas and projects do not evolve into innovation and competitive advantage without entrepreneurship. Innovation creates value when it comes together with entrepreneurship. One fourth of the overall difference between slow and fast-growing markets in the world stems from entrepreneurship (Elçi, 2006).

Conclusion

The process of developing a new product is a complex and difficult one. Successful entrepreneurial leaders can contribute to the formation of innovative culture through motivating their personnel in order to utilize their personal skills and work in a determined and systematic manner.

Being a key figure in the process of creating the idea of a new product and sharing the idea with the team members, the entrepreneurial leader plays an important role in motivating the team members through his/her access to human resources and the budget. The leadership attitude adopted by the entrepreneur shapes his/her effectiveness as well as the success of the company. An entrepreneurial leader will be successful with a new product through employing new technologies without ignoring that both the sector and the market constantly change, utilizing his/her knowledge in the market and following the preference and demands of the customers.

References

Akpınar, S. (2009). *Girişimciliğin Temel Bilgileri*, Kocaeli: Umuttepe Publications

Baker, W. E. & Sinkula, J. M. (2005). Market Orientation and The New Product Paradox, *Journal of Product Innovation Management*, 22, 483-502

Bowen, H. K., Clark, K. B., Holloway, C. A. & Kent, H. (1994). *The Perpetual Enterprise Machine: Seven Keys to Corporate Renewal Through Successful Product and Process Development*, New York: Oxford University Press

Bozkurt, Ç., Kalkan, A., Koyuncu, O. & Alparslan, M. A. (2012). The Development of Entrepreneurship in Turkey: A Qualitative Research on Entrepreneurs, *Journal of Süleyman Demirel University Institute of Social Sciences*, 8 (15), 229-247, Retrieved from http://edergi.sdu.edu.tr/index.php/sbed/article/view/3355

Bradley, F. (2002). *International Marketing Strategy*, İçlem Er (Trans.). İstanbul:Bilim Teknik Publications

Büyükbalcı, P., Can, E., Bal, Y. & Ertemir, E. (2016). *Günümüz İşletmelerinin Yönetimi*, İstanbul: Beta Publications

Chorda, M. I., Gunasekaran, A. & Aramburo L. B. (2002). Product Development Process in Spanish SMES: An Empirical Research *Technovation*, 22 (5), 301–312

Cooper, R. G. (1979). The Dimensions of Industrial New Product Success and Failure, *Journal of Marketing*, 43, 93-103

Crant, M. (1996). The Proactive Personality Scale as a Predictor of *Entrepreneurial Intentions, Journal of Small Business Management*, 34 (3), 42-49

Dinçer, Ö. & Fidan, Y. (2011). *İşletme Yönetimine Giriş, İstanbul: Alfa Publications*

Doyle, P. (2008). *Value- Based Marketing: Marketing Strategies for Corporate Growth and Shareholder Value*, Chichester, England:Wiley Publication

Elçi, Ş. (2006). *İnovasyon- Kalkınmanın ve Rekabetin Anahtarı*, Ankara: Nova Publications

Evans, J. R. & Berman, B. (1992). *Marketing*, 5th Edition USA: MacMillan Publishing Company

Freeman, C. & Soete, L. (2003). *The Economics of Industrial Innovation*, Ergun Türkcan (Trans). Ankara: TÜBİTAK Publications

Gerber, N. E. (1996). *The E-Myth Revisited*, Tayfur Keskin (Trans.), İstanbul: Sistem Publications

Gupta, V., Macmillan, I. C. & Surie, G. (2004). Entrepreneurial Leadership: Developing and Measuring A Cross-Cultural Construct, *Journal of Business Venturing*, 19(2), 241-260

Güney, S. (2015). *Girişimcilik: Temel Kavramlar ve Bazı Güncel Konular*, Ankara: Siyasal Publications

Hisrich, D. R. & Peters, P. M. (2002). *Entrepreneurship*, USA: Mc. Graw-Hill Irwin

İnce, A. R., Erdem, H., Deniz, M. & Bağlar, M. (2015). Investigating The Relationship Beyween Entrepreneurial Personality Traits and Entrepreneurship Skills Through Potantial Entrepreneur Candidates, *The Journal of Academic Social Science Studies*, 41, 399-416, Retrieved from Doi number:http://dx.doi.org/10.9761/JASSS3182

İraz, R. (2010). *Yaratıcılık ve Yenilik Bağlamında Girişimcilik ve Kobiler*, Konya: Çizgi Kitabevi

Kara, Y. (2017). Eğitimde sınırsız araştırma ve bilimsel yöntem. *Sınırsız Eğitim ve Araştırma Dergisi*, 2 (1), 35-47.

Kılıç, S. (2016). *Yeni Ürün Geliştirmede İnovasyon: Yeni Ürün İnovasyonu*, Ankara: Seçkin Publications

Kotler, P. & Armstrong, G. (2012). *Principles of Marketing*, England: Pearson Education Limited

Leenders, R. T. A. J., Engelen, J. M. L. & Kratzer, J. (2003). Virtuality, Communication, and New Product Team Creativity: A Social Network Perspective, *Journal of Engineering and Technology Management*, 20, 69-92

Linan, F. (2008). Skill and Value Perceptions: How Do They Affect Entrepreneurial Intentions? *International Entrepreneurship and Management Journal*, 4(3), 257-272

Morris, M. H., Davis, D. L. & Allen, J. W. (1994). Fostering Corporate Entrepreneurship: Cross-Cultural Comparisons of the Importance of

Individualism Versus Collectivism. *Journal of International Business Studies*, 25 (1), 65-89.

Perreault, W., D., Cannon, J. P. & McCarthy, E. J. (2013). *Essentials of Marketing*, Trans. Ed: Asım Günal Önce, Ankara: Nobel Publications, New York: McGraw Hill & Irwin

Reus, T. H. & Liu, Y. (2004). Rhyme and Reason: Emotional Capability and The Performance of Knowledge-Intensive Work Groups, *Human Performance*, 17, 245–266

Rosenau, M. D. & Moran, J. J. (1993). *Managing the Development of New Products: Achieving Speed and Quality Simultaneously Through Multifunctional Teamwork*, Van Nostrand Reinhold, New York

Schumpeter, J. A. (1934). *The Theory of Economics Development*, Oxford, UK: Oxford University Press

Stolper, W. F. (1994). *Joseph Alois Schumpeter: The Public Life of a Private Man*, New Jersey, USA: Princeton University Press

Varela, J. & Benito, L. (2004). New Product Development Process in Spanish Firms: Typology, Antecedents and Technical/Marketing Activities, *Technovation*, 25(4), 395-405

Yıldırım, R. (1998). *Yaratıcılık* ve Yenilik, İstanbul: Sistem Publications

Zimmerer, T. W. & Norman, M. (1998). Essentials of Entrepreneurship and Small Business Management, Second Edition, New Jersey: Prentice Hall, Inc.

Socio-Economic Determinants of Health

Neda Hashemi Khosroshahi

Introduction

Health is the main source of life and an essential need of the individual. Without health, wealth or belongings of the individual do not matter. There are many definitions in relation to the concept of health. Health is directly in interaction with various factors. However, the definition of health which is accepted worldwide was made by the World Health Organization (WHO). In the text accepted by the World Health Organization in 1948, health is defined as follows: *"Health is a state of complete physical, mental and social well-being and not merely the absence of disease or infirmity"*.

Healthcare services concern the entire population in a country. In the case of certain contagious diseases, all related countries are included within the scope of such concern. It is not certain when and where a need for healthcare services may occur. Similarly, the costs for treatment of a disease cannot be predicted. Healthcare services are not deferrable. Deferring such services would cause higher risks. Finally, healthcare services are services with great external benefits. For that reason, presenting the socioeconomic determinants of healthcare services is of great importance.

Factors of health

The factors of health are generally addressed within 3 groups:

a. Surveillance

Surveillance is an important factor of health and it is the study of obtaining and evaluating information regarding the contagious disease incidents reported by countries or various units and disclosing such information to the public. Surveillance of contagious diseases on the international level is also addressed as public property since it has full public properties (Zacher, 1999: p.268).

b. Control and prevention

Control can be briefly expressed as preventing, when noticed, the spread of incidents such as contagious diseases. Control and elimination practices are two phenomena which are intertwined and complementary most of the time. From a humane perspective, the importance of control and prevention practices is clearly visible.

c. Information

By means of information and technology, significant advantages were obtained in healthcare services in terms of both competition and efficiency. Considering the investments of developed and developing countries in recent years, the share of healthcare expenditures among these investments has increased. It is seen that a significant portion of these expenditures is used within the scope of information and technology.

Classification of healthcare services

Healthcare services are classified as general protective healthcare services, therapeutic healthcare services and rehabilitative (recuperative) healthcare services.

a- Protective healthcare services

It includes all kinds of measures and efforts taken before the disease occurs. For that reason, it is a healthcare service with social benefits higher than special benefits. Examples of protective healthcare services may include services such as maternal and paediatric health, family planning, vaccination of groups susceptible to diseases, balanced diet and food control. Another protective healthcare service is eliminating the factors which affect the environmental health negatively and creating a healthy environment. Vaccination, adjusting nutrition, controlling excessive fertility, personal hygiene and health education services are also among important services.

b- Therapeutic healthcare services

It forms an upper level of protective healthcare services and contains more special benefit compared to the protective healthcare services on the lower level. These are the services which include the diagnosis-treatment process of the disease after the occurrence of the disease or symptoms.

c- Rehabilitation services

Rehabilitation services include the elimination of restrictive conditions that prevent using the body's organs effectively such as accidents and mental disorders. The purpose of these services is to adapt the individuals who have such restrictions to life with their current status and reduce the pain they and their families suffer (Hayran & Sur, 2005, p.67).

Medical Rehabilitation Services include various medical services (prosthesis, strengthening, etc.) implemented to reduce the dependency of individuals, who have lost a part of their organs due to diseases or accidents, on other people in relation to their vital necessities. Social and occupational rehabilitation services refer to all kinds of services which improve the occupational skills of people who have lost or cannot fulfil their occupational abilities due to physical or mental disorders and who have been alienated from society due to their disabilities. The goal is to be enabling them to have a job and exist in society as an individual with the purpose of adapting to social life.

Socioeconomic factors which affect health

Apart from genetic and environmental factors and nutrition, human health is affected by various social and economic factors. It is seen that studies are carried out in different disciplines on this topic. There are numerous studies carried out in various disciplines such as medicine, sociology, psychology, education and economics.

a- Education and health

Studies which address the different variables regarding the impact of education on health stand out in the literature. Most of the studies have used national statistics and the data obtained from survey studies. While some studies appointed health indicators such as mortality and number of applications to healthcare units as direct variables, some studies addressed variables that affect health negatively such as smoking and drug abuse as health indicators.

In her study, Silles (2009) investigated whether there is causality between the amendments in compulsory education laws in England and the health indicators. In the conclusions of the study, it was concluded that there is a casual relationship between the academic year and health indicators. Fonseca and Zheng (2013) have investigated the casual relationship between education and health indicators for 13 OECD member states over 50 years old. In the estimation results obtained with the data collected based on the survey study, the prevalence of diabetes and hypertension decreases as the number of education years increases. Vogl (2012) has investigated the relation between education and health in developing countries. Various discussions in the literature were included in the study. In the conclusions section of the study, it was suggested that education is one of the several factors which are effective in leading a healthy life for individuals. Huang (2016) has investigated the impacts of the compulsory education laws on health in China using temporal and geographical differences. According to the estimation results, education has positive effects on health by reducing the smoking rates significantly and increasing cognitive abilities. Similar results were also obtained in different studies (Winkleby et al. 1992, Arendt 2005, Knesebeck et al. 2006, Walque 2007, Heckman et al. 2010).

In some studies, mixed results were obtained in relation to the impact of education on health. Kemptner et al. (2011) have investigated the relations between education duration and various health indicators in their study on Germany. According to the results of the study, the susceptibility of men to have long term diseases decreases as the duration of education increases. However, this result could not be obtained for women. The impact of education duration on weight gain and smoking is weak. Clark & Royer (2010) suggested that education has a quite limited impact on health indicators in their study which addresses the relations between adult health and mortality in England and education. Mazumder (2008) has investigated the impact of compulsory education laws on long term health indicators of society. According to the results of the study which was conducted for the USA, the changes in compulsory education laws do not have a significant impact on mortality in the long term. Moreover, the changes in the compulsory education laws are correlated only to diabetes among various health indicators that were addressed and they have an impact in reducing diabetes. Groot and Brink (2007) used the survey data in their study on the Netherlands and addressed various medical problems, primarily diabetes that people experienced as health indicators. In the study, the education indicator was the number of education years. According to the estimation results, the increase in education years has a significant impact on improving health indicators. Park and Kang (2008) used the health statistics on adult males in their study on South Korea. In the study, health indicators were regular exercising, regular check-ups and smoking and drinking alcohol. In the results of the study, the tendency towards regular exercising and regular check-ups increases as the education level increases. However, education level does not have a significant impact on smoking and drinking alcohol. Webbink et al. (2010) used the survey study data in their study on Australia. The aim of the study was to investigate the impact of education on weight gain and obesity. The results of the study suggested different results for men and women. According to this, gaining excessive weight and obesity decreases in men as the education level increases. However, no evidence was found that education has a significant impact on gaining weight and obesity. In a study conducted by Tenn et al. (2010) on the USA, national health and tobacco statistics were used. The impacts of education on smoking were investigated in the study. According to the results of the study, no results were found indicating that education duration reduces smoking. In the study conducted by Lange (2011), the data obtained from a survey conducted every year in the USA were used. The aim of the study was to reveal whether well-educated individuals make more conscious decisions. In the study, it was concluded that educated individuals make more cooperation to reduce the personal cancer risks when they are informed about such risks. Again, educated individuals are more interested in activities such as cancer scanning. Maralani (2014) has used the data obtained from a field study conducted on genes in North Carolina State of the USA. According to the results of the study, the education policies implemented by schools and the friendships among young people have impacts on smoking behaviour. However, it was suggested that education inequalities have more impact on smoking behaviour rather than the impact of education on this behaviour. Another conclusion of the study was that the desire to have university education does not have a significant impact on smoking.

b- Income and health

The impacts of income on the health of an individual and society have been one of the topics discussed in the literature especially for the last 40 years. When discussing the impact of income on health, it is seen that the impacts of income variations are investigated first. In these studies, it was suggested that it becomes easier to access various goods and services related to health as income increases and it becomes more difficult as income decreases. Studies conducted in later stages have claimed that "relative income" is important rather than the increase in income. In other words, the relative deprivations, relative incomes and relative social statuses of the people in a society are important (Wagstaff & Doorslaer, 2000: p.543).

Preston (1975) has investigated the per capita income and life expectancy relation among countries for three time periods in the 20th century (1900, 1930 and 1960) and found that life expectancy increases as the per capita income increases. Similar results were also obtained by Rodgers (1979), Prichett and Summers (1996), Jen et al., (2009), Nilsson and Bergh (2012) and Edvinsson et al., (2013).

The later studies in which income distribution is prioritized rather than income stand out. Studies conducted in the 1970s addressed the relations between income inequality on population level and health indicators using the Gini coefficient. Recently, the data of various field studies conducted in countries and the number of studies conducted have increased. There are various studies in the literature indicating that income inequality affects health negatively.

Holcman et al. (2004) indicate that infant deaths concentrate around childbirth and the first week in poor populations. In the study conducted using the data of OECD countries, Wilkinson (1992) has found income inequality to be a strong explanation of the health differences among developed countries, not per capita income. In a study conducted for 47 countries, Flegg (1982) has concluded that the increase in income inequalities increases the deaths during childbirth. Leigh and Jencks (2007) have found that mortality rates decrease with increasing per capita income. Similar results were also obtained by Kaplan et al., (1998), Fiscella and Franks (2000), Deaton (2001), Lorgelly & Lindley (2005) and Edvinsson et al., (2013). However, Jen et al., (2009), Undurraga et al (2016) and Bakkeli (2016) have concluded that income inequality does not have a significant impact on individuals' susceptibility to health problems. Bozma et al. (2017) have obtained mixed results in their study and concluded that there is a negative correlation between the income distribution inequality and life expectancy for OECD countries and there is a positive correlation between the income distribution inequality and life expectancy for non-OECD countries.

c- Unemployment and health

According to this opinion, unemployed people are more likely to have deteriorated health. The impact of unemployment on health may occur as physical discomforts and psychological discomforts. Both health variables were emphasised in the literature, but psychological impacts were more prioritized.

In many studies on psychological hazards, it is suggested that the following problems may occur in the individuals who lost their jobs. Unemployed people lose their confidence, their satisfaction from life is reduced and depressive emotions and stress levels increase (Prussia et al., 1993).

Beland et al. (2002) have presented that the negative impact of unemployment on health is statistically significant. Karsten and Moser (2009) have reviewed the impact of unemployment on psychological health by addressing 237 cross section studies and 87 spatial studies with meta-analytic methods. Studies indicate that unemployed people have more psychological problems than employed people. According to the results of the study conducted by Schmitz (2011), unemployment causes negative impacts on health indicators. Marcus (2013) has concluded that the psychological impact of unemployment also affects the spouses of unemployed people negatively to the same extent.

d- Social Networks and social supports

Social networks refer to the social relationships and connections that surround an individual. People with strong social networks obtain better health aids and medical care by means of accessing new social relations and obtaining services and advice. Some social networks may offer better services to their members independently from professional healthcare services by providing financial and moral aids and other direct benefits. This may be effective on the individual's health. In social networks, group control and peer pressure may cause that individuals in a network to act like other members. For that reason, health values of the individuals, who communicate with groups which smoke or drink alcohol or on the contrary groups which care about their health, may be affected by the group behaviour. People who lack social connections are under stress because of not being able to make friends, feel the sense of belonging, obtain physical and mental care opportunities and have deficiencies in terms of feeling valuable.

Berkman & Syme (1979) have used marital status, connections with close friends / relatives, group memberships and church attendance as social integration variables. In the results of the study, it was concluded that improvements in social integration variables reduce mortality rates. Kawachi et al. (1996) have concluded that social integration reduces mortality rates by decreasing cardiovascular diseases, accidents and suicides. Similar results were also obtained by House et al. (1982), Welin et al. (1982) and Orth-Gomer & Johnson (1987).

Conclusion

Health is a variable which directly affects human welfare. For that reason, health is the most important asset in people's lives. Knowing the determinants of health is important data in relation to what to do about health. For that reason, it is seen that various studies are conducted in various disciplines to determine the factors that affect health. It is seen that studies have been conducted recently on the determinants of health in social sciences in addition to medical sciences. The studies which investigate the impact of education on health indicate that educated individuals care about their health more in general. It can also be said that income and income distribution have significant impacts on health. Especially it becomes easier to access goods and services related to health as income increases. Unemployment on the other hand may affect human health negatively especially since it causes psychological problems. Social integration creates positive impacts on people's psychology and causes positive impacts on health. Joint projects and studies to be carried out by scientists working on the determinants of health in different disciplines might contribute to obtaining more effective results.

References

Arendt, J. N. (2005). Does education cause better health? A panel data analysis using school reforms for identification. Economics of Education Review, 24 (2), April, 149-160.

Bakkeli, N. Z. (2016). Income inequality and health in China: A panel data analysis. Social Science & Medicine, 157, 39-47.

Béland, F., Birch, S. & Stoddart, G. (2002), Unemployment and health: contextual-level influences on the production of health in populations. Social Science & Medicine Journal, 55, 11, 2033-52.

Berkman, L. F. & Syme, S. L. (1979). Social networks, host resistance, and mortality: A nine-year follow-up study of Alameda County residents. American Journal of Epidemiology, 109,186-204.

Clark, D. & Royer, H. (2010). The Effect of Education on Adult Health and Mortality: Evidence from Britain. NBER Working Paper Series, Working Paper 16013.

Deaton, A. (2001). Relative deprivation, inequality, and mortality: National Bureau of Economic Research.

De Walque, D. (2007). Does education affect smoking behaviors? Evidence using the Vietnam draft as an instrument for college education. Journal of Health Economics, 26, 877–895.

Edvinsson, S., Lundevaller, E. H.& Malmberg, G. (2013). "Do unequal societies cause death among the elderly? A study of the health effects of inequality in Swedish municipalities in 2006". Global health action, 6.

Fiscella, K. & Franks, P. (2000). Individual income, income inequality, health, and mortality: what are the relationships? Health services research, 35 (1 Pt 2), 307.

Flegg, A. (1982). Inequality of income, illiteracy and medical care as determinants of infant mortality in underdeveloped countries. Population studies, 36(3), 441-458.

Fonseca, R. & Zheng, Y. (2013). The Effect of Education on Health: Cross-Country Evidence. Cahier de recherche/Working Paper 13-25

Groot, W., Van den, B., Henriette, M. (2007). "The health effects of education", Economics of Education Review, 26, 186–200.

Hayran, O. & Sur, H. (2005). Sağlık İşletmelerinde Yönetim, Sayed Publications, Istanbul.

Heckman, J. J., Urzua, S. & Veramendi, G. (2010). The Effects of Schooling on Labor Market and Health Outcomes. http://www2.um.edu.uy/dtrupkin/Veramendi_paper.pdf, Accessed on 01/07/2017.

Holcman, M. M., Latorre, M. R. & Santos, J. L. F. (2004). Infant Mortality Evolution in the Metropolitan Region of Sao Paulo (Brazil), 1980-2000. Rev Saude Publica; 38:2.

House J. S, Robbins, C. & Metzner H. L. (1982). The association of social relationships and activities with mortality: Prospective evidence from the Tecumseh Community Health Study. American Journal of Epidemiology, 116, 123-140.

Huang, W. (2015). Understanding the Effects of Education on Health: Evidence from China. IZA Discussion Paper, 9225.

Jen, M. H, Jones, K. & Johnston, R. (2009). Global variations in health: evaluating Wilkinson's income inequality hypothesis using the World Values Survey. Social science & medicine, 68(4), 643-653.

Kaplan, G. A., Pamuk, E. R., Lynch, J. W., Cohen, R. D. & Balfour, J. L. (1996). Inequality in income and mortality in the United States: analysis of mortality and potential pathways. Bmj, 312(7037), 999-1003.

Karsten, I. P. & Moser, K. (2009). Unemployment impairs mental health: Meta-analyses. Journal of Vocational Behavior, v74 n3 p264-282.

Kawachi, I., Colditz, G. A., Ascherio, A., Rimm, E. B., Giovannucci, E., Stampfer, M. J. & Willett, W. C. (1996). A prospective study of social networks in relation to total mortality and cardiovascular disease in men in the USA. Journal of Epidemiology and Community Health, 50, 245-251.

Kemptner, D. A., Jürges Hendrik, B. & Reinhold, S. (2011). Changes in compulsory schooling and the causal effect of education on health: Evidence from Germany. Journal of Health Economics 30 (2011) 340–354.

Knesebeck, O., Pablo, E. & Dragano, N. (2006). Education and health in 22 European Countries. Social Science & Medicine, 63 (5), September 2006, Pages 1344-1351.

Lange, F. (2011). The role of education in complex health decisions: Evidence from cancer screening. Journal of Health Economics, 30 (2011) 43–54.

Leigh, A. & Jencks, C. (2007). Inequality and Mortality: Long-Run Evidence from a Panel of Countries. Journal of Health Economics, 26, 1-24.

Lorgelly, P. K. & Lindley, J. K. (2008). What is the Relationship Between Income Inequality and Health? Evidence from BHPS. Health Economics, 17:249-265.

Maralani, V. (2014). Understanding the links between education and smoking. Social Science Research, 48, 20–34.

Marcus, J. (2013). The effect of unemployment on the mental health of spouses – Evidence from plant closures in Germany. Journal of Health Economics, 32, 3, 546-558.

Mazumder, B. (2008). Does education improve health? A re-examination of the evidence from compulsory schooling laws. Economic Perspectives, 2Q/2008, 1-17.

Nilsson, T. & Bergh, A. (2012). Income Inequality and Individual Health: Exploring the Association in a Developing Country: IFN Working Paper.

Orth-Gamer, K. & Johnson, J. (1987). Social network interaction and mortality: A six-year follow-up of a random sample of the Swedish population. Journal of Chronic Diseases, 40, 949-957.

Park, C. & Kang, C. (2008). Does education induce healthy lifestyle? Journal of Health Economics 27 1516–1531.

Preston, S. H. (1975). The Changing Relation between Mortality and Level of Economic Development. Population Studies, 29:231–48.

Pritchett, L. & Summers, L.H. (1996). Wealthier is Healthier. Journal of Human Resources, 31(4): 841–68

Prussia, G. E., Kinicki A. J. & Bracker J. S. (1993). Psychological and Behavioral Consequences of Job Loss: A Covariance Structure Analysis Using Weiner's (1985) Attribution Model. Journal of Applied Psychology. Vol: 78(3).

Rodgers, G. B. (1979). Income and Inequality as Determinants of Mortality: An International Cross-Section Analysis. Population Studies, 33:343–51.

Schmitz, H. (2011). Why are the unemployed in worse health? The causal effect of unemployment on health, Labour Economics, Vo18, 1, 71-78

Silles, M. A. (2009). The causal effect of education on health: Evidence from the United Kingdom. Economics of Education Review, 28, 122–128.

Tenn, S., Herman, D. A. & Wendling, B. (2010). The role of education in the production of health: An empirical analysis of smoking behaviour. Journal of Health Economics, Volume 29, Issue 3, 404-417.

Undurraga, E. A, Nica, V., Zhang, R., Mensah, I. C. & Godoy, R. A. (2016). Individual health and the visibility of village economic inequality: Longitudinal evidence from native Amazonians in Bolivia. Economics & Human Biology, 23, 18-26.

Vogl, T. S. (2012). Education and Health in Developing Economies. http://www.princeton.edu/~tvogl/vogl_ed_health_review.pdf, Accessed on 30/06/2017.

Wagstaff, A. (2002). Inequalities in Health in Developing Countries: Swimming Against the Tide? World Bank, Washington, DC, Policy Research Working Paper, No. 2795.

Webbink, D., Martin, N. G. & Visscher, P. M. (2010). Does education reduce the probability of being overweight? Journal of Health Economics, Volume 29, Issue 1, 29-38.

Welin, L., Tibblin, G., Svärdsudd, K, Tibblin, B., Ander-Peciva, S., Larsson, B., Wilhelmsen, L. (1985) Prospective study of social influence on mortality: The study of men born in 1913 and 1923. Lancet, 1, 915-918.

Wilkinson, R. G. (1992). Income Distribution and Life Expectancy. British Medical Journal, 304 (6820), 165–8.

Winkleby, M. A., Jatulis, D. E., Frank, E. & Fortmann, S. P. (1992). Socioeconomic status and health: how education, income, and occupation contribute to risk factors for cardiovascular disease. American Journal of Public Health, 82 (6), 816-820.

Zacher, M. (1999). Global Epidemiological Surveillance: International Cooperation in Monitoring Infectius Diseases, in Inge Kaul, Isabelle Grunberg and Marc Steren (eds), Global Public Goods; International Cooperation in the 21st Century, Oxford: Oxford University Press, 266-283.

STRATEGIC COST MANAGEMENT

FATMA TEMELLİ AND ÖMER ÇINAR

Introduction

The world is experiencing a rapid change in economic and technological circles. Everyone is influenced by this change; however, the rapid change that has taken place undoubtedly also significantly affects production technologies. As a result of this situation, new approaches and techniques have emerged in business managements. For example, classical approaches to the calculation of costs have begun to give place to modern cost approaches (Bekçi & Özal, 2010: p.78). Many of the companies in developed countries use advanced cost management systems for effective cost management. After the 1980s, the extreme diversity in customer demand and the need for more creative and diverse products have been a guide for the change in the production systems of enterprises. Businesses close to each other in terms of quality, price and technology levels can find a place in the market. Businesses are looking for new ways to reduce costs in order to maintain or increase their market share. And with the change of production systems, they also needed to change existing cost systems (Alkan, 2001: p.177). Along with the increase of global competition, production systems have changed and therefore businesses have had to change the cost of the system. As a result of this change, traditional cost systems were inadequate for businesses (Altınbay, 2006a: p.141) and more modern strategic cost management approaches were required. Strategic cost management is a modern cost management approach consisting of changing cost and management accounting systems, depending on the change of production systems in a highly competitive environment. These approaches, which are expressed as modern cost approaches in the strategic management decisions to be taken, are composed of instruments such as Activity Based Costing, Target Costing, Kaizen Costing, Lifetime Costing, Full Time Production and Full Time Costing, Total Quality Management, Balanced Scorecard, Theory of Constraints, and Value Engineering.

Cost management concept

The concept of cost is the sum of all kinds of sacrifices incurred to achieve something (Savcı, 2000: p.9). Cost is the whole of sacrifices made to reach a goal in its broadest sense. As it is clear from these definitions, every activity by a person or a business has a cost. There are costs for many activities such as taking education by a student, producing tables by a firm, making the sale by a store, etc. (Gürsoy, 1999: p.23). The cost of the product is the value of various production factors measured by money that the businesses spend to obtain the products and services that make up their business activity (Bursal & Ercan, 2000: p.3). In recent times, businesses have been trying to maintain production and sales activities under increasingly competitive conditions. These developments in increasing competition and businesses have required changes in the information systems of businesses (Gürdal, 2007: p.92).

Today, along with globalization, industrialization and technological development leading to improvements in production systems led to a reduction in the direct production costs share within the production costs and a shortening of the life span of the products. Significant changes in production and value creation activities have resulted in technological development and intense competition in logistics, production planning, and quality and testing (Gökçen, 2004: p.58-59).

The distribution of indirect costs by traditional methods leads to misleading information about the cost, which has led to the increasing importance of effective cost control and performance measurement in the product cost. Until recent years, producers considered cost management and cost accounting separately. In fact, cost accounting is conducted to provide information to cost management. Although cost management requires both cost accounting and management accounting knowledge, it differs from the purposes and methods of cost and management accounting in terms of purpose and methods used. Therefore, the concept of cost management is a broader concept than cost and management accounting (Altınbay, 2006b: p.47). While traditional cost accounting deals with cost calculation and distribution, it includes resolution procedures for problems that may arise for profit planning in processes such as cost management, planning, controlling costs, and reducing (Gökdeniz, 2002: p.61).

Cost management is defined as the management and control of activities to accurately determine product costs, improve operations, prevent waste, define cost drivers, plan activities and establish business strategies (Berliner & Brimson, 1988: p.152). Cost management is the provision of information that will assist the manager in efficient use of resources in the production of competitive products or services in terms of timing, cost, quality and functionality in global markets (Şakrak, 1997: p.65; Acar, 1999: p.11). Cost management is to provide information to assist the administrator for the efficient use of resources in the production of competitive products or services in terms of timing, cost, quality, and functionality in global markets (Gürdal, 2007: p.20). According to another definition, cost management is exchanging information with other functions in the enterprise and should strive for an integrated system understanding by providing coordination between production, raw material management, research and development, engineering and financing functions in the business (Acar, 2005: p.42).

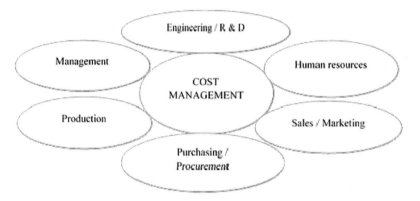

Figure 1-2. Relationship between Functions
Source: Acar, D. (2005). *Küresel Rekabette Maliyet Yönetimi ve Yaklaşımları: Tekstil Sektörü İle İlgili Bir Araştırma.* Ankara: Asil Publishing Distribution, p.43.

Thorough cost management in business provides information for the following four main management functions (Gürdal, 2007: p.21):

- Strategic management,
- Planning and decision making,
- Management and activity control,
- Preparation of financial statements.

The objectives of cost management are described as especially ensuring cost transparency and the acquisition and protection of competition power (Sorg, 1999: p.39). Another goal in cost management is to provide timely and appropriate information to the management. This information enables better use of business resources in product production and service provision and increases the competitiveness of the business in terms of cost, quality and profitability (Karcıoğlu, 2000: p.66). Cost management information is also important for commercial enterprises where warehousing, distribution and customer service management are very important, as well as for industrial enterprises that manage production costs, as well as for service businesses that need to know what services they provide and how those costs are managed. Users of cost management information can be small businesses as well as large businesses. The degree of importance of cost management for a business depends not on the size of the firm but on the nature of the competition strategy (Basık, 2012: p.14-15).

Concept of strategic cost management

The world economy today has become globalized with the influence of many developments including technology. The competition area of businesses is outside of countries' borders. These and similar changes and developments have significantly affected businesses that are ultimately aimed at achieving profit and/or increasing economic added value. As is known, businesses have to either increase their incomes or decrease their expenditures in order to increase their profits. The opportunities to increase profits by increasing the incomes of businesses are often limited by such factors as capacity and demand. Under these circumstances, the issue that needs to be emphasized is to take measures to ensure expenditure control. In sum, the condition of today's businesses to stay on the market is that they can get better quality products at lower cost (Yazarkan, 2012: p.42).

Strategy for businesses is a very important concept. Decisions in business activities are of great strategic importance (Özer, 2004: p.123). In order to meet the expectations of the risk owners, the strategy can be defined as compliance with the environment, resources, and areas of activity of the organization (Johnson and Scholes, 1993: p.5-10).

Strategic management approach can be defined as the science of the precise and explicit presentation of functional decisions that will enable the organization to achieve its goals, the completion and evaluation of integrity. As can be seen from the definition, strategic management focuses on the integration between management, marketing, finance/accounting, production activities, research and development and information-processing systems to achieve organizational success (Yüzbaşıoğlu, 2004: p.389). Strategic management is the whole of decisions and activities to develop and implement effective strategies, to check and evaluate their results. According to this definition, in strategic management, (1) research, review, evaluation and selection efforts are necessary for the planning of strategies; (2) in order for the planned strategies to be implemented, all kinds of internal measures in the business are taken and put into effect; and (3) it covers activities related to the evaluation of the efforts shown (Dinçer, 1992: p.22).

The strategic cost management approach has evolved parallel to the heightened importance of the strategy concept. One of the important roles of accounting information is to facilitate the development and implementation of business strategies (Bekçi & Özal, 2010: p.82). The company that wants to be successful and grow in the long term has to adapt to ever-changing market conditions without deviation from its aims, to develop its capabilities and resources in a stable manner and to protect its competitive advantage in this direction. In order to be able to identify and develop such strategies that will provide a continuous competitive advantage, it is necessary to develop and use strategic information on various financial and non-financial factors. Discipline, which provides this information within the company and enables management to make the right decisions within the framework of long-term plans, is called strategic cost management (Basık, 2012: p.19).

Strategic cost management is the preparation and analysis of management-related cost accounting information in terms of the overuse of all resources of the enterprise and the relative level of cash flow, market shares, quantities, prices and actual costs (Yüzbaşıoğlu, 2004: p.401).

Activity based costing

Activity Based Costing (ABC) is a cost accounting system that focuses on the various activities undertaken in an enterprise and brings costs together based on the scope and characteristics of these activities (Raiborn et al., 1994: p.183). The ABC system is a cost and management approach with the understanding that products consume the business' resources on an activity basis and therefore acting with the understanding that indirect costs should be classified on the basis of activities and between the product and the indirect costs that establish linear relationships at various levels, independent of the volume of production (Öker, 2003: p.32). ABC is a cost accounting system that calculates the cost of activities and reflects these costs in products, services and customers (Gökçen, 2004: p.61). The data obtained by ABC are used to more accurately determine the costs of goods and services, to determine the causes of general production costs, to diagnose the causes of costs and to explain the cost reasons (Brandt et al., 1999).

Target costing

At the most basic level, the target cost is a long-run cost estimate that will ensure that a product or service is profitable when it is sold (Horngren et al., 1994: p.454). According to another definition, the target cost is a market-based cost calculated by using the target sales price to reach a predetermined market share (Drury, 1992: p.305). Target costing is a product development strategy focusing on customer expectations and market opportunities and is defined as a strategic profit and cost management process (Yükçü, 1999: p.923). Target costing initiates cost management during the product development and design phase and continues throughout the product lifecycle by actively participating in the entire value chain (Yükçü, 2014: p.382). The target costing process, which focuses on the design and development of products and services by addressing customer needs, has a very simple nature and application process, although it is complex and versatile (Hacırüstemoğlu & Şakrak, 2002: p.118).

Kaizen costing

Kaizen costing is called continuous improvement in terms of costs, i.e. cost reduction approach. Kaizen cost is the planned cost to be reduced (Civelek & Özkan, 2004: p.276). Kaizen costing is a kind of kaizen or continuous improvement application that is used specifically to reduce costs. The cost reduction objective is addressed specifically for the manufacturing process, and value engineering / analysis is used to achieve this aim (Cooper, 1996: p.24). Achieving Kaizen costing goals focuses on continuous reductions in activities and costs that do not add value to the product, elimination of waste, and continuous improvement in the production process (Yükçü, 2014: p.504).

Lifetime costing

Another dimension that comprehensive cost management brings to business success is the acceptance of a life-cycle phenomenon related to the product. The success of the product depends on its success in the design phase. While the traditional management approach deals with the products in the stages of maturity and decline, today's technology costs reveal that the life cycle must also be focused on the first steps (Basık & Türker, 2005: p.55). Lifetime cost is the total cost of planning, designing, obtaining and maintaining costs that arise during the life course of a product and other costs that can be directly related to the product to obtain or use the product (Otlu & Karaca, 2005: p.249). So, this is all costs involved from product design to production; purchase and use of the product by the customer; and the time it takes to dispose of it (disposal) (Basık, 2012: p.391-392).

Just in time production and full-time costing

Just in Time Production (JIT) is a working philosophy. The main idea is that the products are produced only when necessary, when the customer orders them. The business only manufactures to meet the customer's order (Karcıoğlu, 2000: p.31). The JIT system is a system that enables the elimination of wasted and non-value-added activities and the reduction of costs. JIT is also an approach that focuses on continuous improvement and customer satisfaction (Gürdal, 2007: p.147). The goal in JIT philosophy is to put waste prevention techniques into practice. On the basis of these efforts lies the philosophy of removing waste and human respect (Demir & Gümüşoglu, 2003: p.717). The target to be achieved in the JIT philosophy can be defined as "Zero Stock" and "Zero Error" (Firuzan & Ayvaz, 2004: p.20; Schniederjans & Cao, 2000: p.113; Funk, 1995: p.61; Christensen, 1996: p.7; Giunipero et al., 2005: p.52).

Total quality management

Total Quality Management (TQM) is a structured system with a set of philosophies, techniques, and tools designed to meet customer expectations and overcome these expectations, designed to create an organizational culture that is customer-focused with employee involvement and continuous improvement (Tatikonda & Tatikonda, 1996: p.5). TQM is an effective system combining quality improvement, quality preservation and quality improvement efforts in order to realize marketing, engineering, production and service at the most economical level by considering customer satisfaction of different groups in an organization (Karcıoğlu, 2000: p.106). TQM is a management model that focuses on quality and is based on the involvement of all staff, aiming at achieving long-term customer satisfaction, benefiting both for their own staff and society. In other words, TQM is a modern form of management that cuts costs as well as an approach that best meets customer needs (Yükçü, 2014: p.518).

Balanced scorecard

The balanced performance card is a dynamic performance measurement system or management technique that aims to improve and optimize in-house activities within the framework of customer focus, customer and shareholder expectations within the framework of future customer satisfaction, as well as physical (financial) values based on past experience and aims at implementing strategic approach and strategy, which provides strategic feedback to ensure balance and integration between dimensions, based on non-physical values (dimensions) such as learning and development on the basis of in-house methods in order to adapt to change (Can, 2002: p.238). A balanced scorecard is a strategic approach involving the measurement, documentation and control of its activities in terms of the vision and strategy of a company or institution (Kaplan and Norton, 2009: p.1). The balanced scorecard allows a business' mission and strategy to be expressed in terms of understandable performance metrics, thus creating the framework for a strategic measurement and management system (Ölçer, 2005: p.89). The balanced scorecard method is a measurement-based strategic performance management system that creates a framework for strategic performance measurement and management, transforming the organization's mission and strategies into a comprehensive set of performance indicators (Kaplan & Norton, 1996: p.2).

Theory of constraints

The Theory of Constraints is a management philosophy developed by Eliyahu Goldratt in the early 1980s as a series of books and articles aimed at managing constraints and continuously developing through synchronized production, which can be defined as the cooperation and harmonization of production processes to achieve the objectives of the operator (Büyükyılmaz & Gürkan, 2009: p.178). The theory of constraints focuses on system development. The system is defined as running processes as interdependent. These processes, which are linked to each other in the theory of constraints and which aim to achieve the goal, are defined as a chain. The constraint in this process is the weak link of the chain (Nave, 2002: p.75).

Value engineering

This concept, which was originally expressed as value analysis, was later expressed as value management, value improvement, function analysis, and value control, but eventually it changed to the name value engineering and started to be used in this way (Yükçü, 2014: p.414). Value engineering is an interdisciplinary and intensive problem-solving activity focused on improving the value of the functions required to achieve the goal of an organization, service, process or product (Wixson, 2004: p.60). Value engineering is a technique for producing cost-cutting ideas without lengthening the product development process and without compromising the desired characteristics of the product (Yükçü, 2014: p.414).

Conclusion

As a result, with the change and development of information and communication technologies, there has also been a change in the field of management, and they have begun to look for alternatives to be able to calculate their operating costs more accurately or to the nearest extent. Within the scope of strategic cost management, some approaches have emerged in line with the needs of enterprise. These cost approaches should be able to renew themselves or maintain an update to provide alternatives to decision makers and information users. For this purpose, approaches such as Activity Based Costing, Target Costing, Kaizen Costing, Lifetime Costing, Just in Time Production System and Costing, Total Quality Management, Balanced Scorecard, Theory of Constraint, and Value Engineering approaches have been examined from strategic cost management approaches. In the strategies to be followed within the framework of sustainable competitive approach, adoption of strategic cost management approaches in complementary integrity may provide cost leadership advantage to businesses. The application of strategic cost management approaches in a highly interactive way, rather than a stand-alone implementation for businesses, will be able to respond more to needs and help management to make healthier decisions based on costs.

References

Acar, D. (1999). *Maliyet Yönetiminde Yeni Yaklaşımlar ve Tekstil Sektörü İşletmelerinin Uygulamaları ile ilgili Araştırma.* (Unpublished Associate Professor Thesis), Isparta.

Acar, D. (2005). *Küresel Rekabette Maliyet Yönetimi ve Yaklaşımları: Tekstil Sektörü İle İlgili Bir Araştırma.* Ankara: Asil Publishing Distribution.

Alkan, H. (2001). İşletme Başarısında Maliyet Yönetiminin Rolü ve Maliyet yönetiminde yeni yaklaşımlar. *Süleyman Demirel University Journal of Forestry Faculty,* A (2), 177-192, ISSN: 1302-7085.

Altınbay, A. (2006a). Etkin Bir Maliyet Yönetim Sistemi Olarak Hedef Maliyetleme Sistemi ve TMMT Uygulaması. *Dumlupınar University Social Science Journal*, 16, 141-164.

Altınbay, A. (2006b). *Stratejik Maliyet Yönetimi Yaklaşımlarından Yasam Seyri Maliyetlere Sisteminin Tasarımı ve Bir uygulama.* (Unpublished PhD Thesis), Dumlupınar University Social Sciences Institute.

Basık, F. O. & Türker İ. (2005). Stratejik Maliyet Analizi ve Yönetimi. *V. National Production Research Symposium, İstanbul Trade University, 25-27 November 2005, 53-58.*

Basık, F. O. (2012). *Rekabet Stratejisinde Maliyet Yönetimi.* İstanbul: Türkmen Bookstore.

Bekçi, İ. & Özal, H. (2010). Stratejik Maliyet Yönetiminin Sağlık Sektöründe Uygulanabilirliğine Yönelik Bir Araştırma. *Journal of Academic Researches and Studies*, 2(3), 78-97.

Berliner, C. & Brimson, J. A. (Eds.). (1988). *Cost Management for Today's Advanced Manufacturing: The CAM-I conceptual design.* Boston: Harvard Business School Press.

Brandt, M. T., Levine, S. P. & Gourdoux, J. R. (1999). Application of Activity-Based Cost Management, *Professional Safety*, Januray, 22-27.

Brimson, J. A. (1991). *Activity Accounting: An Activity- Based Costing Approach.* New York: John Wiley and Sons. Inc.

Bursal, N. & Yücel, E. (2000). *Maliyet Muhasebesi.* İstanbul: Der Yayınları

Büyükyılmaz, O. & Gürkan, S. (2012). Süreçlerde En Zayıf Halkanın Bulunması: Kısıtlar Teorisi. *International Journal of Management Economics and Business*, 5(9), 177-196.

Can, A. V. (2002). *Maliyet Yönetiminde Pazara Dayalı Bir Yaklaşım: Hedef Maliyetleme.* (Unpublished PhD Thesis), Sakarya University Social Sciences Institute.

Christensen, L. (1996). JIT Sensitive Distribution – Cutting Waste and Serving the Customer. *Logistics Information Management*, 9(2),7-9.

Civelek, M. & Özkan A. (2004). *Temel ve Tekdüzen Maliyet Muhasebesi.* Ankara: Detay Publications.

Cooper, R. (1996). Look out, Management Accountants. *Strategic Finance*, 77(11), 20-26.

Demir, M. H. & Gümüşoğlu, Ş. (2003). *Üretim yönetimi.* İstanbul: Beta Edition Publishing Distribution Inc.

Dinçer, Ö. (1992). *Stratejik Yönetim ve İşletme Politikası,* 2nd Edition. İstanbul: Timaş Publishing Inc.

Drury, C. (1992). *Management and Cost Accounting.* London: Chapman & Hall Ltd.

Firuzan, A. R. & Ayvaz, Y. Y. (2004). Yeni bir felsefe ışığında yan sanayilerden beklenenler ve tam zamanında üretim. *The Journal of Management and Economics*, 11(1):19-26

Funk, J. L. (1995). Just-in-time manufacturing and logistical complexity: a contingency model. *International Journal of Operations & Production Management*, 15(5), 60-71.

Giunepero, L. C., Pillai, K. G., Chapman, N. S. & Clark, A. R. (2005). A longitudinal examination of JIT purchasing practices. *The International Journal of Logistics Management*, 16(1), 51-70.

Gökçen, G. (2004). Faaliyet Tabanlı Maliyetlemenin İşletme Kararlarında Kullanılması. *Journal of Accounting and Finance*, 23, 58-67.

Gökdeniz, Ü. (2002). Etkin Bir Maliyet Yönetiminde Prensipler ve Performans Ölçümlemesinin Rolü. *Istanbul Chamber of Certified Public Accountants. The Journal of Financial Solution*, 68, 54-65.

Gündüz, H. E. (1997). *Dünya Klasındaki İşletmelerde Bir Maliyet Yönetimi Aracı Olarak Faaliyetlere Dayalı Maliyet Sistemi ve Bir Uygulama*. CMB. Publication Number: 99, Ankara: Tisamat Printing Industry.

Gürdal, K. (2007). *Maliyet Yönetiminde Güncel Yaklaşımlar*. Ankara: Siyasal Bookstore.

Gürsoy, C. T. (1999). *Yönetim ve Maliyet Muhasebesi*. 2nd Edition. İstanbul: Beta Publishing Distribution Inc.

Hacırüstemoğlu, R. & Şakrak, M. (2002). *Maliyet Muhasebesinde Güncel Yaklaşımlar*. İstanbul: Türkmen Bookstore.

Horngren, C. T., Foster, G. & Datar, S. M. (1994). *Cost Accounting*. New Jersey: Prentice Hall, Inc.- Englewood Cliffs.

Johnson, G. & Scholes, K. (1993). *Exploring Corporate Strategy*. London: Prentice Hall.

Kaplan, R. S. & Norton, D. P. (1996). *Using the Balanced Scorecard as a Strategic Management System*. Harvard Business Review, 74, I,75-85.

Kaplan, R. S. & Norton, D. P. (2009). *Der Effektive Strategie- Prozess: Erfolgreich Mit Dem 6-Phasen-System*. Germany, Bielefeld: Campus Verlag.

Karcıoğlu, R. (2000). *Stratejik Maliyet Yönetimi: Maliyet ve Yönetim Muhasebesinde Yeni Yaklaşımlar*. Erzurum: Aktif Publisher.

Nave, D. (2002). How to Compare Six Sigma, Lean and The Theory of Constraints. *Quality Progress*, 35(3), 73-78.

Öker, F. (2003). *Faaliyet Tabanlı Maliyetleme-Üretim ve Hizmet İşletmelerinde Uygulamalar*. İstanbul: Literatür Publications.

Ölçer, F. (2005). Dengeli Stratejik Performans Ölçüm ve Yönetim Sistemi'nin (Balanced Scorecard) Tasarımı ve Uygulanması. *Public Administration Journal*, 38 (2), 89-134.

Otlu, F. & Karaca, S. (2005). Maliyet Yönetimi ve Yaşam Seyri Maliyet Analizi. *Süleyman Demirel University Journal of F.E.A.S.*, 10(2), 245-270.

Özer, A. (2004). Pazarlama İle İlgili Karalarda Faaliyet Tabanlı Maliyetlemenin Etkisi, *The Journal of Overview on Accounting and Auditing*, September 2004. 123-138.

Raiborn, C. A., Barfield, J. T. & Kinney, M. R. (1994). *Managerial Accounting*. Ohio: Sout-Western College Publishing.

Sakrak, M. (1997). *Maliyet Yönetimi: Maliyet ve Yönetim Muhasebesinde Yeni Yaklasımlar*, Publication Number: 080, ISBN 975-367-028-4, İstanbul: Yasa Publications.

Savcı, M. (2010). *Maliyet Muhasebesi*. 11th Edition. Trabzon: Murathan Publications.

Schniederjans, M. J. & Cao, Q. (2000). A Note on JIT Purchasing vs. EOQ with a Price Discount: An Expansion of Inventory Costs. *International Journal of Production Economics*, 65(3), 289-294.

Sorg, W. (1999). Meilensteine der Kostenrechnung, Gertrud Scheld Fachbibliothek Verlag, Büren.

Tatikonda, L. U. & Tatikonda, R. J. (1996). Top Ten Reasons Your TQM Effort Is Falling to Improve Profit. *Production and Inventory Management Journal-Third Quarter,* 37(3), 5-9.

Wixson, J. (2004). *Value analysis/value engineering: the forgotten lean technique,* University of Idaho, Industrial Technology Program, PTTE434, available at: www.if.uidaho.edu/ ,wixsjr/LeanVE2.pdf

Yazarkan, H. (2012). *Bir Stratejik Maliyet Yönetimi Aracı Olarak Sahipliğin Toplam Maliyeti Yaklaşımının Tedarikçi Seçimindeki Rolü: 500 Büyük Sanayi İşletmesinde Bir Uygulama,* (Unpublished PhD Thesis).

Yükçü, S. (1999). Herkes için *Muhasebesi.* 2nd Edition. İzmir: Altın Nokta Publisher.

Yükçü, S. (1999). *Yönetim Açısından Maliyet Muhasebesi.* İzmir: Cem Offset.

Yüzbaşıoğlu, N. (2004). İşletmelerde Stratejik Yönetim ve Planlama Açısından Stratejik Maliyet Yönetimi ve Enstrümanları. *Selçuk University Journal of Social Sciences Institute,* (12), 387-410.

THE IMPORTANCE OF SOCIAL MEDIA IN MARKETING COMMUNICATION

HAKAN IRAK

Introduction

In the changing and developing world, the processes related to marketing have substantially changed. One of the remarkable aspects of this period is that marketing communication has become an important issue. Marketing communication is one of the major research topics of this study, and it plays a supporting role in determining the current status of marketing.

The acceleration of technological developments and the widespread use of the internet have introduced social media. Social media, which turned out to be a large part of people's lives, has become a regularly monitored platform. As a result of becoming more and more popular in people's lives, social media has also shown its presence in fields such as marketing.

The interaction between social media and marketing has shown its effect by the widespread use of marketing activities in the social media. This study will focus on the place and importance of marketing communications in social media. The interaction between these two concepts is the focus of this study.

This study will be prepared to explain the importance of social media in marketing communication. Progress will be made in the study by using a literature review method. After the separate explanation of marketing communication and social media concepts, it is planned to conclude the study by giving information about the place and importance of marketing communication in social media.

The definition of marketing communication

Marketing is concerned with determining and meeting human and social needs (Kotler, 2002: p.1). Marketing refers to a discipline in which both short-term tactical programs are prepared and long-term strategies are developed (Goi, 2009: p.2). Upon the transformation of marketing into an increasingly dynamic process, the concept of marketing communication has emerged.

One of the issues that needs to be mentioned before the definition is that marketing communication should be considered as a whole. To address marketing communication as a whole means that it is necessary to use all possible means and media in marketing communication. This is an issue related to the content of marketing communication, as well as the beliefs of the consumers towards the individuals or organizations that carry out marketing (Yılmaz, 2006: p.54).

Marketing communication is a concept which involves communication between the producing and consuming parties. It is defined as "all of the communication efforts that will enable an organization to communicate with all associated or to be associated parties about its presence, products and services, and what it commits and can offer" (Durmaz, 2001: p.238).

Development of Marketing Communications

The development of marketing communication has been in line with the other developments in the world. The development of economies, the change of the market, the increase of competition, the change of consumer expectations come forefront among these developments (Dinçer, 2009: p.39). All these developments have brought a positive acceleration in terms of improvement of marketing communications.

The development of the marketing communication in history has been realized as shown below.

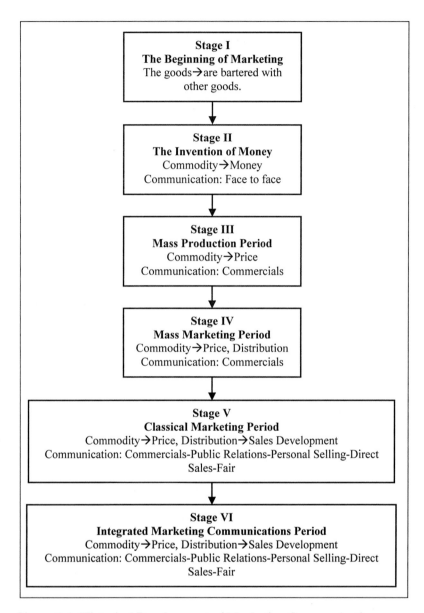

Figure 1-3. Historical Development of Marketing Communication
Source: Başok Yurdakul, 2003: 60.

As shown in Figure 1-3, the historical development of marketing communication has occurred in six stages. These stages are the beginning of marketing, the invention of money, mass production, mass marketing, classical marketing, and integrated marketing communications, respectively. As the relationship between marketing and communication shows that marketing and communication are on par with each other, it makes the above data much more important.

The factors affecting marketing communication

"Marketing communication is an integrated structure which includes all of the communication functions used in marketing a product such as commercials, public relations, direct sales, sales promotion, etc." (Kavoğlu, 2012: p.3). From this perspective, it would not be wrong to mention the functions such as advertising, public relations, sales, and promotion among the factors that influence marketing communication.

The other factors affecting marketing communication are listed as follows (Yılmaz, 2006: p.67-68):

I.   Markets in which power balances change,
II. Increasing competition,
III. The differentiation in consumer trends,
IV. Globalization and the new economic order brought by globalization,
V.   Technological advances and the loss of impact of traditional commercials,
VI. Creation of databases becoming easier and cheaper.

As can be seen above, there are many factors that affect marketing communication, and each of them has different content. This can be interpreted as the factors affecting marketing communication having an original content and that marketing communication has a broad scope.

New communication technologies and marketing communication

The developments in information technology have made internet marketing the fastest growing direct marketing technique and led it to be characterized as the new understanding of marketing in the digital age (Odabaşı & Oyman, 2014: p.325). The emergence of new communication technologies has led to the consideration of marketing methods. In the end, changes occurred in marketing communications, and the level of use of public relations in marketing has increased (Dinçer, 2009: p.40). The relationship between new communication technologies and marketing has shown itself primarily as a change in marketing methods.

Within the context of the interaction between the development of marketing communication and new communication technologies, it is necessary to mention the fact that mobile devices are taking up a large part of human life. In line with the development of mobile devices, marketing communication has begun to change and many businesses have preferred to include mobile marketing in their programs (Bozkurt & Ergen, 2012: p.43). Since it shows that the new communication technologies may have an indicative role in the progress in marketing, this example has an important role. And also, it is possible to mention different examples that will support this change in the way of using marketing communication and its frequency of use.

After the interaction of new communication technologies and marketing communication, the scope of marketing communication has become as shown below.

As seen in Figure 1-4, the scope of marketing communication is directly interacting with technological developments, and the technological developments constitute the context of marketing communications.

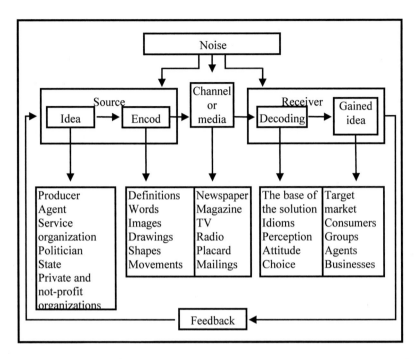

Figure 1-4. The Scope of Marketing Communications
Source: Ralph M.Gaedek & D. H. Tootelian, Marketing: Principles and Applications, (St Paul: West Pub. Co., 1983), p.381.

Definition of social media

As a widely-used media environment today, social media is both a blessing and a malicious tool (Bank & Tat, 2014: p.1188). The decisive factor in this point is the purposes for which the people use social media. In terms of marketing communication, social media may be a blessing as well as a potential source of harm.

"Social media is a new online source of information created, initiated, distributed and used by consumers to inform other individuals about products, brands, people, and subjects" (Barutçu & Tomas, 2013: p.8). Online resources are at the forefront of the definition of social media. Also, this definition includes data implying the rapid interaction between the individuals in the social media.

Another definition describes social media as "a form of human communication in which sharing and discussions can be made without time and space limitation (mobile based)" (Akıncı Vural & Bat, 2010: p.3351). This short and simple definition draws attention to the most basic features of social media. The absence of time and space limitation is the major characteristics of social media and it is one of the reasons why social media is preferred. The importance of personal sharing and discussions are the other issues to be included in the definition of social media.

Various definitions can be made for social media. For this reason, it is preferred to examine other topics instead of giving more definitions of social media to make it clearer.

Social Media Tools

The new opportunities offered by the Internet have made the social media and social media tools increasingly familiar. Social media tools provide people not only with opportunities for communication but also for business activities (Özgen & Doymuş, 2013: p.93). For this reason, being familiar with social media tools seems to be an important issue.

The major social media tools that should be known are as follows (Akıncı Vural & Bat, 2010: p.3356):

I.   Blogs,
II.   Micro blogs,
III.   Forums,
IV.   Photo sharing sites,
V.   Video sharing sites,
VI.   Social networks,
VII.   Wikis,
VIII.   Content tagging sites,
IX.   Chat sites and Podcasts.

Social media such as blogs, podcasts, and videos, has been changing in the way of disseminating and consuming the news. Social media offers online and mobile communication for no or very low cost; therefore, it has become an ideal channel for emergencies or emergency communication (Cambié & Ooi, 2009: p.207).

The comparison of social media and traditional media

The main differences that distinguish social media from traditional media (newspapers, magazines, televisions, radio, etc.) are the increase in consumer activity, openness for participation, participation (voting, commenting and sharing), two-way communication between sender and receiver, and the possibility of forming different communities with different interests quickly. The major difference between social media and traditional media is that the user can start communication and interactions at any time through social media (Barutçu & Tomaş, 2013: p.8). The traditional media does not have such a possibility. Being one of the major factors that increase the frequency of preference of social media, it eliminates the time and space barriers for access.

Social media is different from traditional media because only in social media can all the members make comments and upload their information. Social media is a World Wide Web tool that allows users to be active content creators, to actively communicate with the others, to create various information, and to exchange this information. Also, social media helps users to increase their social interaction with people. This is something they would not do otherwise because people have the opportunity to experience the broader world, such as diversity of people, opinions, and cultures in social media. The main principle of social media is the democratization of content through creating and sharing of information by the same users. User-generated content is open to comments and criticism, and it can be easily accessed by other users. The traditional forms of media operate with the principle of "single information provider for many people" but social media is suitable for the model of "many people to many people." For this reason, it changes people's ways of exploring, reading, and sharing information (Solis & Breakenridge, 2009). Taking into account the apparent impact of Web 2.0 on the global marketplace - or more accurately, the world market - social technology is now considered to be "the given" in the business world (Evans & Mckee, 2010: p.3).

The differences between traditional media and social media are as shown in the following table.

According to Table 1-14, it can be said that social media and traditional media are separated from each other by four themes: time and space limitation, experience sharing, online community building and expert advice. The data in the above table also reveals the advantages of social media over traditional media.

The information given in this part of the study, according to the comparison of traditional media with social media, shows that traditional media is lagging behind today's conditions and has lost its former significance. In today's conditions, in which the significance of time factor has been increasing day by day, the level of using social media tends to increase.

Table 1-14. The Comparison of Social Media and Traditional Media

Social Media	Traditional Media
Two-way communication	One-way communication
Open System	Closed System
Transparency	Opacity
One on one marketing	Mass marketing
About you	About itself
Content generated by a brand and person	Professional content
Free platform	Paid platform
Unofficial wording	Official wording
Unstructured communication	Controlled communication
Social decision making	Decision making based on the economy
Active participation	Passive participation

Source: Taşdemir, 2011: p.651.

The Place and Importance of Social Media in Marketing Communication

Technological changes in society affect social changes. While the communication between the majorities of community members is taking place on the virtual platform, people use social media more actively. It was social media that enabled people to create new, attractive, and innovative ways to communicate on a virtual platform, to participate in communities, and to share important information in time (Indro & Jnjrato, 2014: p.490). Social media is one of the marketing tools used to persuade consumers. Although using social media as a marketing tool is a new development, it seems to be an area developing quite rapidly. Online communities, social networks, blog marketing and many other tools are used within the context of marketing communication and social media relations (Neti, 2011: p.3). As there are many different alternatives in the formation of social media in marketing communication, the tools mentioned here needed to be known.

Today, businesses include social media tools in their marketing communication (Barutçu & Tomaş, 2013: p.11). Thus, social media can be used as a message channel. This becomes a significant detail of the importance and role of social media in marketing communications. The presence of social media in marketing communication in this way can also be associated with public relation activities.

Social media is a tool of marketing communication, and it can change over time (Sevinç, 2012: p.167). Within the context of marketing communication and social media relations, it should be noted that the communication activities in social media should be used as a whole rather than in parts in marketing communication (Taşdemir, 2011: p.658). This issue seems to be one of the main determinants of social media's role and importance in marketing communication. It can be said that the use of social media in this way is a prerequisite for the achievement of the goals.

The presence of social media in marketing communication has become inevitable with the spread of social media. This is because there is a progress in marketing in line with the trend of demand. The marketers who are aware of this fact have started to use social media more in marketing communication. As it would not be a reasonable option for this new media to have a role in marketing communication, this use is inevitable (Sevinç, 2012: p.23). In other words, as the absence of social media in marketing communication would harm the process, the presence of this interaction is a necessity.

As a general assessment, it has been found that changing circumstances must be considered in identifying the role and importance of social media in marketing communication. Besides this, technological developments, particularly in marketing, are the major factors to be considered within the context of marketing communication and social media relations. All these facts have caused the expectations that social media's role and importance in marketing communication will be at higher level.

Conclusion

The study, which examines the importance of social media in marketing communication, reveals that social media's role in the processes and activities related to marketing communication, is inevitable.

All the tools that the companies use to convey their commitments about their products or services to be marketed make up marketing communication. Therefore, it has been concluded that marketing communication has the potential of developing from day to day and that the concept of marketing communication is a result of marketing having the same meaning as communication. The new communication technologies are one of the determinants of developments in marketing communication. As new communication technologies emerge, they will be used in marketing communication.

Social media has become an integral part of human life today. The widespread use of the Internet and the development of technology, have led to the start of such a big role of social media in human life. Compared to traditional media, social media has become an increasingly preferred platform due to the fact that there are no time and space limitations because it can be accessed anywhere with internet connection. The advantages of social media over traditional media are one of the main factors in the spread of social media. The presence of social media in marketing communication has been identified as an inevitable situation, and it can be said that the rapid rise of social media brought this result. If today's conditions continue, the level of this interaction is expected to increase day by day.

The role of social media in marketing communication needs to be considered as a whole. Since it is one of the major findings explaining the role and importance of social media in marketing communication, which is the main research topic of this study, it is important to understand this result clearly. It is necessary to know that social media is used as an effective marketing tool and steps should be taken accordingly. The presence of social media tools in marketing communication should be considered as a whole. Due to the expectation that the relationship between social media and marketing will enhance in the future, proper actions should be taken for the future.

References

Akıncı, V. Z. B. & Bat, M. (2010). Social media as a new communication medium: A research on Ege University Communication Faculty. *Journal of Yaşar University, 20* (5), 3348-3382.

Bank, N. Z. & Tat, U. (2014). Social media and its effects on individuals and social systems. *Management Knowledge and Learning International Conference,* Slovenia: 25-27 June, 1183-1190.

Barutçu, S. & Tomaş, M. (2013). Sustainable social media marketing and measurement of the effectiveness of social media marketing. *Management Journal of Internet Applications, 4* (1), 5-23.

Başok Yurdakul, N. (2003). The Measurement Process of Integrated Marketing Communication. [Ph.D. Thesis], Ege University Social Sciences Institute.

Bozkurt, F. & Ergen, A. (2012). A new mobile marketing tool in marketing communications: 2D barcodes. *Journal of Marketing and Marketing Research,* 9, 43-64.

Cambié, S. & Ooi, Y. (2009). *International Communications Strategy.* UK, London: Kogan Page.

Dinçer, C. (2009). The importance and role of Public Relations in marketing: A study on SMEs. *Journal of academic researches and studies,* 1 (1), 38-46.

Durmaz, M. (2001). Marketing communications. *Journal of Istanbul University Communication Faculty,* 11, 237-242.

Evans, D. & Mckee, J. (2010), *Social Media Marketing: The Next Generation of Business Engagement.* US, Indiana: Wiley Publising.

Gaedek, M. R. & Tootelian, D. H. (1983). *Marketing: Principles and Applications.* US, St Paul: West Publishing. Company.

Goi, C. L. (2009). A review of marketing mix: 4Ps or more. *International Journal of Marketing Studies,* 1 (1), 2-15.

Indro, J. & Jnjrato, M. (2014) Peculiarities of social media integration into marketing communication. *Procedia - Social and Behavioral Sciences*: 156, 490 – 495

Kavoğlu, S. (2012). New approaches in marketing communications: Commercials Based on Game and Sample Applications. *Academic Journal Overview,* 29, 1-14.

Kotler, P. (2002). *Marketing Management, Millenium Edition.* Upper Saddle River, New Jersey: Pearson Custom Publishing.

Neti, S. (2011), Social media and its role in marketing. *International Journal of Enterprise Computing and Business Systems,* 1 (2), 1-15.

Odabaşı, Y. & Oyman, M. (2014), *Marketing Communication Management.* Turkey, İstanbul: Mediacat.

Özgen, E. & Doymuş, H. (2013). A communicative approach to content management as a distinctive element in social media marketing. *Online Academic Journal of Information Technology,* 4 (11), 91-103. doi: 10.5824/1309□1581.2013.1.006.x

Sevinç, S. S. (2012). *Social media in marketing communication.* Turkey, İstanbul: Optimist Broadcast Distribution.

Solis, B. & Breakenridge, D. (2009) *Putting the Public Back in Public Relations: How Social Media Is Reinventing the Aging Business of PR Hardcover.* US, New Jersey: FT Press.

Taşdemir, E. (2011). Social media on the basis of integrated marketing communications. E-Journal of New World Sciences Academy, 6 (3), 645-665.

http://dergipark.ulakbim.gov.tr/nwsahuman/article/viewFile/50000624
43/5000058708

Yılmaz, Y. (2006). An integrative aspect of marketing communication:
Integrated marketing communications. *Electronic Journal Of Social
Sciences,* 5 (18), 54-75.
http://www.acarindex.com/dosyalar/makale/acarindex-
1423879331.pdf

LOGISTICS IN TERMS OF BUSINESS AND ECONOMICS

SİBEL İSMAİLÇEBİ BAŞAR

Introduction

Natural resources are not distributed equally between countries and regions. In the same way, the places where the goods and services are produced and the places they are consumed are not the same. Besides, people visit different regions for various reasons and they are on the move. With these and other reasons, transportation services have always been an important issue.

Logistic activities are as old as human history. The word of logistics originates from the ancient Greek logos (λόγος), which means "ratio, word, calculation, reason, speech, and oration". There are many definitions of logistics. According CSCMP (Council of Supply Chain Management Professionals), *"logistics is the process of planning, implementing and controlling the efficient, cost-effective flow and storage of raw materials, in- process inventory, finished goods and related information from point of origin to point of consumption for the purpose of conforming to customer requirements"*.

Philip Kotler defines logistics as "planning, implementing, and controlling the physical flows of materials and finished goods from point of origin to point of use to meet the customer's need at a profit".

On the other hand, it is considered that the first application area of logistics is military fields. Particularly during World War II, the importance of logistics emerged and began to be regarded as a science in the post-war period. In the post-war period, many businesses in the US especially noticed the importance of logistics. In summary, many scientific studies and researches related to logistics activities were carried out in the 1960s.

Globalization has begun to feel its impact more and more since the 1990s. As a matter of course, there has also been a great increase in the mobility of goods and services. With the increase in demand for transportation and logistics activities, the multi-model system (at least two overflow systems) has been introduced from the uni-model system (one transport system option) for long distance transportation. With the development of multi-choice transport systems, the control of firms on their own logistics activities has weakened. With the increase of sales on the Internet, delivery of products to customers in time has emerged as a competitive element and the "speed factor" has become important in logistics. As a result, businesses are now beginning to see logistics activities as strategic. As a result, the concept of 'supply chain and logistics management' emerged, which included all the stages of transport and logistics actions.

The Council of Supply Chain Management Professionals defines logistics management as follows: "Supply Chain Management is the systemic, strategic coordination of the traditional business functions and the tactics across business functions within a particular company and across businesses within the supply chain for the purposes of improving the long-term performance of the individual companies and a supply chain as a whole".

Logistics aims to managing the supply chain. It is also a science of managing the flow of goods, information and other resources in order to meet producers' and customers' requirements. Logistics involves the integration of information, transportation, inventory, warehousing etc.

Logistics is important both in terms of business and economics. This study focuses on the basic issues of logistics and puts emphasis on business and economics sciences.

Objectives of logistics

Logistics can have multiple purposes. According to the literature, logistics generally has the following objectives:

- Reduction of inventory affects the profit of an enterprise to a great extent. Logistics helps in maintaining inventory at the lowest level. Thus, logistics helps achieving the customer goal.

- Economy of freight: Freight is an important source of cost in logistics. This cost can be reduced by selecting the proper mode of transport, route planning etc.

- Delivery performance: Goods required by the customer must be delivered on time. Proper planning of the transportation channels, availability of inventory, and use of appropriate communication technologies will ensure this performance.

- Protecting products: Products may be damaged due to several reasons. This damage increases the logistics cost, especially reverse logistics costs. The use of proper logistical packaging, advanced technology and training personnel will reduce this damage.

- Faster response: A firm must transport its goods to the customer in the shortest time frame. By utilizing the latest technologies in processing information and communication, firms can improve faster decision making.

Principles of Logistics

Logistics principles are important factors for all logistics activities. It can be said that these principles are common to all logistics activities. According to logistics literature, the most common logistical principles are as follows:

- Standardization: It is important that logistics services are standard. Standards should be provided in materials, services and procedures.

- Economize: According to this principle, logistics services should be minimal cost for suppliers, producers and consumers.

- Sufficiency: Rather than having too much inventory in logistics activities, it is essential to be able to deliver goods in a short time.

- Elasticity: Logistics activities should be in a structure that can adapt to changing situations and tasks.

- Simplicity: Simplicity must be taken into account in the planning and execution of logistics. In this case it is possible to increase effectiveness.

- Efficient Monitoring: All operations must be carried out using all means and tools and possible problems should be eliminated in a short time.

-Coordination: Coordination is a very important factor in ensuring effectiveness in logistics activities. Coordination between logistics planners, performers and customers must be ensured.

- Planning: It is important to determine the reasons for the difference between planned and actual. This will make it easier to identify and resolve problems.

Types of logistics

Logistics activities can be classified as follows:

- Procurement Logistics: This type of logistics includes the process of providing the firms with material resources, the allocation of resources in the warehouses of the enterprise, storage and delivery into production.

- Industrial Logistics: Industrial logistics includes materials management, raw materials for the primary source of finished products and management of these.

- Distribution logistics: This type of logistics deals with the distribution of raw materials and finished goods and services to the relevant units.

Transport logistics: This is the most common type of logistics. This type of logistics deals with the link between supply, production and marketing of products.

Outsourcing in logistics (PL)

Outsourcing in logistics has changed over time. As a result, some terms have emerged that reflect these stages.

1) 1PL means that logistics, manufacturing or trading companies carry out their logistics activities within the companies. In other words, firms do not receive outsourced assistance for their logistics activities. These functions are carried out by the company's own specialized departments. Companies have logistic equipment such as warehouses and transport vehicles. Companies need specialized people and units to be successful in 1PL implementation. In addition, machinery and equipment must be sufficient.

2) 2PL refers to the management of traditional logistics vehicles such as logistics, companies transport and warehouse. Companies that do not have such tools and infrastructure can go for rent. The most important reason is to reduce cost or capital investment. Firms lease a carrier or warehouse manager as a subcontractor for the operational execution. Operations are clearly defined and detailed. The logistics company is acting in accordance with the instructions of the customer.

3) Third party logistics (3PL / TPL) are known as freight logistics or contract logistics. Murphy and Poist in 2000 (pp.121) defined 3PL as "A relationship between two parties or more which, compared with basic logistics services, has more customized offerings, encompasses a broader number of service functions and is characterized by a longer-term, more mutually beneficial relationship". "The manufacturer outsources a package of transport and logistic activities. The third party logistic service provider organizes these activities and may hire third parties for the specific execution (subcontracting)". The producer issues a demand list for transportation and logistics activities. The 3PL logistics service provider is organizing these activities. The 3PL logistics service provider can rent different subcontractors for these activities. The 3PL service provider communicates with both the supplier and the manufacturer. As a third

party, it arranges logistics between two successive actors in the supply chain. The customer usually establishes a long-term business relationship with the logistics provider. In this commercial relationship, the customer measures the performance of the service provider and moves accordingly.

4) Fourth party logistics: In 4PL logistics, the manufacturer transfers the organization of logistics missions to the third party. In addition, logistics management is also outsourced. Third party logistics service providers often control the whole supply chain process. Organizational and executive activities are often carried out by different parties. Third-party logistics service providers often lack warehouses, transport vehicles, and other equipment. Fourth party logistics requires intensive participation of the service supplier in the business activities of the customer. The manufacturer is not out of the process. There is an intensive observation activity here. Logistics costs are again important. But quality of service plays a primary role. Risk and benefits are common.

5) E-commerce is an important trading instrument today. Millions of goods are sold every day on e-commerce sites, and the transportation of these goods to customer increases logistics volume. The fifth logistics (5PL) was developed to serve the e-commerce market. Information technology and systems are very important in 5PL activities. A fifth logistics service provider manages their supply chain networks. Manufacturers are working with companies specializing in e-commerce to provide innovative logistics solutions and concepts. Delivery time in e-commerce is very important for companies. Often the same products are sold on different e-commerce sites. One of the most important determinants of e-commerce is logistics quality. For this reason, 5PL services are getting more and more important every day.

Logistics management

Logistics management is the maintenance, monitoring and development of logistics activities in a certain order. Activities that concern logistics management can be summarized as follows:

- Transportation: This includes the management of all forms of transport and transport service selection.
- Inventory Management: This includes the regulation of stocking policies of raw materials and finished products, and the determination of Just-In Time production strategies.
- Order Processing: This includes all activities related to order taking and recording.

- Storage: This includes activities for determining the location and order of the warehouse. Importance is attached to costs and infrastructure in storage operation.
- Handling: This includes activities related to the identification of the tools necessary for the loading and unloading of materials and the establishment of order.
- Supply: This activity includes the selection of the procurement source, the time of procurement and the determination of the procurement amount.
- Protective Packaging: Protective packaging includes activities necessary to protect finished products or raw materials and materials during their storage and handling.
- Information Management: This includes activities related to the collection and analysis of information.

Logistics and economy

In the science of economics, the perfect competition market is defined as the ideal market. It is impossible to meet the conditions of a perfect competition market. Nevertheless, it can be said that a market is effective as it approximates the perfect competition market. One of the assumptions of perfect competition is that the transportation cost of goods and services is zero. From this, we can deduce that the factors that reduce the transportation costs of goods and services will help effectiveness. For this reason, it is important that logistics activities help to reduce the transportation costs per unit. However, as a result of the diversification of logistics activities and the increase of competition, decrease in the costs causes increase of the firm's profits.

Logistic activities are also important from a macroeconomic point of view. First of all, logistics activities become an "Economic Sector". In this case, it is expected that logistics investments will increase and unemployment of countries will decrease. As a result, increased logistics activities are positively impacting GDP. Moreover, the decrease in the carrying costs of goods can also positively affect the overall level of prices in an economy. The increase in the number of international transportation companies in a country can also positively affect foreign trade indicators.

In recent times, China has become a production centre of the Far East region. In this region, goods are shipped to various parts of the world, especially to the USA and the EU. Transportation costs, both for production and for consumption, have become an important issue for businesses. Transport and logistics costs in both domestic and international trade have become an important factor in the competition of businesses. For this reason, companies have started to give importance to transportation and logistics activities. This competition has also been felt in particular in terms of foreign direct investments. Countries that are advantageous in the field of transportation and logistics have started to use these factors to attract foreign direct investment.

Since 2007, the World Bank has published the Logistics Performance Index (LPI) on countries' logistics activities. The LPI is based on a worldwide survey of operators on the ground. The LPI 2016 allows for comparisons across 160 countries. This index is calculated with the help of data from the 6 subcomponents. The six core components are:

- The efficiency of customs and border clearance,
- The quality of trade and transport infrastructure,
- The ease of arranging competitively priced shipments,
- The competence and quality of logistics services,
- The ability to track and trace consignments,

The frequency with which shipments reach consignees within scheduled or expected delivery times.

According to overall LPI scores, Germany, Luxembourg and Sweden have the best logistics performance. The worst scores belong to Somalia, Haiti and Syrian Arab Republic. When all LPI data are analysed, developed countries have higher logistical performances and less developed countries have lower performance.

Conclusion

Logistics is an interesting subject for today's economic activities. Logistics is primarily important for companies in terms of cost and competition. In addition, it is important to diversify, accelerate and provide various advantages among logistics activities among the countries. The World Bank has published the LPI index since 2007, indicating a country's logistics performances. LPI scores allow comparison between countries. LPI also reflects the performance changes of countries over time. For this reason, each country should analyse their scores well and take precautions about the components that reduce their scores.

References

Acquisition Logistics Overview
http://www.acqnotes.com/acqnote/careerfields/acquisition-logistics-overview

Barlas, D. (2002) Outsourcing logistics: As 3PL increases in importance, providers are expanding e-business services, *Line 56 Magazine*, February.

Bowersox, D. V., Closs, D. J. & Cooper, M. B. (2007). Supply Chain Logistics Management, Mc Graw-Hill, Irwin.

CSCMP Supply Chain Management Definitions, www.cscmp.org

Christopher, M. (2016) Logistics and Supply Chain Management, Fifth Edition, Pearson, UK. http://www.logisticsglossary.com

Emmett, S. (2012). A switch Guide to a Systems View of the Supply Chain, Cambrigde Academic Press, Cambridge Academic Press.

Erdal, M. (2005), Küresel Lojistik [Global Logistics], UTIKAD Publications, Istanbul.

Langley Jr., C. J., Allen, G. R. & Tyndall, G. R. (2001). Third-Party Logistics Study: Results and Findings of the 2001 Sixth Annual Study. Cap Gemini Ernst and Young. pp.1-28.

Mangan, J. & Lalwani, C. L. (2016). Global Logistics and Supply Chain Management, 3rd. Edition, Wiley.

Murphy, P. R. & Poist, R. F. (2000). Third-party logistics: Some user versus provider perspective", *Journal of Business Logistics*, vol. 21, no.1, pp. 121-134.

Wong, Y., Maher, T. E., Nicholson, J. D. & Gurney, N. P. (2000). Strategic alliances in logistics outsourcing. *Asia Pacific Journal of Marketing and Logistics*, 12 (4), 3-21.

https://lpi.worldbank.org/

MULTICULTURALISM

İSMAİL DURSUNOĞLU AND HAYRİYE ŞENGÜN

Introduction

Culture is derived from the Latin word 'colere' and means to cultivate the land, to plough the field and to farm. The term "culture" which appears as the word "cultura/culture/culture" in Western languages, was defined by the French thinker Voltaire as the "formation, development, [to] be improved and exaltation of human intelligence". Culture was used in the sense of civilization, and its content was further expanded in the Enlightenment period and the 19th century. Culture is the whole of human-specific knowledge, belief and behaviour and the sum of the material and spiritual values that are the parts of this whole. It is the whole of elements such as language, tradition, thought, law, rule, moral values, science, philosophy and works of art that enable individual and communal living to occur. In this sense, culture is expressed as the sum of the accepted values that are formed jointly by all the individuals of the society (Çüçen, 2005).

Multiculturalism Concept

According to Taylor, culture is a complex structure that includes knowledge, art and similar talents, skills, and habits that human beings have learned as a member of society (Durugönül, 2012). As it is seen, there are many definitions of culture. According to Kymlicka, culture is the nation. This nation represents a collection of separate languages and values that have been institutionally perfected, with a certain historical background in a region or country (McDonald, 1997). Raymond Williams describes culture as a lifestyle that constitutes certain meanings and values in ordinary behaviours and institutional structures; according to T.S. Elliot, all the characteristic activities and interests of a nation are considered to be culture (Tekinalp, 2005).

The concept of multiculturalism was used by Jimmy Carter in the United States in the 1970s when the melting policy failed, and it has found its scientific, social and political ground in the West since the early 1980s. It is the society where many cultures can live side by side which is emphasized by postmodernism and expressed by multiculturalism. According to Wagner, multiculturalism, as it is used today, means a multi-ethnic society. Ethnic groups are not assimilated even if they are in a minority in a society because they maintain their traditions, cultural values, and distinctive features that shortly distinguish themselves from the rest of society. Baumann points out that multiculturalism has a threefold basis, and ranks them as culture as nationalism, culture as ethnicity and culture as religion. According to Doytcheva, multiculturalism is a political program, an intellectual debate and practice that rises with the thought of bringing up different cultures by allowing them to reform the institutions of modern democracies, to improve and convey their differences (Durugönül, 2012). The concept of multiculturalism is not about individual differences and identities, but about differences and identities that are integrated and fed from cultural elements such as language, religion and ethnicity. In other words, it is necessary to consider collective beliefs, lifestyles and social practices, which are fundamental foundations, in order to talk about multiculturalism (Bhikhu, 2002). The concept of multiculturalism has been interpreted with different points of view. For instance, Rawls and Walzer tried to explain multiculturalism with the concept of justice, Young with the emphasis on diversity, Kymlicka with a minority rights and multi-national state view, Barry with individual rights discourse, Habermas with constitutional citizenship and Taylor with the concept of recognition (Mesut, 2012).

Multiculturalism is a multi-faceted structure that includes many cultural concepts such as race, ethnicity, language, sexual orientation, gender, age, disability, religious education and social status. In the concept of multiculturalism, it is a matter of thought that each culture is valuable, and therefore the comparison between cultures is wrong, and that every culture should be evaluated within the framework of its own truths. Because every culture has its own special conditions, it is very wrong to compare these conditions with different cultures (İlhan & Eylem, 2012).

In the process of globalization, nation-states are weakened from the top by supra-national structures and from the bottom by separatist local dynamics. The greatest criticism of the multicultural discourse to nation-states is the existence of its homogenizing feature. However, multiculturalists stay silent in the face of this criticism as to how social integration can be achieved. In nation-societies, it is supported to close the intersocietally cultural distance through the integration around the standard/dominant culture. The upper identity in multicultural social structures is aimed at social integration on the ground of emphasis on political commitment (citizenship). Multiculturalism means that cultural diversity is right and all cultures are respected rather than participation of individuals in the dominant culture. Multiculturalists think that intercultural equality should not renounce the cultural values of minorities and that cultural freedom is a right (Akça & Vurucu, 2010).

The policy of multiculturalism is regarded as the end of the monocultural modern society. There is the influence of postmodernism in reaching this point. Postmodernism has a mission to protect the differences. However, this thought system aims to integrate with communities rather than to separate from others. Different dimensions of multiculturalism have been revealed in this framework. These are factual, ideal and normative dimensions. Multiculturalism as factual refers to the societies created by individuals with social, religious, ethnic and national origins. Multiculturalism with its ideal dimension means that the cultural multitude in one place is praised and encouraged. Lastly, normative multiculturalism is defined as the state's abandonment of assimilation policies, its recognition of different cultures and its support for their development (Cevat, 2009).

Multiculturalism, seen as a dream of the democratic contemporary world in the 1960s and the following years, is now perceived as a threat to some communities. In particular, the concept which is thought to damage the homogenous structure of the nation-states has an understanding which is discussed in the intellectual framework in this respect but is practically avoided. Multiculturalism, expressed in the recognition of cultural differences, is, according to some analysts, transformed into a political project that allows the nation to be reformed by interrogating the moral foundations of the society in favour of different cultures, not ending the nation-state (Milena, 2013).

Multiculturalism may lead to cultural conflict and change. For instance, people migrating from rural areas to cities or to countries other than their home country, are mixed up in an affair between the cultures they are carrying and the culture they are acquainted with, and there are cross-cultural conflicts (Durugönül, 2012). However, multiculturalism is a concept that essentially guarantees lifestyles and advocates that differences should be treated with tolerance. In a multicultural society, inequalities and racist attitudes are rejected. The concept accepts the institutions necessary for the modern state and also considers the norms and values of minorities. This is an important step in the formation of a democratic culture.

National identity is one of the important elements of the modern period. However, it can be argued that this primary position of national identity for almost two centuries has been changed by the changing and corrosive effects of historical and social conditions. According to the new order, cultural identities that emerged at a more local level appear to erode national identities in the framework of globalization (Vatandaş, 2001). Along with globalization, there are those who think that national identity has lost its importance and nation-states have completed their lives. The differences attempted to be dissolved in the face of national identity reactively revealed multiculturalism. The recognition and tolerance of different cultural identities have been the product of this new idea (Taylor, 1996). Christian Joppke regards multiculturalism as a reflection of the homogenization of nation-state and defines it as a form of ethnic and cultural difference in migration from the neighbouring countries to the centre countries (Chiristian, 1996).

As a consequence of ensuring social harmony and stability and developing different policies with it as of today, the idea of unity on the basis of differences which is based on the principle of multiculturalism has gained importance. It is necessary to examine the concept of assimilation closely in order to correctly understand the policy of multiculturalism. Assimilation is defined as the attempt by others who are different from the dominant culture of society or those who participate in society for special reasons to be challenged in social harmony and to provide similarity with the dominant culture. Terms such as dissolving and swallowing are factors related to the concept of assimilation. Since this negative situation draws reaction, it is desired to define the process encountered with new concepts. Social integration is one of these concepts (Vatandaş, 2001). Multiculturalism is the idea that the dominant culture is motivated by social and political means, as well as concerns arising from the tendency to dissolve or even annihilate the cultural elements of minority groups and immigrants and upholds cultures as much as possible against assimilationist attitudes and politics (Akça & Vurucu, 2010).

Cultures do not exhibit a static state and are constantly developing. Historical developments are shaping cultures, and this situation changes from country to country. Even if there is more than one culture in every country, the presence of a dominant culture is a fact that is widely accepted by everyone. In addition to this, the existence of other cultures living in peace can be considered multiculturalism. However, this definition contains deficiencies. The coexistence of different cultures is not enough for multiculturalism; they need to be recognized by law and their cultural rights need be accepted. From this point of view, multiculturalism should be considered as a struggle and a culture fight.

From the late 1960s onwards, the democratic culture against the growing unease and movement of small groups in the West has encountered new experiences and these are defined as multiculturalism. These experiences are;

- Recognition of land and autonomy for native populations,
- Strengthening regional autonomy and official language status of subgroups,
- Determination of compromising policies for nomadic groups (Will, 2014).

Nation-states aim to create a common culture around the dominant culture by keeping together different cultures they have in their embodiment. Multiculturalism, on the other hand, expresses that each culture is important and needs to be kept alive rather than as a common culture with its intellectual system (Polat & Kılıç, 2013). In some multinational states, the national identities that constitute the structure demand political autonomy or forms of government based on principles of territory to ensure full development. If more extreme instances are examined, these groups even bring their own right to self-determination. Although the right of self-determination adopted by the United Nations is in fact intended for overseas colonial countries, discussions about the concept continues in multinational states (Will, 1995). In theory, there are three main topics of group rights on the basis of multiculturalism, which are self-government, multi-ethnicity and special representation. These groups are moderately approaching the state, etc. Systems so they can build their own self-governments under a federal framework. What is meant by multi-ethnicity is that any group is not to impose the religious, cultural, political, ideological arguments of another group. For instance, people living in Canada with Sikhism beliefs demand that they do not wear helmets when using motorcycles because of their headwear which is particular to them. The special representation is that these groups are adequately represented in the national parliaments and that their wishes and complaints are expressed from the first person.

There are those who oppose it as well as those who support multiculturalism. For instance, Jos de Beaus, professor of political culture at the University of Amsterdam stated that the multicultural model has collapsed in practice, and that subcultures need to be weakened for the future of democracies (Tekinalp, 2005). As indicated, multiculturalism is criticized by many authorities, and it is expressed that it is the source of some social problems and also causes division, conflict and confusion. According to opponents of concept, multiculturalism policy provides categorizing and defining people instead of uniting them under the roof of a nation, which leads to cracks on the ground of social unity. This situation means the end of politics, culture and civilization. It should be reminded that the promise of multicultural life has created division, separation and us/the other dilemmas in the background, and it stands in front of us as one of the biggest problems of the 21st century with this aspect. According to sections who criticize multiculturalism, this concept is a new trap of global capitalism. It is also against the spirit of national unity and solidarity. These are the discourses that these people put forward about multiculturalism (Polat & Kılıç, 2013):

- The multicultural society brings with it intercultural conflicts. Social reconciliation around these conflicts is a distant and contradictory situation.
- Cultural differences make it difficult for ethnic groups to adapt.
- Immigrants keep themselves out of the dominant culture and excluded from society because they are overly committed to their own culture.
- It is difficult for Western culture to establish mutual relations and integrity with other cultures in its structure because it identifies itself as a superior and exemplary culture.
- Complete or limited assimilation is required for integration. Because of this, immigrant or minority groups should comply with the values and norms in the public area.

Multiculturalism supporters have suggested that citizenship should be cleared from the nation and restructured on the basis of multiculturalism. According to this idea, citizenship for participation in national integrity is considered to be the source of all evil; citizenship stresses linguistic, religious and ethnic identities. In other words, multicultural citizenship is presented as a means of solving all political-social problems. However, multicultural citizenship policies have the potential to threaten social and political existence. As Habermas points out, the livelihood and survival of local cultures will bring conflict with the majority culture within the nation-state structure. This struggle will eventually turn into a struggle for cultures to establish dominance over one another and to annihilate the other. Moreover, the division of the society into autonomous units in itself will reveal the risk of becoming a state. The efforts to protect social differences and to treat them with respect as stipulated by multiculturalism are seen as natural. However, the politicization of differences threatens the existing social entity. It is also impossible to fully meet the demands of the differences that arise within the nation-state. States, of course, should be sensitive to social demands coming from the sole. The ideal way to do this is that the state tries to address the society and the social sections to integrate with the state. The practical experience of multiculturalism policy weakens social existence rather than strengthens it. Although it is a fact that societies are multicultural, equal political representation of all societies is also impossible. Political citizenship in modern nation-states maintains its existence as a means by which historical-cultural differences can express it. Therefore, a system that is independent of the nation-state model making multiculturalism possible has not emerged today (Gürsoy & İkbal, 2010).

Conclusion

Globalization is the spreading of social and intercommunal relations across the world in economic, political and cultural terms by removing national borders in the wake of science, mass communication and technological developments and the turning of the world into a common market; in short, it is the world becoming a big global village. Globalization has brought with it many concepts and left many social values or elements on the past pages of history. Globalization foresees a two-way process at the point of promising international integrity on the one hand and activating culture and identities at the local level on the other hand. The concept of multiculturalism which concerns both the societies and the states emerging in the second dimension of this process has been one of the topics frequently discussed in the field of politics and sociology. Multiculturalism is the coexistence of many different cultures protecting their self-identities. There is a parallel relationship between globalization and multiculturalism. Multiculturalism's anticipation of unity in the axis of differences has not got meaning mutually much in the practice. Multiculturalism poses a threat in terms of the nation-state, which is still the most realistic and valid state model today even though its former importance has disappeared. It should not be forgotten that in nation-states with a strong unitary structure, including Turkey, even if the emphasis of multiculturalism and ethnic differences in recent years is a discourse or a policy expressed in order to raise democratic values, it threatens national unity and integrity. There is a need for scientific studies in the literature foreseeing field research related to this. This study forms the theoretical basis for other studies to be carried out in the related field.

References

Akça, G. & Vurucu, İ. (2010). Çokkültürlülük Tartışmaları, Toplumsal Bütünlük Kaygısı ve Yeniden Milletleşme, Sosyal Bilimler Dergisi, 24,18-19.

Çüçen, A. K. (2005). Kültür, Uygarlık, Evrensellik ve Çok-Kültürlülük, Uludağ Üniversitesi Felsefe Dergisi: S:4 KAYGI, (pp. 111-115).

Doytcheva, M. (2009). Çokkültürlülük, çev: Tuba Akıncılar Onmuş, İletişim Yayınları, İstanbul, Turkey.

Durugönül, E. (2012). Redefining Multiculturalism: The Case of Germany, Contemporary Online Language Education Journal, 2(2), (pp.17-28).

Hazır, M. (2012). Çokkültürlülük Teorisine Çağdaş Katkılar ve Bireysel Haklar-Grup Hakları Ekseninde Çokkültürlülüğü Tartışmak, Akademik İncelemeler Dergisi, C:7 S:1, Turkey

Kymlicka, W. (1995). Multicultural Citizenship-A Liberal Theory of Minority Rights. Oxford University Press, 84-117.

McDonald, L. (1997). Regrouping in Defence of Minority Rights: Kymlicka's Multicultural Citizenship. Osgoode Hall Law Journal, 34, (2), 294-309.

Cortigiani, M. (2013). La persona en el centro. la profesión de asistente social en un país en transformación. Humanismo Y Trabajo Social, (12), 33-53.

Özyurt, C. (2009). Toplumu Yeniden Düşünmek: Kozmopolitanizm ve Çokkültürlülük, Sosyoloji Derneği, VI. Ulusal Sosyoloji Kongresi, Adnan Menderes Üniversitesi, Aydın, Ekim-2009, (pp:75-78), Turkey.

Parekh, B. (2002). Çokkültürlülüğü Yeniden Düşünmek: Kültürel Çeşitlilik ve Siyasi Teori, çev: Bilgi Tanrıseven, Phoenix Yayınları, Ankara, Turkey.

Polat, İ. & Kılıç, E. (2013). Türkiye'de Çokkültürlü Eğitim ve Çokkültürlü Eğitimde Öğretmen Yeterliliği, YYÜ Eğitim Fakültesi Dergisi, 10 (1), Turkey.

Taylor, C. (1996). Tanınma Politikası, Çokkültürlülük, der: Amy Gutmann, Yapı Kredi Yayınları, İstanbul-1996 Joppke C. (1996), Multiculturalism and Immigration Acomparison of the United States, Germany and Great Britain, Theory and Society, C:25 S:4, (pp.451-453), Turkey.

Tekinalp, Ş. (2005). Küreselleşen Dünyanın Bunalımı, Çokkültürlülük, Journal of İstanbul Kültür University, Turkey.

Vatandaş, C. (2001). Çokkültürlü Yapıda Ulusal/Etnik Kimlikler (Kanada Örneği), http://www.aku.edu.tr/aku/dosyayonetimi/sosyalbilens/dergi/III2/vatan das.pdf

Will, K. (2014). The Essentialist Critique of Multiculturalism: Theories, Policies, Ethos, European University Institute Robert Schuman Centre for Advanced Studies Global Governance Programme, http://www.raison-publique.fr/IMG/pdf/Kymlicka.Essentialist_critique _of_multiculturalism.Paris.pdf

THE SOCIAL MARKETING

ENES EMRE BAŞAR

Introduction

The term social marketing was conceptualized by Kotler and Zaltman (1971) to refer to the application of marketing to the solution of social problems. As is known, marketing has played a very important role in encouraging people to buy products (MacFadyen et al., 2003). Social marketers, on the other hand, are trying to market concepts such as social fraternity, friendship, peace, healthy lifestyle and struggle with poverty.

This chapter examines these ideas. It begins with definitions of social marketing. It then explains how social marketing has developed. The chapter then handles how products/services-based marketing adapt to the practice of social marketing through segmentation and social marketing mix.

Definitions of social marketing

Social marketing is concerned with the societal or ethical implications of marketing activity (MacFadyen et al., 2003). So, "the 'social marketing concept' encourages firms to market goods and services that will satisfy consumers under circumstances that are fair to consumers and that enable them to make intelligent purchase decisions, and counsels firms to avoid marketing practices which have dubious consequences for society" (Schwartz, 1971: p.32).

According to Andreasen's (1995, p.109) definition "social marketing is the application of commercial marketing technologies to the analysis, planning, execution and evaluation of programs designed to influence the voluntary behaviour of target audiences in order to improve their personal welfare and that of society".

Newer definitions have begun to debate the role of long-term relationships in social marketing. Dann (2010, p.148), for example, has defined social marketing as "the application of marketing concepts and techniques to exchanges that result in the achievement of socially desirable aims." According to Donovan and Henley (2010, p.41), "social marketing is an attempt to influence consumers for the greater good, and as such, always has an ethical aspect; specifically, social marketing seeks to induce consumer change that is deemed to be inherently good, as opposed to change that is good merely because it increases profits non-profit earnings." Schwartz et al. (1994, p.3), on the other hand, has expressed social marketing as follows "a large-scale program planning process designed to influence the voluntary behaviour of a specific audience segment to achieve a social rather than a financial objective, and based upon offering benefits the audience wants, reducing barriers the audience faces and/or using persuasion to influence the segment's intention to act favourably."

The Development of Social Marketing

The development of social marketing has been accompanied by traditional commercial marketing. Wiebe (1952), firstly, examined the effects of the application of a commercial marketing campaign to a social change campaign. However, this idea was not adopted at that time by notable marketing academicians (e.g. Luck, 1974). Despite these negative perspectives, the use of commercial marketing strategies in health campaigns in the 1960s began to pave the expansion of social marketing (e.g. Manoff, 1985). Kotler and Zaltman (1971) used the term "social marketing" for the first time. They defined social marketing as "the design, implementation and control of programs calculated to influence the acceptability of social ideas and involving considerations of product planning, pricing, communication, distribution and marketing research" (Kotler & Zaltman, p.5). Nevertheless, the concept of social marketing reached its present meaning in the 1990s. The idea that social marketing aims not only to change thoughts, but also to affect behaviour has been accepted by marketing academicians in the 1990s (Andreasen, 1995). After that, it could be said that social marketing takes place increasingly every year in practice. The historical evolution of social marketing is seen in Table 1.15.

Table 1-15. Social Marketing: Seminal Events and Publications

1970s

1971: A pioneering article, "Social Marketing: An Approach to Planned Social Change," in the Journal of Marketing by Philip Kotler and Gerald Zaltman coins the term *social marketing*

1980s

World Bank, World Health Organization, and Centers for Disease Control start to use the term and promote interest in social marketing.

1981: An article in the Journal of Marketing by Paul Bloom and William Novelli reviews the first 10 years of social marketing and highlights the lack of rigor in the application of marketing principles and techniques in critical areas of the field, including research, segmentation, and distribution channels.

1988: An article in the Health Education Quarterly, "Social Marketing and Public Health Intervention," by R. Craig Lefebvre and June Flora, gives social marketing widespread exposure in the field of public health.

1989: A text, Social Marketing Strategies for Changing Public Behavior by Philip Kotler and Eduardo Roberto, lays out the application of marketing principles and techniques for influencing social change management.

1990s

Academic programs are established, including the Centre for Social Marketing at the University of Strathclyde in Glasgow and the Department of Community and Family Health at the University of South Florida.

1992: An article in the American Psychologist by James Prochaska, Carlo DiClemente, and John Norcross presents an organizing framework for achieving behaviour change consider by many as the most useful model developed to date.

1994: A publication, Social Marketing Quarterly, by Best Start Inc. and the Department of Public Health, University of South Florida, is launched.

1995: A text, Fostering Sustainable Behavior, by Doug McKenzie-Mohr and William Smith, provides an introduction to community based social marketing.

1999: The Social Marketing Institute is formed in Washington, D.C., with Alan Andreasen from Georgetown University as interim executive director.

2000s

2003: A text, Social Marketing: Principles & Prectice, by Rob Donovan, is published in Melbourne, Australia.

2005: The 10th annual conference for Innovations in Social Marketing is held.
2011: A book, Social Marketing: Influencing Behaviors for Good, by Nancy R. Lee and Philip Kotler, is published in California, USA.
2011: An article in the Journal of Marketing by Philip Kotler, "Reinventing Marketing to Manage the Environmental Imperative."
2016: An article in the Journal of Marketing Management by Christine Domegan et al., "Systems-thinking social marketing: conceptual extensions and empirical investigations"

Adapted from Lee and Kotler (2008)

Segmentation in social marketing

The particular characteristics of social marketing create a need for specialized segmentation criteria. Traditional marketing is generally segmented according to three criteria. These are personal characteristics, behavioural characteristics and benefits sought by consumers. Although all of which are relevant to social marketing, some additional attributes which have specific relevance to social marketing should be outlined (MacFadyen et al., 2003) (see Table 1.16).

Table 1-16. Major Segmentation Approaches

Characteristics		Attributes	Social marketing
Personal characteristics	Demographic	Age, Gender, Social class, Ethnicity, Family profile, Income, Employment	Health status
	Psychographic	Lifestyle, Personality	Health beliefs, motivation, locus of control
	Geodemographic	Geographical area, Neighbourhood type	Residence in disadvantaged area
Behavioural characteristics		Usage, Loyalty, Response, Attitudes	Health behaviour, Stage of Change
Benefit characteristics		Benefits sought	Barriers

Source: MacFadyen et al., 2003

Demographic segmentation is broadly accepted in segmentation of social marketing. The reason is that many social problems continue to be demographic. Compared to demographic characteristics, the application of psychographic segmentation in social marketing is less established. However, the complex psychosocial determinants of health behaviour are adopted as segmentation approaches by social marketers (Slater, 1995). On the other hand, applications of geodemographic to social marketing are determining channels for healthcare advertising and mailing (Mac Fadyen et al., 2003).

Behavioural characteristics include volume of product usage, readiness to use, responsiveness, and attitudes towards usage (Wilkie, 1994). "The concept of readiness to change" is an important behavioural characteristic in social marketing. The basis of the transtheoretical model of behaviour change is based on the idea that the emergence of behaviour is a process that occurs through five stages: pre-contemplation, contemplation, preparation, action and maintenance. The model is explanatory in two ways. First, it stresses that behavioural change is very complex and multi-levelled. Second, it supplies a framework for scheming suitable messages and support interpositions (Bitirim, 2014).

Segmentation by benefit characteristics is specific to the particular product being marketed. This type of segmentation seems at first sight to have slighter connection in social marketing than the others three types. However, social marketing researchers nevertheless need to think in terms of consumers and the benefits they search rather than products (MacFadyen et al., 2003).

In summarizing, social marketers should segment their markets in terms of need. According to MacFadyen et al. (2003, p.713) "as well as bringing the standard segmentation benefits, this will ensure that limited resources are used most efficiently".

The Social Marketing Mix

The marketing mix has to be modified for use in social marketing (see Table 1-17).

Table 1-17. The Social Marketing Mix

Tool		Types
Product	The offer made to target adopters	Adoption of idea (belief, attitude, value) Adoption of behaviour (one-off, sustained) Desistence from current behaviour Non-adoption of future behaviour
Price	The costs that target adopters have to bear	Psychological, emotional, cultural, social, behavioural, temporal, practical, physical, financial
Place	The channels by which the change is promoted and places in which the change is supported and encouraged	Media channels Distribution channels Interpersonal channels Physical places Non-physical places (e.g. social and cultural climate)
Promotion	The means by which the change is promoted to the target	Advertising Public relations Media advocacy Direct mail Interpersonal

Adapted from Kotler and Roberto (1989)

Product

The product, in social marketing, is not just an object with a concrete counterpart. The product in social marketing can be concrete, abstract, or a combination of both. Undoubtedly, in social marketing, product concept and design are more complex than product concept and design process of traditional marketing. Some researchers describe the product as the results of social campaigns, while others describe the product as the tools used during the campaigns (Peattie and Peattie, 2003).

Price

Price, in social marketing, is the monetary costs incurred to change. Although the price emphasizes monetary costs in social marketing, it also involves spending time/effort and psychological costs to change cultural practices by influencing attitudes and behaviours behaviour (Lefebre & Flora, 1988).

Place

Place in social marketing involves channels that transmit information to target groups, and facilities the acceptance of social marketing products. Individuals, institutions or organizations can be evaluated among intermediaries within the distribution channel (Kotler, 2002).

Promotion

In the scope of social marketing, two main priority issues are emerging, in order to ensure effectiveness of promotional activities. First is the establishment of the message strategy, and second is the choice of media tools and techniques. In social marketing, the message strategy involves the development of the right messages to support the behaviour desired by the target groups (Velioğlu & Çoknaz, 2008).

Social marketing researchers have long sought to adapt the established marketing mix model to the social marketing. This is illustrated in Table 1-18, which describes the four Ps of the social marketing mix (Gordon, 2012, p.124).

Table 1-18. The Four Ps Social Marketing Mix

Four Ps	
Product	In social marketing represents the behavioural offer made to target adopters and often involves intangibles such as adoption of an idea or behaviour. Tangible product offerings such as condoms to encourage safe sex can also be present
Price	In social marketing price relates to the costs that the target audience have to pay and the barriers they have to overcome to adopt the desired behaviour, and these costs can be psychological (e.g. loss of de-stressing effect from smoking), cultural, social (e.g. peer pressure to drink), temporal, practical (e.g. cancelling the school run to reduce car use), physical and financial (e.g. cost of joining a gym to get fit)
Place	Place in social marketing are the channels by which behaviour change is promoted and the places in which change is encouraged and supported
Promotion	In the social marketing context promotion is the means by which behaviour change is promoted to the target audience, for example advertising, media relations, direct mail and interpersonal

Gordon (2012), on the other hand, has proposed re-tooling the social marketing mix. It is argued by Gordon (2012, p.124) that re-tooling the social marketing mix can offer emancipation from the narrow confines of the four Ps framework. Gordon's illustrative social marketing mix model outlines how such a new social marketing mix might encompass the features of contemporary social marketing (see Figure 1.5).

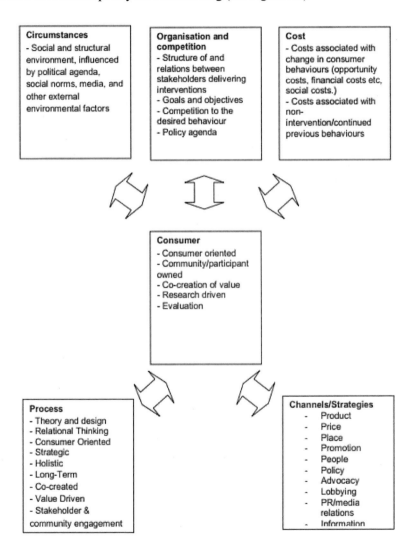

Figure 1-5. Gordon's (2012) Social Marketing Mix

According to Gordon (2012, p.125) "A new social marketing model that includes the other strategies employed in social marketing beyond product, price, place and promotion, and is also able to incorporate a more consumer-oriented approach in which relational thinking, and a strategic and holistic approach to behaviour change, would be beneficial to the field."

Conclusion

Over the last 30 years, social marketing has resolved major social problems, taking traditional marketing principles. In this respect social marketing made itself a consistent and valuable discipline. Its unique characteristics of social marketing mean that the occurring strategies are constantly implemented in distinct ways.

Social marketing must overcome three main challenges in the near future. First, it must proceed to improve its theoretical base. Second, it must successfully tackle real social problems. Third, it should need to provide more educational opportunities in social marketing.

Finally, it would be useful for social marketing to pursue a parallel process of re-tooling the marketing mix. Further research will be needed to upgrade to meet the challenges of the future understanding of social marketing.

References

Andreasen, A. R. (1995). *Marketing Social Change: Changing Behavior to Promote Health, Social Development, and the Environment*, San Francisco: Joses Bass.

Bitirim, S. (2014). Toplumsal Faydanın Yaratılmasında Sosyal Pazarlama ve İletişim. *Unpublished Doctorate Thesis*, Ege University Social Sciences Institute.

Craig Lefebvre, R. & Flora, J. A. (1988). "Social marketing and public health intervention", *Health Education Quarterly*, 15(3), 299-315.

Donovan, R. & Henley, N. (2010). *Principles and Practice of Social Marketing: An International Perspective*. Cambridge University Press.

Gordon, R. (2012). "Re-thinking and re-tooling the social marketing mix", *Australasian Marketing Journal*, 20, 122-126.

Dann, S. (2010). "Redefining social marketing with contemporary commercial marketing definitions". *Journal of Business Research, 63* (2), 147-153.

Kotler, P. (2002). *Marketing Places*. USA: Simon and Schuster.

Kotler, P. & Lee, N. (2008). *Corporate Social Responsibility: Doing the Most Good for Your Company and Your Cause*. USA: John Wiley & Sons.

Kotler, P. & Roberto, E. L. (1989). *Social Marketing. Strategies for Changing Public Behavior*. New York: Free Press.

Kotler, P. & Zaltman, G. (1971). "Social marketing: an approach to planned social change", *Journal of Marketing*, 35, 3–12.

Lee, N. R. & Kotler, P. (2008). *Influencing Behaviors for Good*, 3rd Ed., USA: Sage Pub.

Luck, D. J. (1974). "Social marketing: confusion compounded", *Journal of Marketing*, 38, October, 70–72.

Manoff, R. K. (1985). *Social marketing: New imperative for public health*, New York: Praeger.

Peattie, S. & Peattie, K. (2003). "Ready to fly solo? Reducing social marketing dependence on commercial marketing theory", *Marketing Theory*, 3(3), 371-380.

Peattie, S. & Peattie, K. (2003). "Ready to fly solo? Reducing social marketing's dependence on commercial marketing theory", *Marketing Theory*, 3(3), 365-385.

Schwartz, B., Middlestadt, S. & Verzosa, C. (1994). "Social marketing for gender equity in Bangladesh", *Social Marketing Quarterly*, 1(1), 3-3.

Schwartz, B., Middlestadt, S. & Verzosa, C. (1994). "Social marketing for gender equity in Bangladesh", *Social Marketing Quarterly*, 1(1), 3-3.

Schwartz, G. (1971). *Marketing: The Societal Marketing Concept*, University of Washington Business Review, 31, 31–38.

Slater, M. D. (1995). Choosing audience segmentation strategies and methods for health communication, in Maibach, E. and Parrott, R. L. (eds), *Designing Health Messages. Approaches from Communication Theory and Public Health Practice*, USA: Sage.

Velioğlu, M. N. & Çoknaz, D. (2008). *Güncel Pazarlama Yaklaşımlarından Seçmeler*, Ankara: Detay Yayıncılık.

Wiebe, G. D. (1952). Merchandising commodities and citizenship in television. *Public Opinion Quarterly*, 15, Winter, 679–691.

Wilkie, W. L. (1994). *Consumer Behavior*, 3rd edn, New York; Wiley.

CHAPTER TWO

LINGUISTICS AND LITERATURE

WOMEN CAUGHT BETWEEN TRADITION AND MODERNITY IN NEZİHE MERİÇ'S STORIES[*]

AYHAN BULUT

Introduction

Nezihe Meriç, one of the first female storytellers of the Republican era, is an author who uses innovative methods to address the stages of social change and freedom experienced by the country and contributes to the renaissance of our literature by keeping in line with transformations and developments brought about by modernism in the social structure. Dwelling upon women's issues that are crystallized in Turkey by the ongoing debate on women's social status in Europe and America, Nezihe Meriç puts women's social, economic, class and cultural position in the centre of her novels and stories. She creates new images of women who break down the rules set by the patriarchal social structure.

Meriç focuses on social conditions when creating her images of women. She considers social conditions and obsolete customs to be the greatest obstacles to the development of women's freedom. She believes that customs impeding women's social status should definitely be done away with so that Turkey caught between tradition and modernity can at last be modern. Describing in her stories the inner loneliness and conflicts of women oppressed and shunned by patriarchal structures of society, Meriç argues that the relationship between individual and society is ultimately imbalanced due to obsolete customs, the prevalence of which is always detrimental to women. As an intellectual, Nezihe Meriç never turns a blind eye to issues of women raised under the yoke of patriarchal structures. The issues she points out are the issues of educated or uneducated, conscious or unconscious, and deeply hurt women who are the victims of male domination and obsolete traditions and customs (Doğan, 1980: p.50). Meriç tries to guide oppressed women by exalting women protagonists who have the courage to oppose those obsolete

---

[*] In this section " Life, Art and Works of Nezihe Meriç " has been derived from the master thesis of author

traditions and customs. Portraying unhappy middle-class intellectuals, mostly women, Meriç (Önertoy, 1984: p.268) focuses on women's identity and makes various social, political and cultural issues integral to her stories. She tries to give an intense narration of political aspirations, individual orientations, internal and external conflicts, and women's political and individual achievements, failures, griefs and sorrows.

Women are the focal point of Nezihe Meriç's stories. Except a few stories, all her stories address social issues and critiques of traditions and false customs from the perspective of women, who fulfil an important function in the way stories, achieve their objectives and are well understood. Women are presented as positive figures in the face of all negative values. The portrayal of women being oppressed by men bestowed with power by traditional societies is favored by Nezihe Meriç, as it triggers the development of a critical approach by women to the male-dominated power structure of patriarchal society. It is more than natural that the author, also a woman, evaluates things from women's point of view and stands in favour of women as she is not exempt from restrictions of social traditions. She even depicts women who do not have the courage to stand up to society as kind hearted characters. They are portrayed as women who never give up on having positive perspectives of life, despite their oppression by society. Since the author tries to reflect the perspectives of women on her works, she pays great attention to the details of women's inner worlds and psychological motives. Almost all of the women portrayed in her works are poor and middle-class urban people from every walk of life such as teachers, lawyers, doctors, engineers, retirees, drivers, grocers and university students who are drawn to their inner world filled with pessimism in the face of the overwhelming power of city life. The growing feeling of loneliness, that women protagonist's experience, is exacerbated also by social pressure. Nezihe Meriç tries not to ignore the relationship of the women characters with their environment. *"She performs introspection and extrospection together. She depicts her protagonists' appearance and inner feelings together, through which they come into existence not only with what they say or do but also with what they think and hear"* (Bezirci, 1999: p.85). Hamdi Olcay describes this technique, which portrays women's emotionality more clearly, as: *"Women's hearts can only be learned through women's hearts... But unfortunately, most of our women authors have all along refrained from revealing their emotions loud and clear. The reason for this could be the sense of constraint engendered by the veils they covered their bodies with, the loose robes they put on, the burqas they wrapped themselves up in or the cages they lived in. They have forced themselves to think and write as others would like them to. In short, they have not been able to be sincere. This is why we do not even have a woman artist alive today. We will see many "beauties" that perpetuate their love, suffering, compassion"* (Olcay, 1951: p.81).

The issues that she addresses in her stories such as man-woman relations, marriage, affairs and adaptation problems that young women face when migrating from the village to the city are accounted for by both social as well as individual reasons. As Önertoy (1984: p.268) states; *"Meriç wants to say that social disorders can be solved with a number of individual efforts. Thus, she has the characteristics of an author whose realism is limited to observations and whose focus is on the individual"*. While she reflects the existential venture of women in social dilemmas on the basis of individual situations, she poetically expresses women's search for identity, positions in conflicts and disintegration from which they suffer. The fact that the characters in her novels and stories are predominantly women and that it is only the women characters that experience inner conflicts bring her works closer to a feminist line of thought. Her stories deal with problems posed by ossified values that orbit around the lives of modern women and address the relationship between free women and society in a feminist context. The modern woman in her stories chooses to rebel, though sometimes passive, rather than submit to her fate. Thus, Meriç, compared to the past, appears to have taken on the changing responsibilities of women.

This study examines the main women characters in Nezihe Meriç's stories and classifies them as "Enlightened Women," "Housewives," "Young Girls," "Old Women" and "Downtrodden Prostitutes" depending on gender, age and social status.

1. Enlightened Women

Enlightened urban middle-class women are mostly educated in academics and have such occupations as teachers, lawyers, doctors and engineers. Oppression of women in social and cultural life by the patriarchal structure and impeding nature of false customs that prevent women from developing an independent gender identity bring women to the brink of conflict. Coexistence of the values of the modern world and traditional values, and the conflict of traditional values with the values of the modern world idealized by the republic are always detrimental to women, at which point the search for identity begins. The search for identity ends up with the protagonists suffering from inner loneliness.

In the story titled *Öğretmen*, a teacher, the protagonist, is positive, affectionate and profound. The main theme of the story is the feeling that the teacher, who is a young girl, has which was brought about by the coming of spring. This feeling is sometimes associated with longing for a world embodying all kinds of charm associated with spring which triggers an unconditional love for all people. This sometimes leads the teacher to adopt a critical perspective of society through recalling. The story depicts the lives of different people, who belong to the world we live in and to a world longed for. Despite the portrayal of the lives of different people, the author has no negative thoughts in the name of love for those people. People created by the author's imagination filled with the joy of nature do not need to know each other to love each other (Meriç, 1998: p.64):

A young man who passes by her while she is picking each petal off a daisy, and his brown eyes beaming like those of a child, he speaks the phrase: "He loves me, he loves me not. He loves me, he loves me not. The teacher frowns but she laughs up her sleeve. In fact, even if that young man came up to her and kissed her on the cheeks, she would think to herself. So, what? It is spring now. It was just a brotherly kiss".

However, society is not ready for such thoughts.

Nezihe Meriç portrays a woman teacher named Meli, the character of the stories titled *Susuz IV, Susuz V* and *Susuz VII* in her storybook titled *Topal Koşma* to underline her sociological observations regarding the social status of women. Meli is an idealistic literature teacher educated with the values idealized by the Republic. She is a selfish, strong, conceit and pessimistic woman who adopts the fight against ignorance as a principle. She pays a visit to a friend of hers whom she had not seen for a long time. The conversations Meli has with her friend, married with children, and the repercussions of those conversations on Meli set the course for the story. Meli's friend appears as a character who maintains the continuity of the concept of family which is at the brink of disintegration due to men cheating on their wives. The dialogues further emphasize Meli's pessimistic identity. The effect of city life on Meli's mood, her self-centeredness and lack of a purpose to fight exacerbate her pessimism. "*I am defeated again. I just cannot understand and I am in doubt. I do not know what to hold on to* (Meriç, 1998, p.130)".

In the story titled *Susuz V*, the teacher Mahmut and his friend have a conversation and mention Meli, who struggles to be an individual. Different from her friends, Meli has not been defeated by life. Unlike her friends, who have resigned themselves to the values of society, Meli has adopted the high values of individuality. "*Love is the physical and spiritual unity of meaning attributed to life or in the understanding of life by men and women*" (Meriç, 1998: p.140). This definition belongs to Meli. This attitude reduces Meli "*to one of those who saved their skin in the eyes of society*" (Meriç, 1998: p.140). Such portrayal of Meli is a criticism to the strict rules of traditional society which downplays and ignores Meriç's image of women. Asım Bezirci describes Meli, who makes reappearance in *Susuz VII*, as an isolated, alienated and perturbed middle class intellectual and an idealist teacher (Bezirci, 1999: p.91). Meli experiences a conflict between individual and social values. This conflict is conveyed by Meli's thoughts. The conflict arises from Meli's personality which refuses to adopt and attempts to fight against the ideas, world-views and lifestyles imposed by society because she belongs to a generation in which, with her own words, "*My contemporaries chanted 'My Kemal!' and 'My Turkey!' on the one hand and wrote poems on the other hand.*" Expressing the situation of women who fail to resist societal norms, Meli conveys her critique of society as "*Social rules are there to make people happy. We are the new dough being kneaded on the old kneading trough. There is no room for us on it*" (Meriç, 1998: p.166). Meli does not keep up with the times and resists and challenges the disciplinary power of traditions and customs. This image corresponds to the image of women idealized by Meriç, who gets Meli to state: "*I am an opinionated and breezy soul. I duly obey the social rules. I turn something I don't like into something I like... My thirst is not able to find anything to hold on to* (Meriç, 1998: p.158-159)". However, her failure to change things she wants to change deepens her unhappiness and uneasiness. "*Meli is defeated after all but she sets a positive example of how to put an intellectual fight against traditions and customs which one does not like*" (Bezirci, 1999: p.91-92). "In this way, Meriç revives Hayriye in Bozbulanık in the personality of Meli, which shows that she has not yet made the transition from individual understanding to collective insight" (Bezirci, 1999: 92).

Addressing the issue of inequality between men and women from the perspective of an affectionate and idealist teacher, *Susuz IX* tells the story of the loneliness and misery of a mother who struggles to stop her family from falling apart for her child (Bezirci, 1999: p.92). The story which "*includes conversations revolving around poverty and wealth, and taking place even during pre-performance rehearsals, which are supposed to be the happiest times of children at the play age* (Kırzıoğlu, 1996: p.136)", reveals what mothers who want their children to be well-educated have to go through. In this way, the social system that is contemptuous of women is criticized.

Susuz VIII deals with, around the theme of loneliness, the conflict between the aspirations of an intellectual woman and values of traditional societies. Ayşe, the main character of the story, is a well-educated young teacher with a critical perspective in a stereotypical, closed and traditional society. Meriç constructs Ayşe's identity as a means of presenting the responsibilities that should be undertaken by the generation of the Republic. Ayşe is portrayed as a type who tries to understand and interpret the zeitgeist and who fights false customs. However, although the younger generation receives a good education, it fails to move beyond the narrow confines of society, which causes Ayşe to feel lonely, unhappy and downbeat. The inconsistency between social norms and her ideas leads her to alienation from society and family. The sense of being trapped by society and being at variance with social norms are Ayse's source of misery: "*First of all, I am not happy. Here lies the problem. Oh, that's me it is me who is not happy. I am not alive. I cannot breathe. This is what is important. I am not happy. I am Powerless* (Meriç, 1998: p.186)". The feeling of weakness brought about by the limitedness of the individual effort and failure of the new generation to fulfill its mission turns into a general feeling of rebellion: "*It has been a couple of years since you finished faculty. What did you do? It is yourself and humanity you don't believe in. You all are a disgrace to the Republic. You all are making Ata [Mustafa Kemal Atatürk] turn in his grave. Yet, it is all in our hands. We have to stand strong. You are swamped by feelings. It is a sickening sentimentality* (Meriç, 1998: p.185)". With Ayşe's expressions of self-criticism, Meriç points out the conflict between the intellectual and society and criticizes the individual power of the new generation of the Republic which does not turn that power into action. Having been excluded by society, Ayşe tries to forget her misery by thinking about her uncle's daughter, Nil, who escaped to America. Nil's escape hints at leaving for countries where the issue of gender is considered important. However, Ayşe has no power to break the back of this corrupt order, which has caused her to become alienated from herself and her surroundings.

A high school headmistress introduced to the reader by Ayşe's thoughts is the antagonist of *Susuz VIII*. Nil has to enroll in her old school to be able to go to America to study. However, the headmistress refuses to issue the document on the grounds that Nil was a bad student. Therefore, the headmistress, trying to prevent a young person's education, represents the antagonist of the story: "*The headmistress is a brunette. The dull and dopey darkness of lack of comprehension in her eyes... A fourteen-year-old sooty stub walks like a spoon... The same darkness is in her eyes twenty years ago* (Meriç, 1998: p.180)". With the expression "*twenty years ago,"* Meriç criticizes the mentality of the National Education which does not adapt to the conditions of the day because Ayşe and Nil, who are integrated into the zeitgeist of their generation, are more conscious about education than the headmistress. To emphasize her criticism, the author portrays the headmistress as an inconsiderate person who makes people's lives difficult.

Nurhan, the protagonist of the story titled *Tedirgin,* is a middle-aged member of the urban-aristocratic class who has a happy marriage after a happy childhood. She is affectionate and broad-minded. She has an innate and deep desire to find herself and understand life. However, due to inadequate education, she cannot fully understand some things that she questions. Drawing attention to the importance of education for self-fulfillment, Nezihe Meriç portrays Nurhan as a person who sympathizes with activist youth, yet has difficulty comprehending their cause. Nurhan does not know exactly why young people, whom she believes are educated and therefore right, participate in demonstrations. This reveals the clash of generations between Nurhan and the young people: *"...our lives have no meaning, I understand that, but it is the way these children handle matters. They have an approach to the meaning of human life this cannot be explained by ignorance and have moved beyond us, we have never existed in the way they think* (Meriç, 1998: p.56-57)". Active rebellion triggered by education becomes a passive rebellion in Nurhan.

In the story titled *Umut'a Tezgah Kurmak,* Mrs. Nesrin is an idealist literature teacher. Her morbid state of mind stems from an unhappy childhood in an aristocratic family environment. Her family's indifference to society also had an effect on her mental state. The attraction of the scientific aspect of teaching was considered a solution to the unhappiness of the young girl who was sensitive to social issues. Her teaching experience turns into a critique of the dilapidated education system. The education system, which fails to teach Ataturk's principles and to comply with the requirements and values of the era, is a continuation of the old mentality. It has turned into a system that hinders the ability of individuals to construct independent identities and fuels individual crises by preventing individualization: *"I will no longer try to get on the good side of society and raise students who will not be able to comply with it. I made them memorize aruz prosody, authors' biographies etc. Now what to teach them and how to teach it to them...How come I have not sensed the disorder and irregularity of the education system since I was a child? I haven't been able to build values for myself. I just could not figure out what to believe and how to live...Curricula, courses, books and orders that change at governments' request...It gave me nervous aches, nervous aches. I searched for myself in the midst of the ignorance and impasse of this hodgepodge education system* (Meriç, 1998: p.79-80)". Such statements as *"We will fight!"* that Nesrin utters is an expression of the rebellious identity that emerges as a consequence of the lack of communication between society and the education system. Ultimately, Nesrin rebels against all institutions of the system and participates in demonstrations together with the rebellious youth.

In the story titled *İkircim*, Zerrin is a well-educated and well-off college graduate who is aware of her responsibilities for her family and society. She has a world-view according to which living and creating are equivalent. This is especially evident from the meaning she attributes to the furniture at home, which she describes as *"My home is my shell"* (Meriç, 1998: p.157). She is after the happiness of creating new things with her sewing materials, which she refers to as her "friends". *"She feels proud of having all the qualities of a good citizen, being useful to society and living an exemplary life"* (Meriç, 1998: p.160). Consciousness of social responsibility and democracy coincide. According to Zerrin, rightist and leftist movements that drive Turkey to anarchy is about failure to consolidate democracy. As a response to those who regard Socialism as the solution, she states:

So, you think Atatürk did not know how liberation could be achieved? If it was Socialism that could save us, then don't you think Atatürk would have introduced it to the country? I wonder if they could name one country the people of which were saved by socialism or communism. Yes? On the one end is America, the colonial power and on the other end, Russia. Right! Are Russian people happy? We have passed by and seen those iron curtain countries many times. Nobody is even smiling, let alone be happy" (Meriç, 1998: p.157).

According to Zerrin, the only hope for Turkey is to exert conscious efforts towards democracy. It has to "repulse political reaction and save the country to consolidate democracy. It is not possible with rightist or leftist movements (Meriç, 1998: p.166)".

Güzin is another intellectual protagonist of the same story. Güzin is introduced within the framework of Zerrin's critique of socialism. Güzin and Zerrin are ideologically poles apart. Güzin becomes ideologically obsessed with socialism, which she regards as the only way to liberation. Her friendships and conversations always revolve around socialism. Even when she raises her children, her socialist ideology overshadows her motherhood. Zerrin humiliates socialism identified with Güzin from a critical point of view as she thinks that socialism, which tries to preserve its existence with fashionable words like system of exploitation, is actually the sole source of exploitation, disorder and unhappiness.

The stories titled *Pazar Kurulur Pazar, Bugenvilli Başlangıç* and *Öykücük* tell the tales of the author's writing adventure. The intellectual women protagonists who want to turn their impressions into stories exhibit the personality traits of the author.

Especially, the observational competence of the middle-aged woman protagonist of the story titled *Deli Deli Deli* is striking. In the story titled *Suskun Ezgi,* the protagonist, a mother who has been married for 23 years and has two sons, is a figure of intellect. Her evaluations have a rebellious nature which is directed against traditional norms and practices.

2. Housewives

Nezihe Meriç stresses particularly about the daily lives of urban families and draws attention to contradictions they experience. Social relations in cities are intense and women have to work for a living, which cause contradictions to be seen more clearly in their lives. Since they provide for their families, they are portrayed as good characters. Maternal affection is the most obvious characteristic of these women, who do not hesitate to criticize society.

The story titled Bazıları, revolving around men-women relations, explores the subject of day-to-day relationships of an urban middle-class family in a winter season. The family represents the process of transition from the traditional family to the nuclear family structure due to urbanization as a result of migration from the village to the city. The story focuses on the alienation the family members go through during this process and finally emphasizes the importance of family.

The parents, concerned about their children, try to shape their future with dreams befitting their own small world and the conversations they have with each other drive the plot of the story. Of Rumelia origin, Mrs. Sabiha is a civil servant. She is introduced as a woman who has been married for twenty-five years and put her family at the center of her life. The only thing that gives meaning to the small world that she has created for her is her children. It is possible to see all the subtleties of maternal affection in almost everything she does:

"There is a picture of their daughter, Nevin, on the stills library over the radio: a small and cute green-eyed midge. With the collar of her raincoat turned up, the books in her hand and the smile on her face, it is as if she is saying 'I am freezing, mother, and freezing!' Mrs. Sabiha is thinking about her anyway: 'She never covers her head up, rascal. She

will get sick. 'There is a picture of their son hanging on the wall. She looks up at it and hears his voice: 'Hard to tell but I am a jolly man! It all depends. We will become lawyers before long.' She sighs. 'Ah! Motherhood ah! I would not wish this even for dogs!' Mrs. Sabiha becomes engrossed in her own thoughts (Meriç, 1998: p.54)".

Sabiha's thoughts, narrated by the author, reflect the inner world of a woman who is aware of a difficult task such as motherhood. Her sigh; "*Ah Motherhood ah*" reveals that it is women who have to take tremendous responsibility and bear the burden of family. Unlike her husband, who lives in his own world, Mrs. Sabiha is constantly in touch with the outside world, cognizant of social events and abreast of what is going on around her. She shares them with her husband. Sabiha is portrayed in this way to add dimension to urban family life.

In the story titled *Narin*, the author uses flashbacks to allow us to gain insight into the character Aunt Fehime through the world of thought of a young girl/narrator. Aunt Fehime is a poor, suffering and lonely woman. The reason why she suffers is because her daughter ran away with a soldier. What the daughter did becomes the beginning of a tragic life for a mother who loved her child dearly. The young girl describes the mother's tragedy and suffering as: "*The poor woman has been consumed by pain. She wouldn't talk to anybody about it. She grows okra in her garden and sells it. She is all alone with a sorrowful look on her face. When she sees me, she first smiles and then she puckers her lips and her face becomes all wrinkled and tears start coming down on her wrinkled cheeks*" (Meriç, 1998: p.70). These expressions indicate that the sense of motherhood is intensely experienced.

In the story titled *Özsu*, Hayriye is meticulously introduced to readers by the narrator/protagonist who watches the street on her death bed. Hayriye puts love in the centre of her life. She is cheerful and optimistic, hence the most positive character of the story. She has all the characteristics of a traditional woman. She has unlimited love, which she unconditionally and purely puts at people's disposal. We can see this in all her actions.

"*The colonel's tenant, Mrs. Hasna, didn't have to run errands after she [Hayriye] moved to the neighbourhood. 'That's no bother, for God's sake! I can get for you whatever you need, I am already on my way there' she [Hayriye] used to say. Thus, she [narrator] did not have to see an old jaded woman shuffle the street, which would make her feel miserable.*"

In another part of the story, what Hayriye did for a sick girl is described as follows.

"The woman had such vitality, kindness, compassion and joy that she would share them with us as much as she could. Just because I said that I was sick, she brought me bundles of flowers from her husband's and friend's gardens. As soon as she found some free time, she used to pick Gülsev up and come over to my window to chit chat with me. She would do anything so that I wouldn't get bored" (Meriç, 1998: p.74). The source of Hayriye's behaviours is love and soon she becomes the protagonist of the story with the influence of her acts on people. She becomes the individual symbol of change taking place in the street which becomes a world where everyone can live with flowers and people. The reason the author introduces Hayriye in this way is her belief is that people are not inherently bad. According to the author, the basis of all evil in people is social oppression and patriarchal structures which men use to objectify women. According to Hayriye, the cause of women's unhappiness is exemplified by the mysterious man who brought Mehlika, suffering the pangs of love, to the brink of suicide. Hayriye sums up her conviction with the phrase '*Isn't it just typical of men?*' (Meriç, 1998: p.76)

Using recollection and inner monologue technique, the story entitled *Alaturka Şarkılar* introduces the woman protagonist, Aunt Rana to us. She represents the positive aspects of life. She is a cheerful and happy housewife who has never lost the lucid laughter and innocence of her youth. She has a happy way of life with her garden and animals. She has an all-encompassing love. The narrator describes Aunt Rana, who takes love as the basic principle to interpret life, as: *"But she was always as innocent as a little girl. She loved birds, chicks, cats, small puppies, bitter pepper pickles old mansions, children, young people, old people and tiny apartments"* (Meriç, 1998: p.87). Excerpts reveal that Aunt Rana spent her youth with passion, enthusiasm and love, therefore, she is introduced by the narrator protagonist as the most positive character of the story. Two marriages that ended up in divorce cannot destroy her optimistic attitude towards life and people. *"Aunt Rana, who is still passionate, still a child and still innocent,"* (Meriç, 1998: p.87) has at last a happy family with Mr. Ahmet.

Mrs. Makbule whom we encounter in the story entitled *Keklik Türküsü* is the mother of Oya, who perceives love as a supreme value. Mrs. Makbule represents the traditional Turkish woman who carries the burden of family and of Turkish society on her shoulders. The way she perceives love and chooses a bridegroom for her daughter also conforms to the traditional Turkish woman's mission. She selects her bridegroom according to conventional criteria. The fact that the bridegroom is an engineer is interpreted as one of the most important criteria for marriage.

She vainly tries to persuade her daughter to marry an engineer she does not want to marry. Thereupon, she says to her neighbour, Mrs. Zehra: "*I didn't know what to say to people. She says no to everybody. People are going to think she is love-struck, or she has a fear. You can't stop people from* (Meriç, 1998: p.96)". Mrs. Makbule exhibits the viewpoints of traditional society with the expressions "*love-struck*" and "*she has a fear*" because it is only men who have the right to fall in love in traditional societies while women's fate is to sit at home and wait for their husbands. Mrs. Zehra's function in the story is also representing the traditional Turkish woman. Mrs. Zehra's and Mrs. Makbule's perception of love are not different from each other. Mrs. Zehra also tries to persuade Oya, who is in love with a banker, to marry an engineer. The things she says to Oya also represent the role of the traditional Turkish woman: "*Other girls would kill to marry a doctor or an engineer... Get married already so that we can come to your house and drink your coffee. We just want to feel proud of giving our daughter in marriage* (Meriç, 1998: p.103).

Remziye, the protagonist of the story entitled *Dışarılıklı,* represents thematic power. To escape the impossibilities of village life and to enjoy city life which she dreams of, she marries a man who works in the city. However, she fails to adapt to city life. Knowing little about city culture and imitating other people, she ends up making a mockery of herself. The daughter of the Greek landlord finds Remziye very coquettish. People around her make fun of her because of her new precarious identity. Despite all this, the author does not portray Remziye as one of the members of the group representing opposing forces because she has no negative behaviour other than imitating the lives of others. Remziye sees nothing wrong with people laughing at her on the island ferry and assumes an optimistic attitude by interpreting their sarcastic behaviors as "*I guess they find me friendly enough to be laughing at* (Meriç, 1998: p.107). The way Remziye is portrayed reveals the author's conviction that opportunities senselessly seized only by money bring with them a growing disintegration and that people who believe that "whoever has the money, has the power" fail to conform to social norms. In order to emphasize that change is and can only have a meaning with a social movement, the author gets Remziye to say: "*Apparently, I should have grown up in Istanbul in the first place*" (Meriç, 1998: p.107).

The mother in the story entitled *Susuz IV* is a character who, in the face of changing social order, maintains the continuity of the concept of family, which is on the verge of breaking down due to men cheating on their wives. She constantly struggles with day-to-day life and deals with her husband's infidelity as she loves her children and puts motherhood in the centre of her belief in the grand values of family. The mother describes the responsibilities and status of women in society as: *"It was only for the kids, my dear Meli, only for the kids. I grew up without a father and a mother. I just wanted them to be happy"* (Meriç, 1998: p.131) *"The kids' expenses are raising. We can't make ends meet if I don't work"* (Meriç, 1998: p.132). With these thoughts and behaviours, the mother makes a great sacrifice by putting her maternal instinct before problems that conflict with her own values and norms.

The main theme of the story entitled *Susuz IX* is the mothers who struggle to make sure that their children receive a good education despite economic difficulties. The women protagonists of the story represent the traditional Turkish woman who carries all the burden of family and is oppressed under the patriarchy structure. These women are Hüsniye, Boz, and the Grandmother. Cheated on by their husbands, these women feel humiliated and unhappy. The narrator/protagonist explains the situation of these women with the concept of "oppression" (Meriç, 1998: p.198). Although these women did not acquiesce to the infidelity and disregard of their husbands, their helplessness in the face of traditions prevented them from exhibiting a visible reaction. As a critique of traditional family, the author underscores that women are not regarded by men as human beings. For this, she gets the women to say: *"Why did he make me his wife then? He thinks I'm some sort of animal?"* The continuity of family depends on women. According to the author, mothers perceive high values through maternal instinct, therefore, she exalts them against men who represent oppressive forces of patriarchy. The Grandmother represents women oppressed by traditional society. Boz reacts when her husband cheats on her and the Grandmother says to her: *"Don't push his button... He is a man. Are you crazy or what! Cry...cry...We had men too...They used to swing with broads...We had men too...We used to make lace and spin yarn. Kids, girls, we all used to get together. Cry, cry"* (Meriç, 1998: p.200). The expressions *"Don't push his button"* and *"He is a man"* are important in the sense that they reveal women's desperation and weakness in the face of patriarchal structures securing the power of men over women, and more importantly, they show that women accept their fate and submit to this role.

Another story about the conflicts that women experience is *"Dedi, Ölüm Aklımda."* Nedret, the protagonist, is *"a woman whose life has been confined in four walls"* although she works and goes out shopping (İnce, 1981: p.605). Under the dominance of enclosed spaces, Nedret soon falls to pieces and starts questioning everything, which leads her to self-identification. Ossified social relations and women's social status have their own share of her questioning. Speaking to herself, Nedret says *"One smile or two occasionally! It's the anger that does it. There is this ongoing commotion for two bites of bread. Everybody is struggling to earn a living, everybody is concerned for the future. Everything is messy and broken...Those who hustle, those who know the right people pull the strings! Otherwise, work for pittance... So, what is the point of living! A meaningless life* (Meriç, 1998: p.13)". With these expressions, the author shows that women are crushed under the burden brought about by economic conditions.

The author portrays Nedret as a person who dislikes and questions life because of the responsibilities that social life and oppressive system impose on women. Nedret represents women who have to take all the burden of life in a society based on male domination by stating *"Whereas I keep running here and there. I grin and bear it at the office and at home. I've forgotten that I am a woman, that I am a human being. I'm stuck in-between trying to handle each* (Meriç, 1998: p.17)". This is a mission imposed on women by traditional society and they are obliged to fulfill this mission. This obligation draws its strength from social roles imposed upon men and women. The only thing that women can do is fulfill it: *"Well, we get half a kilo each but he always has his rakı." "He drinks. Don't you know him? There is no money for anything but he always has money for it". "If you act like a donkey, they put a saddle on you. What can we do? That's just the way it goes* (Meriç, 1998: p.18)".

Nedret, oppressed under the pressure of traditions, pours out her grief to a woman who shares the same fate as her and shares her blue devils, internal conflicts and the broken social order. In this way, the woman, whose name is not mentioned, helps readers to understand and gain insight into Nedret's feelings. *"Oh, I almost forgot! Ask me what happened today. Did you see what that old man of yours did* (Meriç, 1998: p.12), *"Tell me about it! I'm coming now, I will tell you what happened, you are gonna be bursting with laughter"* (Meriç, 1998: p.14). These words told by the woman to Nedret show that the woman is not as sensitive as Nedret and does not feel the pain of individual change as much as she does. Despite this, the woman does not accept the norms of society based on male dominance. She has, however, no other choice but to accept the role imposed on women by society. Meriç blames the education system conforming to patriarchal traditions which define women's roles in society by getting the woman to say: *"To hell with them! I always say this; they didn't let me study, they just didn't let me study. I ended up utterly ignorant...Me! I can't change, even if I wanted to. What can I do? My thoughts are refined but I can't make nothing of them"* (Meriç, 1998:

p.18). By getting the woman to repeat the expression *"they didn't let me study"* twice, the author emphasizes the presence of a mechanism which oppresses women's enthusiasm about education. The source of this oppression is ossified false traditions which give men a privileged position and see women as second-class beings.

The story entitled *Giderek Daha Güçlü* criticizes housewives for having the characteristics of traditional social structures, being unaware of the meaning of life and for not having founded modern families. The young girl, the narrator, constantly criticizes these women. These women, *who are afraid of their fathers and uncles*, (Meriç, 1998: p.235) live their lives in the direction of traditional obsessions along with an indifference to nature and innovations. Their impression on the young girl presents the details of projection of society. The young girl, the spokesperson of the author, goes beyond the bounds of criticism by making comments about the women's neglecting their self-care, which, to her, defies the elegance of women. The next-door neighbour who has a bad taste in clothes reminds the young girl of that feeling: *"She must have come to earth to disincline people from fashion."* Lacking in family consciousness and constantly shouting, this woman is the most negative character of the story. However, the neighbours are living in the apartment which the young girl refers to as "the third door", have achieved family consciousness. The woman is smart and has a job. She has adapted to city life. She is described as a positive character that is abreast of the happenings in the country and capable of analysing them.

In *Umut'a Tezgah Kurmak*, Nezihe Meriç criticizes the passive attitude displayed by women towards society and traditions with the words *"Women, who are unaware of what is going on around themselves, have turned into sorrowful senile. If it wasn't for their three months' pensions, they wouldn't even be able to take shelter in their sons' or daughters'* (Meriç, 1998: p.80). Women, who are not conscious of their individual quest and act by their genetic reflexes, are heading for a fall. The author warns women to discover their own raison d'être so that they could give meaning to life and avoid turning into sorrowful senile.

The mother in the story titled *Acıyı Aşmak* is not only a housewife. Her sensitivity to social values is her most prominent characteristic. With her maternal instinct, she reacts to the murder of three young people for being "anarchists" and criticizes the system. Her criticisms are not conscious reactions: *"It's vileness wherever you look... Government offices, bribes...We all know about that. Is there anything that is right in this country? They pillage and plunder the State's wealth. So, are we supposed to keep quiet about it and do nothing* (Meriç, 1998: p.154)?".

This criticism brings with it the emotion that justifies the attitudes of the youth who rebel against the system. Another characteristic of the mother is her self-criticism. She believes that she is ignorant about the system. Her ignorance about the solution of social problems pushes her to search for information. She speaks openly about her ignorance in the face of social problems, solutions to which are not put into practice. She searches for ways to defeat ignorance, which leads to helplessness and weakness. Consequently, the first way she takes is to learn leftist theory.

3. Young Girls

The majority of the young girls in Nezihe Meriç's stories represent the thematic strength. Their conflicts, contradictions, perspectives, and experiences form the texture of the stories. Sexuality, bodily pleasure, man-woman and mother-girl relationships, and different areas reflecting urban culture in traditional society are explained in a way that reveals the psychology of young girls. These educated young girls, who struggle to become an individual against traditional norms, are mostly alone. They are misunderstood and confined into narrow boundaries by society, which leads them to loneliness and isolation. They are reluctant to express their reactions openly because of the stereotypical patterns of male domination. It seems like Meriç's women will not be able to escape their impasse and remain in a state of loneliness unless they maintain a stance against patriarchy and male domination (Oktay, 1962: p.15). The young girls choose to express their rebellion either by sleeping with their loved ones or by leaving home. The author idealizes young girls who develop a critical approach to the oppressive power of the patriarchal society and question the traditions and themselves by challenging social norms. Therefore, they take a stand against men, who represent the repressive mindset of the patriarchy. For this, the author portrays young girls, who do not conform to obsolete customs, to present the conflict between individual and social norms. Most of these girls are well-educated and belong to the intellectual strata of society.

The protagonist of the story titled *Dağılış* is a young urban girl, Meryem, who shows great interest in history. She admires Rome, which gave birth to renaissance, founded open cities and created the Italian spirit. She has always wanted to see Rome since she was a child. One day, she seizes the opportunity to go to Rome. She witnesses unplanned urbanization and a disorganized social structure in Rome and becomes deeply saddened, which indicates her great sensitivity to history. Infuriated by the current state of Rome, she says: "*Then with that weariness, that impalpable but perceivable incompleteness, they were asking. "Which spirit? Italian spirit* (Meriç, 1998, p.62)".

The name of the young girl, Aliye, in the story titled *Öğretmen,* is portrayed as a criticism to traditional society. Aliye is the symbol of an individual who changes in a society which cannot transform itself according to the new world order. As she changes, she develops a critical approach to society. As a child of *"two people who were randomly united without knowing each other and without desire,"* she considers herself a "bastard of bastards" (Meriç, 1998: p.65). The source of this emotion is the repressive and rigid traditions of arranged marriage. Aliye is the child of such a marriage. Aliye' attitude towards this tradition is Meriç's criticism to society. Meriç criticizes the oppressive aspect of traditions and argues that societies must adapt themselves to the era. For this, she offers a modern alternative to traditional society through Aliye. This alternative world entails change and individualization: *"But think about it, if two souls, two bodies who seek and find each other were united...then aside from official documents and signatures, the child born would not be a bastard"* (Meriç, 1998: p.65). However, Aliye is defeated by the strict order and rigid rules of society. Family, which draws its authority from traditions, is an institution that has the power to exonerate itself by seeing Aliye as property. Therefore, the change Aliye goes through has been ineffective in the face of social oppression.

The story titled *Narin* narrates the feelings of a lonely young girl. The loneliness of the young girl originates both from society and from her own nature. The epigraph *"a giant loneliness descending quietly from mountains far far away"* at the beginning of the story and her other expressions in various parts of the story such as *"I am a quiet and insignificant girl"* (p. 68), *"My heart sinks. In fact, loneliness is in me"* (Meriç, 1998: p.69) confirms this. The acceptance of loneliness in this way creates an unhappy character who perceives the world in a pessimistic manner.

The lonely are coming...I recognize them by their eyes on crowded streets, on desolate paved roads, in dimly lit corridors of apartments. I recognize them wherever I run into them. I see cynical men.... their helpless glances stick to me. I know some women, some women who are timid and lonely under their tough and fierce looks and disguised by make-up and fears. Then I hear dimly lit alleys, I hear things that are rotten, stinky, disgusted by and vomited on. I try not to think. I say to myself, they must have lost something. I hear. I cannot tell they have completely forgotten their kids and moms. They can never brighten up and laugh (Meriç, 1998: p.70).

This quote from the story is important as it reveals the level of destruction of loneliness on human psychology and what kind of human it creates. Another girl described in the same story is a gypsy. She is lightly portrayed by the young girl who represents the thematic power. She sells flowers and tells fortunes. That she is good-humored and sings differentiates her from the protagonists who accept the feeling of loneliness as their destiny. She exhibits no behavior which could be interpreted as caused by loneliness. When the young girl buys flowers from her and tells her that she has no one to give these flowers to, the gypsy girls says *"Solitude is only for God."*

The young girl, the protagonist and narrator of the story titled *Özsu*, represents a character who believes that love is necessary, such as water and bread, for a healthy society. She sees herself as imprisoned in an environment where a static lifestyle dominates, people have forgotten to laugh and human relations are weak. She is very unhappy. She likens her situation to that of her dog named Dik that has been locked up in the basement. Someday, a woman named Hayriye moves into the neighbourhood and the pessimistic and unhappy atmosphere of the street changes. The street becomes a place dominated by joy and love. The protagonist/narrator's happiness with the change is an indication that love is very important to her. Despite her sickness, her comments on Hayriye's presence in the neighbourhood reflect the mood of a person who believes in love rather than a morbid mood.

Oh! Dear Hayriye! What a laugh we've had...The potion has kicked in. The street is now ours even though Hayriye is not around. Despite all our daily troubles, problems, sorrows, and conflicts and disagreements between ourselves and our world, waking up in the mornings and coming back in the evenings to this clean and fresh street with flowers and people who get on well with each other grab us by our hearts (Meriç, 1998: p.78).

Another girl who stands out in the story is Mehlika, who is a symbol of pure love. But the man she loves does not reciprocate her love and so Mehlika has nervous breakdowns and thinks about committing suicide. Her pessimistic attitude proves that she approaches love and affection with sincerity.

Alaturka Şarkılar is a story based on the remarks and reminiscences of a young girl named Nezih on her way to pay a visit to her aunt, Rana, who lives in the country at a time when urbanization was intense. Nezih encounters two soldiers on the road and is afraid of them. Her fear is a reference to a social structure that objectifies women and to how women perceive men. Women are lonely in this structure. The reason for this loneliness is the mark left on the deep world of women by the likelihood of men oppressing them in the patriarchal structure. Carrying the deep scars of the patriarchal structure, Nezih suppresses her feelings for the opposite sex in accordance with the traditional image of women:

"So, I'll imagine like it was my lover who has whistled this time. A messy brown-haired man passed through me. He seemed carefree and jokey. I thought what if he lies down right beside me and I pull out some grass and drop it on his face. Though my mind was saying priggishly and solemnly 'My dear, stop acting like the girls in those dime novels, for God's sake! I paid no attention to it and shrugged it off'" (Meriç, 1998: p.190).

Another story that emphasizes the fact that male-dominant society fails to understand women and crushes them is *Kurumak*. The main theme of *Kurumak* is the conflict of a young teacher, Bilge, who on the one hand wants to live everyday life and on the other hand do important things that will affect the ordinariness of daily life. She wants to have an influence on society and the masses and change them for the better. Owing to her nature, she believes that she has some duties that she has to undertake in social life, which are making a difference in society which has succumbed to mediocrity and changing it for the better. However, she fails to actualize her ideals and therefore experiences conflict. She explains her desire to project her own values and ideals onto society as "I want to influence society and the masses and accomplish great things and feel that glorious joy that Socrates defined" (Meriç, 1998: p.92-93). The fact that her wish did not come true plunges her into the shadows of despair and rage. She considers marrying Macit even though he does not understand the trouble she is going through. This shows on the one hand that she is longing for the comfort of the everyday life and a regular family life, and, on the other hand, that she is trapped in the cage of the patriarchal social structure. Despite all this, Bilge possesses a power of an encompassing love, which she describes as follows: *"Please Macit, do not try to find a nervous, desperate or morbid type of girl in me. Quite the contrary, I love life, the air, the water, walking, laughing and so on...I love everything. This thing that I have inside me, it is something I cannot describe"* (Meriç, 1998: p.90). As can be seen, Bilge does not attribute that inner despair to her personality traits. Her despair is external and stems from the patriarchal social structure that does not understand women. Completely ignoring her struggle for existence, Macit responds *"C'mon, it's not that big of a deal. You want to live outdoors. This is some sort of longing for nature and not more than that* (Meriç, 1998: p.117)". His response shows how women are perceived by men and how patriarchal structure is reproduced.

Keklik Türküsü examines man-woman relations in the context of gender. The male dominant cultural concept of what a woman's intra-community roles should be is the theme of the story. The protagonist is a young academy student whose mother wants her to get married. Oya is the daughter of a middle-class urban family. Representing a young person who has values woven with love and feels love passionately; Oya was cheated on by Ahit. Though she feels all the pain of his infidelity in her heart, she does not want to ruin the purity of her feelings for him. She does not let herself be lured by the opportunities offered by other men who want to marry her and tries to stay true to love which she esteems very highly. Her devotion to the sanctity of love constitutes the source of her psychological conflicts and spiritual crises. Her perception of life when she falls in love and after she is cheated on is completely different. The narrator describes this difference as: *"When one falls in love, one sees the whole world as a greenish calmness from behind the closed eyelids... You know those pink hard candies; they have that faint pinkish color, and smell that spreads into one's body. That's what love is like"* (Meriç, 1998: p.97). Suffering from a deep melancholy after being cheated on, Oya describes love as *"Imagine you are jumping from the world and letting out a magnificent scream in the midst of frenzy and breaking into pieces until there is nothing left of you. That is what love is"* (Meriç, 1998: p.101). With this definition of love, Oya criticizes the dominant culture's understanding of love and family. Meriç tries to reveal the difference in perception of love between women who are subordinate to the dominant male culture and Oya. These women are Oya's mother and her mother's friend Mrs. Zehra. In order to talk Oya into marriage, the mother and Mrs. Zehra represent the roles that women in a male-dominated society should take on. Mrs. Zehra advocates her side by saying *"Your husband' bread and butter are for you...Start your own family when you have the time"* (Meriç, 1998: p.96) while Oya's mother says *"We have one foot in the grave, I want to see her settled down. Her father does not care at all"* (Meriç, 1998: p.96). In this way, they try to make Oya adopt a passive identity.

The young girl in *Susuz I* is a law student. With the sense of equality, she has gained through education; she is a self-confident person who claims her rights. In this sense, she is different from women who are oppressed by male domination in traditional societies. She goes to fetch a doctor for a sick child but the doctor refuses to come at first. She says to him *"But you must come. It is a doctor's job. We are losing time. Hurry up*

if something happens to that kid, I will sue you (Meriç, 1998: p.113)."
Thus, Meriç emphasizes that education will help women break the siege
laid by social roles imposed on them by the dominant culture.

Susuz II deals with intergenerational conflict. Dr. Vahit's daughter,
Suzan, is a girl who "*constantly renews and develops in the flow of time*"
(Meriç, 1998: p.121). There are conflicts of value between Suzan and her
family. Nil is introduced by Ayşe's world of thought to readers in the story
titled *Susuz VIII*. Nil is excluded by all relatives except her grandmother
after the death of her mother and her father and goes through tough times.
She is a seventeen-year-old girl with a soulful and deep world. After all
those hardships, she decides to go to America. She is instrumental in the
way Ayşe expresses her critiques of false traditions and society. As a
prerequisite for Nil to stay in America, she has to enrol in a school in
Istanbul. The denial of her request causes a deep sorrow in Ayşe. Initially,
Ayşe's thought focus on Nil and then expands and reveals the inner world
of Ayşe, who suffers from generational conflict in the society in which she
lives.

Another story about young girls who cannot reconcile with society is
Menekşeli Bilinç. A college girl represents the thematic power of the story.
She critically interprets unchanging customs in the face of changing times
and criticizes with her social and cultural capital the lifestyle offered by
customs. For this reason, she is in conflict and disagreement with her
surroundings. However, this conflict and disagreement do not condemn
her to her inner world. She sees individuality as an indispensable element,
which leads her to a conscious rebellion. When her free-spiritedness,
desire to live her own life, and concern for the future and the inertia of
traditions all come together, rebellion becomes a supreme value for her.
Her sister, on the other hand, is a character who feels the weight of
traditions on her shoulders and tries to conform to behaviour patterns
imposed by them. Her personality does not change, just like unchanging
traditions. She accuses her sister, who rebels against traditions and wants
to leave home, of being a member of a "useless generation." She does not
want to understand her sister. In this way, she serves the purpose of
presenting different points of view of the members of the same generation.

Another story that captures the feelings of rebellion of young girls who
cannot reconcile with society is *Hışhışı Hançer*. The young girl in the
story represents a character that is in conflict with a society which frowns
upon romantic relationships. The conflict results in her have sexual
intercourse with a loved one. She has had sexual intercourse with other
men before because she is very beautiful and men lust after her. However,

despite her physical intimacy with her lover, her expectations remain unfulfilled, which leads her to unhappiness. She, in a sense, causes her own unhappiness with her illusion that she is irreplaceable in the eyes of all men. The narrator highlights that the girl's low level of education and superficial perspective of love are the source of her unhappiness. *Varım Diyorum İnanmalısınız* and *Açarda Tutku Gülleri Açar* are the author's other works that tell the stories of young girls who sleep with men they love as an expression of rebellion against society.

Nil, who guides the story *Susuz VIII*, is also in the story *Tedirgin*. Nil fails to question life, looks down on her relatives, puts money in the centre of her life, judges people by their social and economic status and gives no importance to love and friendship. The story emphasizes often that although she is well-educated, she is indifferent to the problems of the society in which she lives and of the youth of which she is a member. Unlike Nurhan, Nil opposes the youth activism. Her indifference to social issues is about the way she perceives the state of things. Her conviction that money is the only power and that conflicts do not have a social dimension shows how superficial she is. She lacks all the profoundness that we observe in Nuran. Therefore, she is portrayed by the author as the antagonist of the story. Most of her behaviour gives away her selfishness, which causes her to be hated and labelled as a snob by society. The story also mentions a country girl, Nebahat, who goes from Antep to Istanbul to stay with her well-off relatives to study. The way she is dressed and talks gives away her origin: "*Country girls, I can recognize them wherever they are...All I have to do is take a peek, then I can tell a country girl from an Istanbulite girl...the way country girls poise, the way they sit are all different...This Nebahat girl is also from the country*" (Meriç, 1998: p.51). Nebahat's values pointed out by the narrator/protagonist change during her stay in Istanbul. The new values give Nebahat a rebellious identity. She aligns herself with the activist youth. The tendency of Nezihe Meriç to portray consciously rebellious protagonists is also evident in Nebahat. While all her relatives regard Mr. Kenan, a member of Istanbul aristocracy, as a legendary hero, Nebahat looks down on her uncle. When she is captured during a rebellion, Nuran asks her "*What will your uncle say to this?*" to which Nebahat responds: *Who gives a shit about him* (Meriç, 1998: .61)".

The wealthy young daughters of an aristocratic family in *Umut'a Tezgah Kurmak* are criticized for their narrow-minded view of life. They believe that happiness comes only with money and ostentation and choose their husbands and friends accordingly. Unlike their sister Nesrin, who is an idealist, the other sisters have no skills of thinking critically about society and system. This gives information about what kind of people are brought about by the corrupt system and also about what kind of people should be raised instead.

Despite the fact that the young girls in Meriç's stories are deceived about love, they do not assume a pessimistic attitude towards life, which is again due to the concept of love itself because these girls hold tightly onto one thing in life: LOVE. The feeling and meaning of love seem to have convinced the girls of Meriç more than cultural endeavor (Oktay, 1962: p.15).

4. Elderly Women

Elderly women in Nezihe Meriç's stories often have the characteristics of traditional society. Therefore, they are in conflict with the next generation because they represent traditions. Apart from them, there are also elderly women who cling to life and stand in favour of change. These women are portrayed as positive characters in the stories. Aunt Safinaz in the story titled *Kurumak* is an example of this. Aunt Safinaz is a happy housewife who lives with her husband Mr. Cemil and her grandchildren. Despite her advanced age, she is the most lively and cheerful character of the story. She is never pessimistic. She always sees the positive aspects of life. Many behaviors perceived by many housewives as torture are perceived as fun for Aunt Safinaz.

Elderly women, who are representatives of traditions, are dealt with in the story titled *Dedi Ölüm Aklımda*. The two elderly women in the story are not only two elderly women but also the representatives of all social traditions and values (İnce, 1981: 607). Therefore, they react to social change by expressing their longings. This is especially true of the grandmother when she scolds her grandchildren, who are reactive to the past, and shows that she does not approve of them criticizing the government. She says "*Good grief, they swear at everything, they read newspaper, they swear. They listen to the radio, they swear. They curse at home from dawn to dusk. We had such people at the time of our Supreme Sultan, Abdülhamit* (Meriç, 1998: p.22)". In this way, elderly women show the distance between the past and the present and become the symbols of a generational conflict and elements that perpetuate the past.

Nedret's mother and mother-in-law are introduced to readers by Nedret's world of thought. Although these two women have the same values, "*the mother-in-law keeps bragging about her lineage and money and regards her royalty as superiority beyond reach. Nedret's mother agrees with her values even though her class position is different but nonetheless the mother-in-law oppresses and dominates her* (İnce, 1981: 608)". There is a direct correlation between this attitude and the power the mother-in-law possesses. Nedret acquiesces to the privilege the mother-in-law possesses and thinks: *"The other one [Nedret's mother] does not even open her mouth! Grandmother [referring to Nedret's mother] is the projection of a melody sung at home since ancient times. She is timid...She crawls into her bed quietly and says 'thank God.' It is the mother-in-law who has the monopoly to shout and groan and pound on the wall to show her anger. She is the mother of a boy. Besides her lineage goes all the way back [to the palace], so she is the Sovereign"* (Meriç, 1998: p.20).

The grandmother, feeling lowly for being the mother of a girl, avoids meddling and constantly curries favour with the mother-in-law as she is the mother of a boy. Nedret cannot tolerate this and describes her mother as "slavishly submissive" and bows to the oppressive power of traditions.

Teknik Arıza tells the story of a traditional Turkish woman who carries the burden of the whole family on her shoulders. Mrs. Nermin is cheated on by her husband and divorces him, which leaves her face to face with a difficult life. Women who have to live under male domination are described more strikingly in *Boşlukta Mavi*. They compare themselves with a young urban woman and pity themselves for not having a social status like she has.

The young girl in *Giderek Daha Güçlü* gets bored of her family, which lives according to traditional obsessions, and decides to leave home, but her grandmother does not understand her decision. The young girl wants to live alone but the grandmother finds this ridiculous. Due to the generational gap, the young girl's wishes and decisions are incompatible with the values the grandmother has.

Symbolized by the grandmother, women oppressed by the traditional values of patriarchy are addressed by Susuz X. Her son cheats on his wife and the wife finds out about it. Grief-stricken, she tells her mother-in-law what happened, to which the grandmother replies: *"Don't push his button... He is a man. Are you crazy or what! Cry...cry...We had men too...They used to swing with broads...We had men too...We used to make lace and spin yarn. Kids, girls, we all used to get together. Cry, cry"* (Meriç, 1998: p.200). The expressions *"Don't push his button"* and *"He is a man"* are important in the sense that they reveal women's desperation and weakness in the face of patriarchal structures securing the power of men over women, and more importantly, they show that women accept their fate and submit to this role.

In *Umut'a Tezgah Kurmak,* we encounter different elderly women.
These are Mrs. Boncuk and Mrs. Hoca. Mrs. Boncuk creates the thematic
power of the story. We learn about Mrs. Boncuk in general terms from the
mental motions of Nesrin, who is in the position of the main thematic
power. Mrs. Boncuk had a happy childhood in a family dominated by
traditional values. She was left alone after her mother and father were
killed. She had two daughters from an unhappy marriage. Unlike people
who are insensitive to social values, she is sensitive enough to hide activist
youths in her house. This sensitivity, which costs her two years of her life,
is clearer with her friendships in prison. Life after release is now an arena
in which any kind of fight has to be put up for happiness. Mrs. Hoca on
the other hand is a prisoner who helps people from every walk of life to
feel comfortable and have sincere friendships in prison. She was arrested
on the grounds that she was involved in political actions. With her ideas
and experiences about life and zeitgeist, she informs other prisoners and
helps them achieve individualization. She is referred to as Mrs. Hoca
(teacher) due to her effect on people. Nesrin's word about Mrs. Hoca
reveals this effect: *"Of course it is Mrs. Hoca that shook her to her senses.
Actually, isn't she the one who has affected and directed all of us? I,
Nesrin Çarıklı, am I the Literature teacher Nesrin Çarıklı of two years
ago? Isn't she the one who held my hand in my struggle to find back my
psychological balance* (Meriç, 1998: p.77)"?
    Another elderly woman who is as sensitive to social issues as Mrs.
Boncuk appears in the story titled *Acıyı Aşmak.* Just like Mrs. Boncuk, the
grandmother in this story hides young rebels in her house. She loses her
life in a police raid carried out to capture the young rebels. The story
especially emphasizes the grandmother's solitude and secluded life-style.

5. Downtrodden Prostitutes

Downtrodden prostitutes are not antagonists in Nezihe Meriç's stories. It is
possible to see Nezihe Meriç's positive view of people in these characters.
Sofiya in the story titled *Uzun Hava* is one of them. Sofiya is a woman
who makes a living through unlawful means. Despite this, she is not an
antagonist in the story because she turns down Sabir's marriage proposal
although their love was reciprocal.
    The reason why Sofia turns down the marriage proposal is because she
is a prostitute. She is not afraid to criticize herself. Her decision about the
marriage proposal arouses sympathy in the eyes of readers and prevents
her from being regarded as an antagonist. She preserves the purity of her
love by rejecting an offer that would be of her benefit and allow her to

have a family. This positive viewpoint is replaced with a critique of women's reckless attitudes towards life. The story titled *Narin* criticizes people who do not take life and people seriously. The women loosely narrated in the story are the victims of loneliness who hide their loneliness with superficial goals and who have forgotten about their kids and mothers. With all these negative traits, these women are regarded as degenerate people who have lost moral values. Combined with the narrator's hatred, these women, who seek happiness on illegitimate grounds, turn into a social critique: *"I know some women, some women who are timid and lonely under their tough and fierce looks, and disguised by make-up and fears. Then I hear dimly lit alleys, I hear things that are rotten, stinky, disgusted by and vomited on. I try not to think. I say to me 'they must have lost something...' I hear. I cannot tell, they have completely forgotten their kids and moms. They can never brighten up and laugh* (Meriç, 1998: p.70).

Conclusion

If we make a general assessment, we can explain the result of this study as follows: Through fictitious women characters, Nezihe Meriç expresses the oppression of women under feudal traditions of a patriarchal society which tries to look modern and progressive. These women who are the protagonists of her works are in constant conflict with contradictions of patriarchal and traditionalist society. The author presents the contradiction between modernity and tradition by making use of dualities such as women-men, women-family, and women-false traditions. Nezihe Meriç puts forward the experiences of oppressed women, disintegration of gender stereotypes in society by a radical questioning, women's struggle to become free individuals in the face of identities forcefully imposed on them by society and *"willy-nilly transformation and moderation, yet, pertinacity of patriarchy"* (Arat, 1998) despite all these efforts. Reading Nezihe Meriç, a contemporary and critical author, means learning about the effect of the political atmosphere of the past on our people and understanding the hidden aspects of women. For readers, Nezihe Meriç is a hopeful author of intellect and eloquence whose works have great depth. Achieving to reflect the psychology of women on her works without fearing society's opinion or disapproval, she is one of the authors who have breathed new life into Turkish literature.

References

Arat, Y. (1998). The Patriarchal Paradox-Women Politicians in Turkey, Fairleigh Dickinson University Pres, 1998, (Cited by Fatmagül Berkay, "Cumhuriyetin 75 yıllık Serüvenine kadınlar Açısından Bakmak", 75 yılda Kadınlar ve Erkekler, Türkiye İş Bankası Yayınları, İstanbul

Aydın, M. (1995). Ne Yazıyor Bu Kadınlar, ilke Yay., Ankara

Bezirci, A. (1999). Nezihe Meriç, Evrensel Basım Yay.,İstanbul

Doğan, M. (1980). "Kendini Sınırlayan Ustalık", Milliyet Sanat, Kasım

İnce, Ü. (1981). Nezihe Meriç'in Bir Hikayesi Üzerine. Türk Dili Dergisi, Nisan, Ankara

Kırzıoğlu, B. (1996). Nezihe Meriç'in Roman ve Hikayeleri Üzerine Bir İnceleme, Atatürk

Meriç, N. (1998). Toplu Öyküleri I, YKY, İstanbul

Meriç, N. (1998). Toplu Öyküleri II, YKY, İstanbul

Oktay, A. (1962). Aydınca Bunalımlar ya da Kadınlar Dünyası. Değişim, p.4, 15 Şubat, Ankara

Olcay, H. (1951). Bir Hikayeci Takdim Ediyoruz. Seçilmiş Hikayeler Dergisi, C. 5, Ankara

Önertoy, O. (1984). Cumhuriyet Romanı Türk Roman ve Öyküsü, Türkiye İş Bankası Kültür Yay., İstanbul Üniversitesi Yay, Erzurum

METHODS OF TRAINING OF FOREIGNERS IN THE PHRASEOLOGICAL SYSTEM OF RUSSIAN IN ASPECT OF REGIONAL GEOGRAPHY AND LINGUOCULTUROLOGY

BAHAR DEMİR AND FISENKO OLGA SERGEEVNA

Introduction

The problem of reflection of national consciousness in the form of a national-cultural component in the semantics of phraseological units involves interest among linguists. This is due to the fact of new methods and techniques of language. It describes the mentality of a purely linguistic object moving in the field of pedagogy, in particular in the field of the method of teaching Russian as a foreign language.

The studying of phraseology in the course of the Russian language as a foreign language has a special relevance - a comprehensive studying of language and culture that is an assimilation of cultural content with the activation of linguistic resources which leads to a higher and deeper level of knowledge with the foreign language. This phraseological system is the core of Russian national identity, imaginative reflection of national traditions, culture, and Russian civilization. Idioms are not only a source of cultural information, but also contain a wealth of linguistic material which allows a basis to study various aspects of Russian morphology, syntax, phonetics and lexemes.

Formulation of the problem

The study of phraseology in a foreign audience - the problem is complex and interesting. Properly organized work on the phraseological system of the Russian language expands the active reserve of students, and it helps correct understanding of the rich Russian language in all its forms and its fluency. A rather-comparative analysis of figurative and semantic content of phraseology and Russian phraseological units in the native language of the students has great importance for the practice of teaching Russian as a foreign language. In the study of Russian phraseology by the foreigners, two languages are involved: Russian and the native language of students, so a productive methodological principle of learning foreign phraseology of the Russian language is the native language of the students account and peculiarities of their culture. The comparison of phraseological units of the language studied with the relevant units of the mother language involves identifying general and specific elements, which are related to the universal nature of logical thinking operations and the national originality of language. This contributes to a more precise understanding of the semantics of phraseological units as an indirectly-derived funds formation concept – sphere of Russian language, their proper use and retention in memory, enrolled emerging associations based on the one hand, and precluding the interfering effect on the other. Features of the comparative study of phraseology of the two languages in a foreign audience in terms of teaching methodology for *RaFl (Russian as foreign language)* as an interesting linguistic-cultural plan, is compared to phraseological units in the learning process, which are introduced with cross-cultural information.

Methodical principles of training of foreigners in the phraseological system of Russian

The linguistic-cultural aspect to the methods of teaching Russian as a foreign language involves the isolation in the lexical content syntactically indivisible holistic linguistic sign general cognitive models of their formation and specifics, which make it difficult to understand Russian foreign idioms.

Submitted phraseological material of foreign students has specific features resulting from the overall specificity of teaching Russian as a foreign language. An analysis of phraseological fund of the Russian language allows you to select 4 groups of phraseological units:

Group I: there are idioms, which have not only identical semantic and stylistic characteristics, but also the identity of images;

Group II: these are idioms, in which there are partial match (proximity) images in the presence of common values and stylistic colouring;

Group III: there are idioms with the same value and stylistic coloration, but in different ways;

Group IV: there are idioms, idiomatic or non-semantic matching in another language.

National coloured phraseology is one of the most difficult to digest by the students, so to create an accurate and complete image of phraseological units it is necessary to give a detailed, exhaustive commentary. For example: phraseological unit *Kazan orphan* – it means a person pretending to be unhappy, resentful, helpless, etc., to soften someone.

Comment: "After the conquest of the Kazan Khanate in 1555 Ivan the Terrible besieged Tatar khans' heavy tribute: every spring they brought their gifts by their carts. But each spring sly khans reduced offerings, hypocritically they were complaining about the shortfalls, decay and so on. To be more convincing they tried to have poor clothes then Moscow boyars. In the days of Ivan, the Terrible, who waged numerous wars, in Moscow there were many orphans: dirty, in rags, they lived by alms, singing songs of the pathetic.

One can't help comparing the cries of the blue Kazan khans with these orphans; citizens of Moscow called them orphans Kazan.

Since then, the expression Kazan orphan designates any showing false modesty person who was complaining of his fate [7, p.57].

At the initial stage of the study of the Russian language only the most essential everyday phrases are used, those widely used in everyday speech: such as sit idly, hang one's nose, etc.

At the advanced stage of learning the Russian language, and especially when the students begin a course of Russian literature, there must be a consistent introduction and consolidation of a large number of phraseological units. It is desirable to have a close relationship with the teacher of the Russian language, with a teacher of literature, as it is possible to avoid dubbing, and to a kind of division of work in the issue of supply of phraseology.

It should be, if it is possible, that the vocabulary of phraseological units is chosen in accordance with the reading course in Russian literature.

Thus, the student meets phraseological units twice: the lectures on literature in Russian and during preparation for classes on literature. That is of course to affect productive assimilation. In a series of exercises, a unit's phraseological assimilation and retention techniques can be offered. For example, the student could:

1) Explain the meaning assigned in the text of phraseology,

2) Insert the missing phraseological units by selecting them from separate data such as a mixed group,

3) Choose two phrases with the same key words within the meaning,

4) Explain the meaning of a phraseological unit.

Exercises can also be built using antonyms, false homonyms (i.e., on the principle of resemblance phraseological units and free combinations) and polysemy.

The above examples do not certainly exhaust all possibilities of supply and retention of phraseological units in the process of learning the Russian language; they can be largely expanded and supplemented, depending on the specific problems of a certain stage of training. An obligatory circumstance of assimilation of phraseological unit is its supply in the context that helps correct design proposal with set phrases.

The national and international in the semantics of phraseology

One of current problems of a modern technique of teaching Russian as a foreign language is the question of volume, selection, training in understanding and practical use of the Russian phraseological units. Being a part of considerable layer of the Russian lexicon, the phraseology represents the huge case of a lexicology, yet not finally limited by a framework of scientific characteristics and, besides, untranslatable literally (without loss of sense) on other languages. There are some difficulties. That in foreign audience representatives of different regions already has knowledge of phraseology of the native language. It reflects both the regional geographic, and culturological national concepts. As a rule, they don't have fully with the similar phenomena in Russian.

According to V.M. Mokienko, interweaving of national and international "happens all the time ... every turn is borrowed from another language, entering into a new environment, somehow it adapts to it and ultimately "nationalized" even when it interferes with incomprehensibility literal sense or another writing system [13, p.8]".

International in semantics of phraseological units it is shown because of phraseological overlapping which arises on identical reconsideration of initial free phrases. Tropes play the major role in development of phraseological overlapping.

If the unequal structural-grammatical completeness and different component structure of the elements which form phraseological units and they don't influence the substantial party and don't change style and the figurative drawing. Then in this case, we can speak about close equivalence of phraseological units with the correlated languages.

It will be noted that conceptualization of the figurative sphere is the most important component of collective consciousness. Phraseological images can be defined as the images of objects and the phenomena of external reality endured as units of content in consciousness for lack of the corresponding relevant stimulation.

The equivalence and non-equivalent phraseological units

When foreigners' philologists train Russian, they have a problem of assimilation of the Russian phraseology. These problems are very relevant. The complex of methodical methods of studying of the Russian phraseological units by foreigners assumes also a method of comparison to phraseology of the native language. Search of an equivalent to the Russian phraseological unit in the native language is process fruitful and useful. Selection of an equivalent does not only help feel more precisely semantics of a set phrase, its co-native sphere, but also to expand associative perception of steady combinations of non-native language.

According to E.M. Solodukho, it is possible to call the phraseological units coinciding on value and stylistic orientation full equivalents. It is possible to call the phraseological units having partial divergences in semantic structure and not coinciding stylistically limited equivalents (Solodukho, 1982: p.25).

The identity and similarity of images and motives are underlying the language nomination. It is not necessarily a consequence of the genetic relatedness of languages. It can be based on the general laws of unrelated languages; thus, comparative and typological methods are interdependent.

Comparison reveals the lines characteristic of this language, and lines having analogues and equivalents in other language, and the typological method. It allows to divide language similarity of the phenomena caused by relationship and to define the common-language parallels, which are a consequence of community of laws, and language thinking and shown in languages of various structure i.e. language universality. In this regard, the typological method is defined by modern science as the method comparing languages on systemically important signs and aiming at identification of isomorphism and an allomorfizm and establishment of their types. "A typology, prerequisite as a method, consists in objective community of a structure and functioning of human languages: the physical community of people, the sign nature of a language code and identical target orientation of language. It means to be the means of communication and information transfers [14, p. 7-8]".

However, though laws and forms of thinking in the essential categories are shown generally equally, in different languages between thinking and language there is no rectilinear and unambiguous interrelation. Language, having got in connection with emergence of thinking, forms rather independent phenomenon and has the internal laws of development, which can't be consolidated to laws of development of thinking. It explains the difference in languages.

The special meaning of typological studying of phraseological structure of various languages is that it allows getting more deeply into essence of process in a forming of phraseological units. Moreover, it is to open the general laws of formation of phraseological units. In some compared languages, the whole groups of phraseological units formed for the same phraseological motive meeting. Emergence of such units can't be explained with neither the general origin of these languages nor influence of one language on another.

Such phenomena occur from identical language perception and judgment of the facts of reality, on identical tendencies of development of folk humour, associative, metaphorical thinking and language forms of his reflection.

The theory and practice of comparative researches of phraseological systems in various languages has already proved illegality of qualification of all phraseological fund of this or that language as national and individual, national and peculiar, i.e. actually in the Interlingua relation of incomparable [11, p.16]. In addition, the "hypertrophy", "absolutization of national exclusiveness phraseology" are "recognized incorrect" [4, p.15], as they obviously contradict objectivity of the fact of comparability both separate multilingual phraseological units, and the whole multilingual phraseological systems [15, p.23]. At the same time, it is necessary to see behind Interlingua communications of phraseological structure of his national originality and to forget that "many phraseological units contain a bright national and cultural component in the semantics" [18, p.92].

As shows experience with foreign students, there are many phraseological units, similar on registration, not only in closely related languages, but also in the languages far on the origin.

It is possible to claim that phraseological image is an essential component of phraseological value. Moreover, it acts as the carrier of national, cultural, and international elements in phraseological units. The similarity and difference in figurative structure of phraseological units has to become an equivalence measure / non-equivalence phraseological unit. Therefore, the main criterion of the comparative analysis of phraseological units of two languages, in our opinion, is degree of figurative proximity.

Comparative research of phraseological units in various languages is an evident linguocultural source (at the same time and it is the native language, in comparison with studied foreign languages). It forms practical base for a technique of teaching phraseology.

Conclusion

Thus, the special meaning in the system of training Russian by foreigners is occupied with phraseology. There is recognition by methodologists in need to consider foreigners in phraseological fund of Russian connect features of linguistic characteristics of phraseological units. It has a particular interest; it has analysis in a mirror of their native language.

The process of introducing in a speech practice of phraseology by the students is enrolled with regard to regional geography and linguocultural information. It provides as the phraseological manner.

Necessary component in a technique in training of phraseology is studying of the phraseological image, which is the cornerstone of phraseological unit. Studying of similarity and difference in figurative structure of a phraseological unit has to be considered as an obligatory preliminary component of linguomethodical system of the presentation of phraseological unit.

Four groups of phraseological units allocated based on semantic, stylistic and figurative characteristics. It can be the basis for this system. In this regard, allocation of the general components in a lexical meaning of two languages –particular importance is studied and native languages.

References

Adonina, L. V., Lazarev, S. V, Fisenko, O. S. & Chernova, N. V. (2015). Universal values: semantic-cognitive approach // Journal of Language and Literature, 6 (4), 393-396.

Ananyev, B. G. (1960). Psychology of sensory perception. – M.: Academy of Sciences of the USSR, pp.486.

Ananyev, B. G. (1960). Psychology of sensory perception. – M.: Academy of Sciences of the USSR, pp.168.

Dolgopolov, Y. A. (1973). Comparative analysis of somatic phraseology: on material of the German and English languages: Avtoref. yew. ... edging. филол. sciences. – Kazan, p.41.

Fisenko, O. S. (2015). Image as consciousness element//Urgent problems of social and humanitarian knowledge. M.: Feather, p.136-142.

Gak, V. G. (1977). Comparative lexicology. (On material of the French and Russian languages). – M.: International relations, p.264.

Gavrin, S. G. (1963). Studying of phraseology of Russian at school. Benefit for teachers. – M.: Uchpedgiz, p.151.

Ivanov, V. V. (1981). Russian – language of international communication of the people of the USSR//linguistics Questions. 4, 3-11.

Kargina, N. V., Fisenko O. S. (2016). Interactive methods of reading the story of A.S. Pushkin "Blizzard" in foreign audience (on the example of the "directed reading" equipment)//Modern science: urgent problems of the theory and practice. Series: Humanities. 3, p.148-151.

Kornilova, T. V., Matveenko, V. E., Fisenko, O. S. & Chernova, N. V. (2015). The role of audio and video means in the training of foreign philologists concerning national vocabulary of Russian language. Journal of Language and Literature, 6 (4), 390-392.

Maslova, V. A. (2001). Cultural linguistics. M.: Academia, p.208.

Maslova, V. A. (2007). Cultural linguistics: studies. benefit for student. high. ducatinal institutions. M.: Publishing center "Akademiya", pp.208.

Mokiyenko, V. M. (1999). Images of the Russian speech: Historical and etymological sketches of phraseology. SPb. Folio-Press, pp.464.

Raykhstein, A. D. (1980). Comparative analysis of the German and Russian phraseology. M.: Vyssh.Shk., pp.143.

Solodukho, E. M. (1982). Problems of internationalization of phraseology. – Kazan: KGU publishing house, pp.168.

Solodyb, Y. P. (1985). The Russian phraseology as an object of a comparative structural and typological research (on material of phraseological units with value of quality standard of the person). Dissertation for Ph.D., pp. 406.

Vereshchagin, E. M. & Kostomarov, V. G. (1980). Lingvostranovedcheskaya theory of the word. M. Russian, pp.118.

Note

The publication was prepared with the support of the «RUDN University Program 5-100»

THE RUSSIAN-CHINESE BILINGUALISM: FACTORS AFFECTING THE ADEQUACY UNDERSTANDING AND THE EFFECTIVENESS OF COMMUNICATION

MYERS G.N., DINEVICH I.A., SMIRNOVA S.V. AND KARPOVA J.V.

Introduction

It is well known that the success of communication is determined by a number of indicators that are largely determined by personality characteristics, i.e. an intellectual level, knowledge, a spiritual experience, value orientations, life priorities, which in turn are determined by the norms and the cultural values; by interpersonal relationships (feelings, psychological traits, reactions, peer evaluation, self-evaluation, etc.); by the interest in the subject of the utterance (the content, attitude to the subject/object of discussion, predictions, motivations, expectations, knowledge sharing, common interests, inter-individual basis of understanding).

In the process of communication, in addition to the mutual evaluation of the psychological qualities of the partners the self-esteem plays an important role. An objective self-assessment provides an adequate understanding of the interlocutor, the subject matter of the question and the possible ways of verbal behaviour. The overconfidence or underestimation of their own capabilities leads to inadequate comprehensive understanding, to errors during the elaboration and adoption of decisions, incorrect assessment of the partner's behaviour that may cause undesirable conflicts (Bozhenkova, 2000).

The understanding of the interlocutor perspective is necessary for the exchange of knowledge about the objectivity of the subject matter content, as the exchange of knowledge contributes to the emergence of interindividual basis of understanding (the themes), while our own experience is important as knowledge, attitude to the subject and relationship to the person as a whole [ib]. In order to the information expressed and the information received were identical, it is necessary for both consciousnesses to comprehend equally this information, to develop the same relation to it and to evaluate it. If the interlocutors want to achieve understanding and mutual intelligibility, the norms, which they orientate themselves, must coincide and form the same linguocultural field [ib].

What way do the above-described factors affect on the success of communication in the Russian-Chinese bilingualism? What difficulties do Chinese students face in the new language environment?

The main text

Students from China are one of the largest groups of foreign students receiving education abroad, so the issues concerning their adaptation have become the most important ones for psychologists. Chinese students who came to study in Russian universities face a number of challenges, which can be divided into several categories:

1) Socio-psychological categories (common problems for young people at this age stage: the changing of students' social role, correcting of their needs and values, clarification of self-esteem, level of self-actualization, the need to display the life stance);

2) Activity ones (common problems for all freshmen, heightened by the diversity of syllabi and models of the relationship among the students and teachers in China and Russia, the adaptation to new physiological stress, learning and cognitive activity);

3) Didactic ones increase of regulated volume of educational information that is common to all foreigners related to insufficient knowledge of the language and culture, prejudices, etc. (Bozhenkova, Bozhenkova & Shaklein, 2015).

Such problems lead to serious difficulties in the adaptation period.

The face-to-face interaction among representatives of different countries and cultures does not lead to understanding, to open confidential relations. Student exchanges do not necessarily lead to positive intergroup perceptions and harmonious relations. Due to the significant differences in cultures, educational systems and value orientations the acculturation of the students is very often slow and difficult. Even under the most favourable conditions of communication, for example in constant interaction, successful collaborative activities, frequent and deep contacts relatively equal status, in the absence of obvious differences, the students may have difficulties and tension when communicating with representatives of the country of residence. Therefore, the problem of intercultural adaptation remains one of the most difficult and the achievement of the compatibility of a person with a new cultural environment depends on its successful solution.

In addition to personal and demographic factors the group ones (the desire of group members to stay in its composition, to fulfil their obligations to the collective), have an impact on weak adaptability of Chinese students. In particular, the Chinese have a culture, where a power of tradition is still strong; the behaviour of individuals is largely ritualized; the difficulties of Chinese students in our country are connected with a large cultural distance between the Russian and Chinese cultures.

The most difficult area of entering a new cultural context is an educational activity that is primarily due to the necessity of learning the Russian language to the extent which will be sufficient for the acquisition of professionally significant knowledge and skills.

In addition to the level of competence in the Russian language, academic success and psychological satisfaction of Chinese students in Russia is influenced by other factors, particularly the behaviours in the University. Consequently, the students to adapt to the new culture must not only learn its behaviours, but also to develop the ability to apply them in specific habitats.

In the questionnaires and essays students from China noted that visiting the first lecture, practical trainings, they experienced the strongest shock due to the unfamiliar nature of the interaction among students and teachers. The reason for such a shock is in intercultural differences, which are based on these "dimensions of cultures" as individualism/collectivism, and the distance between the individual and the "power". The Chinese culture is more collective and hierarchical than the culture of Russia, and that's why students, who graduated from high schools in China, are verbal passive in the classroom, they try not to attract attention to themselves, ask little questions and participate in discussions. The desire of Russian students to "stand out", asking questions, and even more so debating with the teacher, is seen as provocative and insensitive. This behaviour is perceived by the Chinese as disrespectful to the teacher, as an attempt to doubt his/her knowledge that, from their point of view, may lead to "loss of face". Conversely, the respect for the teachers is associated with a formal and distant relationship. For Chinese students, the teacher is the transmitter of knowledge, the authority, and not the organizer of educational process in which they should be the active participants. Their role in the classroom, they see only in hearing and thinking, and not in discussions that make them feel the anxiety and depression because they take the discussions as a confrontation (a conflict). The conflict in Chinese culture is regarded as a violation or disharmony of relations (Bozhenkova & Myers, 2011). The Chinese feel some qualms about its appearing, demonstrating the highest values of avoiding conflicts even in comparison with other representatives of Asian nations. In addition, the Chinese students are not used to analysing theoretical material, to comparing and contrasting different points of view, to choosing the best of several ideas and approaches. A particular problem for them is critical analysis because they mistakenly associate it with criticism of the concepts' creators, leading to their authority damage.

Communicative strategies of Russian teachers in communicating with students cause confusion. Chinese students do not understand the speech and behavioural tactics forming a friendly style, creating a closeness of views strategy, as they are accustomed to the distancing that exists in their cultural traditions.

As a result of these differences there is a misunderstanding between Chinese and Russian students, Chinese students and Russian teachers, who take calm, sober, attentive, non-aggressive Chinese students as passive and indifferent. In fact, the respect and reverence, patience and modesty towards their own achievements are very important for them, they are reluctant to show their emotional state, express their opinions or objections, especially to the people that have a higher status. In this situation, the task of teachers is to show more respect for the educational traditions, which are characteristic of Chinese culture, and gradually to teach Chinese students the norms of interaction in the classroom accepted in our country (Shaklein, 1997).

Therefore, when teaching Chinese students you should create such conditions, choose such tactics of communication, which given their usual methods of teaching, help them gain the ability of new (for them) social communication, to find common ground of their own spiritual experience and knowledge system with the "world view" shared by members of a linguistic community and meet their existential needs through shared code – the language.

Another important factor influencing the effectiveness of communication is the behavioural strategies associated with paralinguistic/extralinguistic manifestations in the process of communication. Nonverbal communication (the movement, facial expressions, gesture, gaze, posture, intonation, timbre, volume and tempo of speech, speech sound, and distance) affects the quality of your message, and accompanies it along the lines of verbal number, or even replaces it. No doubt that listening to the teacher and observing his/her non-verbal behaviour, the learner finds it easier to perceive information, as at the same time he gets it through auditory and visual channels, that is extremely important for Chinese students. Auditory mechanisms of Chinese people are sensitive to the rhythmic pattern of the utterance, and monotonous series of phrases and a quiet tone of voice are perceived as insignificant and unimportant information. It is important to note that the Chinese syllabic tones perform distinctive function and are not used to express intonation differences. In the Chinese language there are two main types of intonation (rising one and falling one), while studying the Russian language Chinese intonation pattern interferes with Russian, and "as a result, the tone of Chinese students has the same static tone without the downturn (PS-1) to the end of the sentence which is typical of the Russian language, the special importance is the duration of the pauses between its lines. PS-3 does not reach the right places of movement of the centre in questions, so the interviewee can make mistakes in the emotional sense and communicative intention of the speaker" (Vagner, 2002, p.100).

Summary

Therefore, teaching Chinese students-philologists of the oral dialogic communication in the Russian language, a special attention should be paid to the suggestive properties of speech as a factor influencing the effectiveness of communication, because understanding the meaning of the word, they are often unable to respond adequately to the intonation which differs from the value message of the speaker, and, as we have noted, that is unacceptable, in their culture, and often leads to an internal conflict.

The possession of the body language o is the possession of the audience attention. Chinese students regard the teacher as the representative of science, a mentor, and a wrong understanding of a gesture, facial movements, and posture may lead to misunderstanding. In turn, the inability of the teacher to read information from gestures, eye movements, postures, entails a lack of understanding in class, the inability to build a productive dialogue with the audience.

Students coming to study in Russia are not confined to communication in the University classroom, therefore, the possession of nonverbal communication is necessary in order to prepare competent professional, able to build a dialogue with representatives of the culture of another country. The incorrect assessment of verbal behaviour can be avoided if we know and consider speech and behaviour tactics of each other. The

Chinese and Russian cultures have equal gestures. For example, when Russian or Chinese shows the thumb raised up, it mean that anyone or anything is appreciated. When Russian and Chinese military salute, they bring to the temple the palm of his right hand with a clenched and fingers extended, palm side forward. The shaking hands are also used in Russian and Chinese communication when meeting or presentation. The Chinese and the Russians usually nod my head and smile when greeting and parting.

However, in non-verbal manifestations of the two peoples there are differences. One of the most common forms of non-verbal communication is the smile. The Chinese often smile, but that not always seems sincere. Their smile is called "enigmatic," and indeed, she often expresses a variety of feelings: friendship, restraint, reticence, embarrassment. The smile in Russian culture is a reaction to positive emotions, and the expression "duty smile" contains a negative connotation.

Thus, when learning the Russian language paralinguistic extralinguistic factors as elements of cultural linguistics play a huge role because a Chinese student begins to perceive the target language not only as a set of necessary rules and norms, but also as a sort of distillation of the flow of a previously unknown culture, which falls on him from the first days of stay in a foreign country (Zhao, 2008). Consequently, one of the most important tasks for a future teacher not only to master the foreign language speech, para/extra linguistic, pragmatic, sociocultural, psychological and other factors expressed both verbal and non-verbal means, but also to teach their future students to understand and use them.

References

Bozhenkova, R. (2000). 'Speech communication as a linguocultural phenomenon and the process of adequate text (on the material of the Russian language)' Ph.D. Dissertation, Moscow, Russia

Bozhenkova, R. Bozhenkova, N., Shaklein, V. (2015). The Russian language and speech culture. Moscow, Russia

Bozhenkova, R., Myers, G. (2011). Revisited the intercultural adaptation of Chinese students in the Philology Universities of the Russian Federation. Izvestia of Southwest State University. Linguistics and Pedagogy, 2, 57-60, Kursk, Russia.

Shaklein, V. (1997). Linguocultural situation and research of text. Moscow, Russia

Vagner, V. (2002). Linguooriented methods of teaching Russian as a foreign language. Traditions and innovations in the professional teacher's activity of Russian as a foreign language. People's Friendship University of Russia, Moscow, Russia

Zhao, Y. (2008). Linguocultural basis of ethnooriented teaching the Russian language and testing (by the example of Chinese studnts). Ph.D. Dissertation, Moscow, Russia

THE SEARCH FOR "THE OTHER KINGDOM" IN THE NOVEL BY I.A. BUNIN "ARSENIEV'S LIFE": BOOK ONE

MARIANNA ANDREEVNA DUDAREVA

Introduction

Contemporary researchers contemplate on the latent nature of Bunin's folklorism, integrating proverbs, sayings, song formulas into their texts, ethnic constants in poetry (Dalgat, 2004). However, the attitude to the early works of the writer and folklorism forms in the works is problematic, and, what is most important, the axiological perception of folklore in poetry is one-sided. For example, V.V. Lyukevich, in some of his articles, criticized the words of M.K. Azadovsky about the dark folklore baseline in Bunin's prose, but himself saw exclusively tragic and dark principle in the perception of the folk by the poet (Lyukevich, 2014: p.50-61). However, what should be implied by the dark, irrational, subconscious? When considering the nature of folklore from a non-materialistic viewpoint, from the positions of archaic understanding (of life and death, the other world, the initiative path), which are present in fairy tales, charms, epics, the irrational and dark comes out with reverse correlative.

The folklore provides the artist with an opportunity to go beyond the boundaries of the ordinary, philistine understanding of the life — this appeal to folklore and myths will become particularly relevant for the aesthetics and poetics of modernism, in which Bunin was involved. Like L.N. Tolstoy, he cautiously and even critically treated the emerging modernist trends, but himself his ideology was closer to the new literature. According to a fair observation of I.B. Nichiporov, it is the sense of the crisis of rationalism in the knowledge of the world, history and the human soul, as well as the formation of new ideas about art that brought Bunin closer to modernism (Nichipirov, 2003: p.232). Thus, the crisis of rationalism pushed writers and poets back to the archaic, mythological, and folklore codes. Such treatment requires the writer to have some kind of reincarnation, to grow into what he describes. Bunin himself reflected on this creative act in Tolstoy's Liberation: "Some kind of people have the ability to feel strongly not only their own time, but also others', past one, not only their own country, their tribe, but also others', foreign, not only themselves but also their neighbours, that is, as commonly said: "the ability to reincarnate," and particularly vibrant and particularly imaginative memory. In order to be among such people, one must be an individual who has passed, in the chain of his ancestors, the long way of numerous existences* and suddenly manifested in himself a particularly complete image of his wild primeval man with the entire freshness of his sensations, with all his imagery..." (Bunin, 2006: p.50).

The poet-symbolist A. Belyy called this the person's attachment to other cultures. For example, in the article "The Emblems of the Meaning" (1909), we can find: "That truly new that captivates us in symbolism is an attempt to illuminate the deepest contradictions of the modern culture with the coloured rays of diverse cultures. We are now experiencing the whole past it was: India, Persia, Egypt, Greece, as well as the Middle Ages come to life, sweep past us, as the epochs that are closer to us are rushing past us" (Belyy, 2010: p.57-58). If we transfer Belyy's thought to the scientific space, we will see that the humanitarian science is also trying to solve the problem of interpreting works of art, especially artistic texts, from different angles. *The concept of entelechy of culture* was put forward by G.S. Knabe who defined this phenomenon as "the absorption by a certain time of the content, nature, spirit, and style of the past cultural epoch on the grounds that they were consonant with another later epoch and capable of satisfying its internal needs and requests" (Knabe, 2000: p.19). Is this how Andrei Belyy considers the art of symbolism and the *art of the future*? How complex and often changeable are the views of the poet on the symbol, its features, on how dialectical his conclusions about romanticism and realism are, but the reflection on the *need to remember* the words of *other epochs by the artist* always remains unchanged, and this problem is closely related to another, the problem of "cosmic", not philistine, not positivist view of art. So, the impending epoch itself was an *entelechy* by its nature and it was expressed in the circulation of the word in folklore and myths, and even the need of the artists in it. Bunin the realist is consonant with this epoch in the aspect of our subject, as well.

Materials and methods

Russian literature of the beginning of the 20th century absorbed the knowledge of folklore, the archaic ideas about the Cosmos, and gave an idea of a man who was attached to the supramundane, the metaphysical.

Of course, the subjects of *Eros* and *Thanatos* so strongly relevant to the national axiology organically entered the artistic world of Russian writers along with this. Neither did I.A. Bunin pass over these subjects. There are numerous works devoted to the concepts of "love" and "death" in Bunin's poetics in literary criticism, in particular, the thanatological motives of "The Dark Alleys" (Konovalov, 1995: p.107-109). *The purpose of* this article is to consider the genesis of the mortal border images in Bunin's poetry, in the first book of the famous novel "Arseniev's Life." *The methodology of* our research assumes the use of historically functional, historically genetic, and systematically typological methods of analysis and application of the experience of folkloric commenting of texts.

Where did the writer bring this tragic, often dark, and elemental image from? Azadovsky, who studied Bunin's folklorism, pointed out that Bunin saw the tragic in folklore, in the people element; all the people's sorrow passed from the verbal-poetic into the artistic: "... in the very folklore tradition, in its rites and everyday manifestations, the writer found wild, gloomy images" (Azadovskiy, 2010: p.131). This makes us think about the genesis of *mortal images* and the nature of thanatological motifs in Bunin's poetics. Here, it is necessary to say about the special type of his works' folklorism. On the one hand, researchers who were the first to develop this problem pointed to the bookish nature of Bunin's folklorism and, mainly, sought to find all sorts of sources that the author could rely on to create a certain image (Pomerantseva, 1973: p.139-152). On the other hand, a number of new works have appeared that state the syncretic latent nature of folklorism. Particularly distinguished are the articles by V.A. Smirnov who drew attention to the opposition "Eros – Thanatos" coming from archaic folklore foundations (Smirnov, 2011: p.162-200). In addition, the theory of literature has singled out various types of folklore a long time ago: recording, it is stylization and borrowing, latent. From these positions, Bunin's work is especially interesting; firstly, Bunin knew various genres of folklore, studied them, and even collected them. Secondly, Bunin creatively reworked folklore. The writer himself strove specifically for artistic comprehension of folklore, rejecting, for example, Remizov's stylizations and alterations (Maltsev, 1994: p.146). In the context of such a theoretical formulation of the issue and Bunin's message, let us turn to the novel of his emigration period, "Arseniev's Life."

Literature Review

Attempts to consider the "Arseniev's Life" novel in the light of the folkloric traditions have already been undertaken and, it is worth noting, very successfully done by the folklorist V.A. Smirnov. The scientist pays much attention to the landscape sketches, coupled, in his opinion, with the "lunar myth." In the turning point for the life of the main character, the Moon appears, which manifests the cosmogonic nature of the situation: The star model of the world, the Moon's motif "in the novel are certain counterpoints that determine its entire tonality" (Smirnov, 2016: p.135). These observations are accurate and fair; they also refer to the formula of *the heavenly fencing*, to the charming poetics. However, it seems to us that from the viewpoint of the folklore tradition functioning, special attention should also be paid to the types of spatial models in the novel that are related to the field, plain, unknown *invisible land*. Researchers have long introduced the concept of a geographical and metaphysical living space in relation to the artistic world of Bunin (Prashcheruk, 2011: p.7-15). Also, the "exit points" into this metaphysical and symbolic space of the novel were revealed, for example, from the viewpoint of special lexical organics (the concepts "soul," "surrounding world," and others were analysed) (Smolentsov, 2012). The metaphysical, transitional space (between "that" and "this" light) is also expressed at the level of the topography, which is set by the model of the field, plain.

The concept of "field," also rather frequent from the standpoint of the work's language, was already appealed to in "Arseniev's Life." Scientists point out that it is in the field where Arseniev draws closer to the Cosmos; a kind of mysterious "power of the space" is exercised over the soul (Gallyamova, 2012: p.124), which makes the main character yearn and feel lonely. But was the motif of loneliness and anguish expressed only in this type of space? It is worth paying attention to Arseniev's attraction to everything *miraculous and inexplicable*, starting, paradoxically, with death: "Are not we born with a sense of death? And if not, if I had not suspected, would I have loved life as much as I love and loved?" (Bunin, 2006: p.7). These thanatological reflections that open the novel set not so much on the gloomy conversation about death, as on the conversation about the *vague, invisible, and wonderful* in life that the main character tries to catch since his young age. Often in Arseniev's reflections, there are lexemes "incomprehensible," "unknown": "The depth of the sky, the distance of the fields told me about something else, as if existing apart from them, caused a dream and yearning for something I lacked, touched with *incomprehensible love* and tenderness to someone and something I don't know..." (Bunin, 2006: p.9). These concepts of the invisible suggest the eidology of the ideal and other-worldly, which Bunin could borrow from the Russian fairy tales. A confirmation of this is the direct mentioning by the main character himself of the fairy tales heard in his childhood: "Recollecting the fairy tales read and heard in my childhood, I still feel that the most captivating were the words about the *unknown and the unusual*" (Bunin, 2006: p.19). Perhaps, this "childish" discovery of the main character also expresses the basis for understanding Bunin's folklorism, whose essence reduces itself to the archaic ideas of humans about the Cosmos, the invisible unknown life, and the desire to learn it. This opens up the special type of Bunin's character: the *man of the threshold*. Is it accidental that through the mind of a little boy, the reader is reminded of stable fairy-tale formulas, rising actions: "In a certain kingdom, in a certain state, beyond the far end of the earth beyond the mountains, beyond the dales, beyond the blue seas? Tsar-Maiden, Vasilisa the Wise..." (Bunin, 2006: p.19). Here are listed the possible models of the *edge of the world*, the limit beyond, which cannot be comprehended by the common way. Actually, Arseniev with his strange teacher seeks such places in his adolescent's daily life. The attic, which is often explored by the characters, embodies in a ritual sense the other world: "And so many times I climbed with Baskakov in the attic, where, according to a legend, some grandfather or great-grandfather's saber was lying about? We climbed there on a very steep staircase, in the semi-darkness, bending over. <...> In the world, there was the sky, the sun, the space, and here only the twilight and something *crushed, drowsy*" (Bunin, 2006: p.30). But the horror and mustiness of the attic attracted the child, rather than repelled. The search for a fairy-tale saber filled his meager, in his opinion, life with superficity.

The craving for the ideal affects not only indirectly the strange searches and hobbies of Arseniev, which he shared with Baskakov, but also his reading preferences. First, the reference to Pushkin's "Ruslan and Lyudmila" is extremely momentous, where the idea of the threshold, the aesthetics of the outer-worldly reality is clearly represented already from the first lines, to which the Bunin's character refers: "It would seem that such a nonsense, some never and nowhere existing seashore, some "booky" cat, who for no reason found itself there, and for some reason is chained to the oak, some wood spirit, mermaids" and "On unknown paths there are traces of extraordinary beasts" (Bunin, 2006: p.33).

And *poetic guessing*, insight does not fail the smart boy here. He is attracted by the inexplicable from the viewpoint of the everyday reality: "But obviously, that is the matter. That nonsense, something ridiculous, unprecedented, and not something reasonable, genuine" (Bunin, 2006: p.33). Obviously, the fact that a scientist seeks and reveals works in poetics through careful analysis is perceived by the poet at another, deeper, unconscious level. And this is the manifestation of the entelechy of culture and thinking. In one case, the researcher needs to draw typologies, identify ethno-poetic constants. In another case, the artist of the word needs to live into another environment, epoch — this was what Bunin wrote in "Tolstoy's Liberation." However, Arseniev appeals not only to Pushkin, but also to world literature, knightly novels, feeling himself a participant in the distant past. This *travesty* expresses the sacred memory, the *mimetic action*. This allows the character to perceive the surrounding reality imaginatively, for him the ordinary gets the status of the Absolute.

Arseniev sees the sensation of the otherworldly, non-domestic current of life in his illness, which he treats as a transition to the other world: "In the last year of our life in Kamenka, I suffered the first serious illness, for the first time I learned the amazing thing that they used to call simply a serious illness and that there is actually a sort of *wandering to some other-worldly limits*" (Bunin; 2006: p.37). It is interesting to see the *room topography* itself, the position of the main character in space during the illness: "Ah, I remember very well those moments when I began to come to myself at times and saw either my mother in the form of some huge ghost, or instead of the bedroom, a dark and gloomy barn, where the candle placed on the floor behind the head of the bed generated thousands of disgusting figures, faces, animals, plants fluttering and trembling in the fiery waves!" (Bunin, 2006: p.38). The design of *the other world* has its own laws, and the main feature is the "inverted nature", ugliness of common things (compare the dream imagery of Pushkin's Tatiana). In addition, the candle in our context refers to the funerary *mortal candle* set for the soul of the deceased, who does not see and can find the way to the *other world with the help of the light* (Tolstoy, 1995: p.189). Arseniev delicately feels the state of the threshold. Not accidentally, Bunin describes the terrible images of the character's drowsiness and puts a candle in his bedhead.

Results

The feeling of death chases the boy especially after Nadya's death, who appears either as a sackcloth puppet, or someone with black terrible lips: "I suddenly realized that I am mortal, that every minute that wild, terrible thing that happened to Nadia could happen to me, and that in general everything earthly, all living, material, corporeal is inevitably subject to death, decay, that purple blackness, which covered Nadya's lips by the time she was taken out of the house" (Bunin, 2006: p.39). In the mind and soul of the main character, death is dialectical: he is either afraid of it, or seems to wish to die, while remaining in the *threshold conditions*: "... my half-mad, enthusiastically bitter dreams of the torments of the first Christians, of the maidens torn to pieces by wild beasts on some courses, of the royal daughters, pure and beautiful like god's lilies, beheaded by their own cruel parents, of the burning desert of the Jordan, where, covering up her nakedness only with her own hair grown to the ground, Mary of Egypt dwelt, entreated her fornication in the world..." (Bunin, 2006: p.40); "I lived only by the inner contemplation of these pictures and images" (Bunin, 2006: p.40). And again, at the turning point of life for Arseniev, he does not have a domestic view of things, but an imaginative one: through the inner image all the surrounding reality is highlighted. Again, there is a feeling of a fabulous, other-worldly life, which the main character consciously seeks: "<...> escaped into his fabulously holy world, revealing with his mournful joys, the thirst for suffering, self-indulgence, self-torture" (Bunin, 2006: p.40).

Conclusions

The first book of the novel reveals to us the secret life of Arseniev the child and the boy. He feels himself on the verge of real and surreal, as indicated by the symbols of the field, attic, book with fairy tales, and his visions. In the most ordinary (for an adult), Arseniev foresees the inexplicable, mysterious and strives to this with all his heart. The identification in the text of archetypal constructions, the folklore commentary, which is connected in this part more with the models of spaces, leads the reader to the *ontological* plan of the narrative.

References

Azadovskiy, M. K. (2010). Folkorism of I. A. Bunin. Russkaya Literatura, 4.

Belyy, A. (2010). The Emblems of the Sense. Andrey Belyy Collected Edition. Symbolism. The Book of Articles. Moscow: Kulturnaya Revolutsiya; Respublika, pp. 57–58.

Bogdanova, I. G. (1999). Artistic Humanization of the Love and Death Topic in Bunin's Works. The Writer, Art: Contemporary Perception: Collection of Graduate, Scientific Articles. Kursk: Kursk State Pedagogical University.

Bunin, I. A. (2006). Complete Works in 13 Volumes, M.: Voskresenye, Vol. 5, 8.

Dalgat, U. B. (2004). Ethnic Poetry in the Russian Prose of the 1920s–1990s (excursuses). M: World Literature Institute of RAS.

Gallyamova, T. A. & Ertner, E. N. (2012). The Image of the Russian Fields in the Novel by I.A. Bunin "Arseniev's Life" // Herald of Tyumen State University, 1.

Knabe, G. S. (2000). The Russian Classical Studies: The Content, Role, and Fate of the Antique Heritage in the Russian Culture. Moscow: Russian University of Humanities.

Konovalov, A. A. (1995). To the Question of Life and Death in the Book by I.A. Bunin "The Dark Alleys". The Issues of Evolution of the Russian Literature of the 20th Century" Proceedings of the Inter-University Scientific Conference. Moscow: Moscow State Pedagogical University, Release 2, pp. 107–109.

Li San, C. (2016). The subject of love and death in "The Dark Alleys" by I.A. Bunin: The Philosophic and Aesthetic Context: Thesis of Candidate of Philology: 10.01.01. Moscow.

Lyukevich, V.V. (2014). The Folklore Element of the Artistic Model of the National World in the Version of the Fairy Tale about Emelya and "Kostsy" by Bunin // The Philological Science and School: Dialog and Cooperation: Proceedings of the VII All-Russian Academic and Research Conference. in 2 volumes. Part 1: The Theory and Practice of the Literary Text Analysis. Reading and Relevant Problems of the Literature Education at Schools and Universities. The Role and Place of Dictionaries in the Improvement of the Contemporary Education. Moscow: Moscow Institute of Public Education, pp50–61.

Maltsev, Y.V. (1994). Ivan Bunin. 1870 – 1953. – M.; Frankfurt: Posev.

Nichiporov, I. B. (2003). The Poetry is Dark and Cannot Be Expressed by Words. The Work of I.A. Bunin and Modernism. – Moscow: Metafora.

Pomerantseva, E. V. (1973). The Folklore in Bunin's Poems. The Literary Heritage. Moscow: Nauka, 84 (2), pp.139–152.

Prashcheruk, N. V. (1999). The Literature World of Bunin's Prose: The Language of the Space. Yekaterinburg: MUMC "RO".

Prashcheruk, N. V. (2011). The Metaphysic Consciousness of I.A. Bunin in the "Arseniev's Life" novel // The Metaphysics of I.A. Bunin: Collection of Scientific Works Dedicated to the Work of I.A. Bunin. Voronezh. Release 2. – Pp. 7–15.

Smirnov, V. A. (2001). Bunin. Smirnov V.A. Literature and Folklore Traditions: Poetics Issues (The Archetypes of the Female Principle in Russian Literature of the 19th–Early 20th Centuries). Ivanovo: Yunona, pp. 162–200.

Smirnov, V. A. (2016). The Problem of Personality Cosmization in the Novel by I.A. Bunin "Arseniev's Life" // Herald of Kostroma State University named after N.A. Nekrasov, 2.

Smolentsov, A. I. (2012). The Novel by I.A. Bunin "Arseniev's Life": the "Contexts of Comprehension" and the Symbolism of Images. Abstract from the Thesis of Candidate of Philology. Voronezh.

Tolstoy, N. I. (1995). The Eyes and Vision of the Dead // Tolstoy N.I. The Language and the Popular Culture. Documentaries about the Slavic Mythology and Ethnic Linguistics. – Moscow: Indrik.

Note

The publication was prepared with the support of the «RUDN University Program 5-100»

TRAINING OF THE RUSSIAN PHRASEOLOGY BY FOREIGNERS: STAGES OF WORK ON PHRASEOLOGICAL UNITS AND DIFFICULTIES IN ASSIMILATION

FISENKO OLGA SERGEEVNA, GOEVA NINA PARLOVNA AND POLYANSKAYA EKATERINA NIKOLAEVNA

Introduction

One of the most important places in the methods of teaching Russian as a foreign language takes phraseology to recognize the same object of study as vocabulary (Shakhsuvarova, 1983, p.92). If the lexis reflects the full number of phenomena, facts, and processes of reality in its entirety, first the phraseology includes the field of experiences and feelings, the psychological conditions of the person (the theme of sadness, joy, love, friendship, conflict and struggle), qualitative and quantitative characteristics of objects and events.

Despite the fact, it is necessary to include learning content of phraseology at an early stage of teaching Russian as a foreign language, that is, in the first semester of preparatory departments many teachers recognize it. There are obvious contradictions with regard to the inclusion of phraseology in learning content at the noticed stage. However, there is a common point of view that according to the initial stage of the phraseological units and should not be given. It is the actual use of phraseological units practical in almost all textbooks and training aids in Russian for foreign students of the elementary level.

Materials and methods

The object of research interest is the phraseological system of Russian, studied by us through the complex linguistic methods.

The teaching method of foreign languages is closely related to pedagogy, linguistics and psychology, so the most methodical principles are based on the laws and regulations of these sciences. If such laws or regulations are used directly (these are just transferred from pedagogy, psychology or linguistics in methodology), usually they tend to become permanently established and the general methodological principles. If the laws or regulations of pedagogy, psychology or linguistics are used indirectly (they are interpreted in methodological purposes), it can be said only about private teaching principles.

The implementation of permanent methodological principles is an indispensable condition for the effectiveness of the educational process and teaching method. The Russian method of training the principles are most often classified based on the basic techniques for the sciences. In this regard, the four groups of principles are considered:

1. Linguistic – these are consistency, concentric distinction of phenomena at the level of speech and language, functionality, stylistic differentiation, minimization, situational and thematic organization of the material, the study of lexis and grammar on the basis of syntax;

2. Didactic – these are awareness, visibility, durability, accessibility, stronger, systematic and consistent, activity, collectivity, distressed, developing education, creativity;

3. Psychological – these are motivation, the gradual formation of knowledge, skills, abilities, and taking into account individual psychological characteristics of the student;

4. Methodological –these are the communicative and accounting features of the native language, complexity, oral lead, interconnected studying of all kinds of speech activity.

The stages of phraseological units in a system of teaching Russian as a foreign language

The generalization of methodological research has shown that there are different ways of organizing work on phraseological material. As a rule, they are one-aspect because they are addressed to an individual party's phraseological units (lexical composition and grammatical characteristics, nominative value of national-cultural component of semantics, etc.). Moreover, these are applicable to a more or less wide range, but there is always a limited range of phraseological unit. In this regard, the inclusion of phraseological unit in speech leads to difficulties. They are caused with the common means of inter-phrase connection, the special means of communication, the lack of compatibility under the general rules, the restriction on the compatibility under the general rules, the individual rules of compatibility, formulation of punctuation, special rules, and failure to include members' offers between components of phraseologies. Many of these challenges are reinforced under the influence intralingual and translingual interference.

A significant role in the successful acquirement of the phraseological system of the Russian language is the formation by students' mastery of phraseology skills: the potential (it is comprehension of unfamiliar phraseological units in the context based on a literal translation), receptive (it is a recognition of previously studied phraseological units), productive (it is the use of phraseological units in a person's speech). The above skills with phraseology may be unconscious or conscious. Unconscious ownership is formed with a positive transfer in the presence of two languages of phraseological unit identical in meaning and formal structure forms. This feature is particularly increased in the study of a closely related language. Comprehension skills can be carried out at different levels: general and special. The realization on a general level is the ability to distinguish the idiom of the available combinations of words as a stable and reproducible unit, to interpret the meaning or to translate into their native language. Other information about phraseological units are special, and their completeness should be determined taking into account the difficulties that they help to overcome, as well as the categories of students.

We believe that the most productive training purpose is a phased description of phraseology. This approach allows more fully taking into account the possibilities of translingual interference. **The first phase** includes:

a) it is a comparison of phraseological units in each set of features that constitute the idiom; b) these are ordering phraseological units by descending number of matched features; c) there is a division of the resulting list of phraseological units in a homogeneous layer; and d) each such naming formation is according with semantic and functional properties of its constituent units.

Consistent application of the procedure is laid to distinguish the following types of structural and semantic associations of phraseological units: idioms, proverbs, sayings, phraseological combinations, phraseological substantive phrases (nominative expression), the formula of speech etiquette, and grammar component expressions. One of the features of phraseological semantics is its predominantly subjective orientation. "Idioms estimate a person at the point of physical, mental, moral and ethical, and intellectual qualities. They describe it in relation to social class, occupation, age and life experience, family ties" (Gubarev, 1980). There is an existing object phraseology related to the characteristics of objects and phenomena of reality and it consists of «Phraseological dictionary» A.I. Molotkova, 4-5% of the total number of phraseology. This suggests that much of the wealth of idiomatic language can be seen as some form of reflection. It reflects human relations (Petrenko, Nistratov & Romanova, 1989, p.27).

The content of **the second stage** is the methodological orientation of the resulting linguistic model. It includes next, the first it is a reformation of such linguistic model that complies with the methodological goals and objectives of a particular stage of education, the second appropriate in terms of the reduction of training tasks typologically similar phraseology layer and the presentation of the test array in the form of idiomatic language field. It consists of the core and the periphery. It exist the importance of the title of the principle in the selection of methodological idiomatic material; it is occurred appropriate as one of the criteria of used phraseological units. We emphasize that the Russian phraseology is hardly subjected to linguistic processing, therefore, without accurate data on the incidence of phraseological units; commonly, we have to implement and use the principle, and to guide with subjective frequency. There is the presence of elected phraseological units in phrasebook, as well as intuition and experience of the informants, which are involved in the sample phraseological units.

Difficulties in mastering of the phraseological units of the Russian language by foreigners

Practical experience has shown the mastering of phraseology. The students face to real difficulties (lexical, grammatical, meaning, cultural) contextual inclusion by foreign students in their mastering.

Lexical difficulties of the mastering of phraseology are idiomatic related to lexis, archaisms, neologisms, stylistically marked words, proper names, terminology, transliterations, and other words of low frequency of use.

The grammatical difficulties are caused with the study of phraseology: phraseologically related word forms, preference for infrequent forms of unfilled positions in the components with obligatory valence, homonymous and repeated forms, unusual word order, predicative structures unknown to students. In addition, for almost all types of phraseology to a greater or lesser level are characteristic differences between formal lexical and grammatical status and categorical meaning.

The solving of the specific issues in linguodidactics is complicated by the fact that the problems of comparative phraseology in Russian and foreign languages are insufficiently developed. Thus, comparative analysis should be based on the characteristics of the system being studied foreign (Russian) language. On this same basis, phraseology training should be built, based on the real conditions and in following with a comprehensive approach in studying Russian as a foreign language. Among the real conditions of learning, it is necessary to determine the level of Russian ownership in phraseology in view of the end goals and objectives of studying Russian as a foreign language.

In general, the level of ownership with the Russian language, and in particular phraseology, it is determined based on testing, questioning, during interviews and observations on practical exercises. One of the formal indicators of the real level of knowledge in the Russian language is the phraseology "negative linguistic material" (according to the words of L. Scherba). The informants make the mistakes.

Among the typical mistakes, due to the complexity of the phraseological system of the Russian language and patterns of use of phraseology in the communication process, these are picked out:

1) Phraseological unit is not perceived as a holistic, sustainable formation, as well as free phrase: *to speak for the eye, to waste breath, the green light, put down roots, to wash dirty linen at home.*

2) A free phrase is used instead of phraseological units. It contains one of the components of the phraseological unit: instead of Russian's *to pull the pieces (lexical meaning of idiom is to judge a person), the foreigners say to touch the bone or to collect the bones; instead of Russian's a cat laugh, the foreigners say cock to laugh, turkeys at laugh, or people at laughed; instead of Russian's gone with the wind, the foreigners say to look for the grain in the field or to look for happiness in the field.*

3) Part of a phraseological unit is used with the other part (contamination) - as a result of mixing two phraseological units: *to count the ribs* and *to pull the pieces*, it occurs mistaking form *to count the bones*; similarly: *there is no law for fools* and *it's still all up in the air* - a pitchfork law does not apply, etc. The ignorance of the semantics of phraseological units leads to the fact that students don't choose the right synonyms for phraseological units: the Russian idiom is from the pure heart (lexical meaning is without malice, treachery, or evil intent; honest; sincere; guileless.) – *Joyfully*, free; to be gone (lexical meaning is being away from a place) – *lost*; stone's throw (lexical meaning is: it usually refers to a distance much greater than one could throw a stone.) – *Easily*;

enough to swear by (lexical meaning is to have great reliance on or confidence in) – *grief.*

4) Of particular note is the weak ownership paronyms by the students (mostly in proverbs and sayings): the mistaken use of *clever head from a distance can be seen the clever idea to paint* – instead, the Russian proverb is *clever head is revered in his youth;* the foreigners say *that written with a pen, the hand cannot write that written with a pen, do not erase* – instead of Russian version is *that written with a pen, do not cut down with an ax (lexical meaning is: if the written words are done and have legal power , it is already impossible to correct it).*

The main difficulty for the students is partially variable idioms: stable comparisons, phraseological combinations and some structural type's impredicative aphorisms (sayings, winged words). They require from the students the knowledge of regularity of its variability. Variability lexemes are observed in phraseological units, word forms, block diagrams, optional components. Thematic grouping of phraseological units also plays under these conditions, an important role in the methodical interpretation of phraseological material for educational purposes in the classroom for the development of speech. With a thematic grouping of phraseological units is also used comparison (comparison) phraseological units of Russian and native language learners; concentric features and aspect actualization of linguistic phenomena on the phraseological material (using material of dictionaries, reference books and fiction texts).

The structure of studying material in thematically principal has both advantages and disadvantages. Polysemous phraseological units have the disadvantages. It is their multifunctionality. Therefore, it is a possibility to refer to a variety of topics. Rather uncertain criteria of thematic correlation are quite a significant number of idiomatic unit. However, the lack given of idiomatic unit (from the point of view of linguistics) can be considered as an advantage (from the point of view of didactics). There is a repeatability of phraseological units in a variety of topics for the development of speech in different speech situations. Thematic lists can be considered as a methodical interpretation of idiomatic material for training purposes.

The lists of phraseological units can be presented in various forms: in alphabetical order by the first word of phraseological units, or in alphabetical order by key words. The activation of phraseological units is carried out in Russian speech of students. There are thematic lists of phraseological units and a base of semantic groups of phraseological units with the same type of components of phraseological units.

Conclusion

Thus, the phraseology takes a significant place in the methods of teaching Russian as a foreign language. It studied at the expense of intralinguistic and interlingual interference makes it possible to better master the system of Russian. When teaching phraseology of teachers of Russian as a foreign language, it is necessary not only to provide students with the necessary minimum common phraseology, but also to teach foreigners the ability to recognize the phraseological units, to pay maximum attention to foreigners on the ways and means of administration of phraseological units in the text and syntax. Inclusion of phraseology in the learning process will give lessons an amusing process. However, training in Russian phraseology is a difficult task, which is associated with the occurrence of a variety of different constraints on the grammatical, lexical, semantic and cultural levels. Overcoming these will not only expand the active vocabulary, but also the formation of the communicative competence.

References

Adonina, L. V., Fissenko, O. S. & Chernov, N. V. (2015). Technique "directed reading" as an interactive method of working on the text in a foreign audience // Actual problems of the humanities and natural sciences, 12 (1), pp.119-121.

Adonina, L. V., Lazarev, S. V, Fisenko, O. S. & Chernova, N. V. (2015). Universal values: semantic-cognitive approach // Journal of Language and Literature. 6 (4), pp. 393-396.

Fisenko, O. S. (2014). Archetypes in a «new religious consciousness» // Сборники конференций НИЦ Социосфера, 14 (13), 53-54.

Gubarev, V. N. (1980). To the problem of semantics steady verbal complexes both word marks and indirect nomination // Semantic structure of words and collocations. Ryazan, pp.40-46.

Kapitonov, T. I. & Shchukin, A. N. (1987). Modern methods of teaching Russian language for foreigners. – M.: Russian Language, pp.232.

Kargina, N. V. & Fisenko, O. S. (2016). Interactive methods of reading the story of A.S. Pushkin "Blizzard" in foreign audience (on the example of the "directed reading" equipment)//Modern science: urgent problems of the theory and practice. Series: Humanities, 3, pp.148-151.

Kornilov, T. V., Matveenko, V. E., Fisenko, O. S. & Chernov N. V. (2015). Components of linguo-didactic system of training of foreign philologists in the national painted lexicon with use of audiovideo means//the Bulletin of the Moscow state regional university. Series: Pedagogics, 3, pp.73-79.

Kornilova, T. V., Matveenko, V. E., Fisenko, O. S. & Chernova, N. V. (2015). The role of audio and video means in the training of foreign philologists concerning national vocabulary of russian language // Journal of Language and Literature, 6, (4), pp.390-392.

Lazarev, S. V., Fisenko, O. S. & Chernova, N. V. (2016). Formation of communicative competence of foreign students on the example of the introduction lesson "Tasks and Functions of Public Relations"//Language and the personality in multicultural space. Collection of articles. It is gray. "The young philologist" under the editorship of L. V. Adonina, O. S. Fisenko. – M.: Feather, pp.21-26.

Patotska-Platek, M. (1992). Training of phraseology in Russian textbooks for the Polish schools: Avtoref.dis. … канд.пед.наук. – M, p.20.

Petrenko, V. F., Nistratov A. A. & Romanova N. V. (1989). Reflexive structures of ordinary consciousness (on material of the semantic analysis of phraseological units)//linguistics Questions, 2, pp.26-39.

Vlasova, N. S. (1990). Practical technique of teaching Russian at the initial stage. Compos – M.: Russian, pp.191.

Shakhsuvarova, E. M. (1983). Linguistic and methodological aspects of the description of phraseology of Russian for training of foreign pupils at the initial stage. abstract. dissertation. Ph.D.– M.

Note

The publication was prepared with the support of the «RUDN University Program 5-100»

CHAPTER THREE

EDUCATION

AN ANALYSIS ON GRADUATE STUDIES IN TURKEY ON COMPUTER-ASSISTED INSTRUCTION FROM DIFFERENT VARIABLES

OĞUZHAN SEVİM

Introduction

Rapid developments in science and technology have influenced education as other social structures. The idea that education has a vital importance for society has made interaction between education and technology more important and revealed that education has to take advantage of new technologies effectively in order to adapt to these rapid developments (Akkoyunlu & Tuğrul, 2002: p.12; Aktümen & Kaçar, 2003: p.340-341). As a result of this obligation, developing technologies have been used at schools.

Many education institutions in the world and Turkey are developing projects and working on creating more effective and creative educational environments by using information and communication technologies. In these studies, ways of utilizing computer technologies for different purposes in education process are sought. Computer based word processors, spreadsheets, databases, hypertext, hypermedia, and multimedia tools are some of these technologies. In addition, "graphic and desktop publishing software used in the presentation of course materials, audio conferencing that creates virtual classroom environments within the scope of communication technologies, and video conferencing applications enable lecturers, students and experts in different regions of the world to exchange views" (Geçer & Dağ, 2010: p.21-22). Through these materials, while the students are trying to access the information, they can act both individually and carry out their studies through a mentor when they need it.

The use of contemporary technology facilities in the classroom environment, besides the textbook, helps the students to acquire what they have learned in a permanent way and also helps to enrich the teaching process. These tools, which are emerging as audio-visual tools, increase both students learning desires and their interest in lessons. For this reason, while planning the course, the teacher should determine where, when and how to use these tools (Demirel, 2003: p.51). Teachers may not find the ideal educational device for their intents and purposes, and even if they find it, financial limitations of their institution may prevent them from obtaining this equipment and utilizing it as a teaching their material. Teachers can overcome this obstacle by preparing teaching materials with the available facilities. The teacher who conducts the course systematically must find answers to the questions about the practicality of the material and its suitability of the students and the course while preparing educational appliance (Demirel, 2003: p.54). Because the effectiveness of materials used for teaching depends on the correct use of certain visual design principles and materials in development. Visual design elements consist of line, area, shape, size, texture and colors, and design principles are listed as integrity, balance, emphasis, alignment and closeness (Yalın, 2003: p.106-118). A teaching material, as a prerequisite, needs to be well-designed for performing its functions (Aydın-Yılmaz & Mahiroğlu, 2004: p.112). A well-designed teaching material not only facilitates the teacher's work but also helps the students to understand the content of the course easily.

Computer-based applications in teaching can be used not only to inform students but also to assess how much information is gained and evaluated by the student. With computer aided assessment and evaluation software, the current situation of the student can be revealed with all the details, student's stages of development in learning environment can be followed, and it is possible to give feedback that the student can instantly see the mistakes he/she has made as he/she transforms his/her knowledge into a skill.

When the literature is analysed, it is seen that many studies have been made in different fields related to computer-assisted instruction (CAI). In these studies, although success and attitude are generally emphasized, it is understood that product evaluation, concept teaching, teacher opinions about the product, and a new model development studies are carried out (Ayvacı et al., 2016).

In the study conducted by Çeliköz (1995), studies on computer-assisted instruction in Turkey are classified as follows:

- The works of the state on CAI
- Studies carried out in universities and science institutes
- Attitude measurement researches
- Researches on model proposals for CAI
- Researches on preparing course software

- Researches on evaluation of course software
- Researches on comparisons of CAI with traditional teaching
- Other researches

When the titles in Çeliköz's classification are analysed, it is understood that they are inclusionary in evaluating the studies related to the CAI which is carried out today.

Depending on the development of computer technology, computers are used in all fields of knowledge (Mathematics, Science, Geography, Social Studies, Music, Turkish ...). Numerous studies have been carried out on the integration of CAI materials into the teaching process both in Turkey and abroad. For this reason, while the literature review was carried out, the studies were classified according to their relation to each other and information was given about each sample study. As a result of the literature review, the studies related to the CAI are summarized under the following headings:

- Studies on teaching Turkish
- Studies on foreign language teaching
- Studies on the development process of CAI materials
- Studies in social sciences
- Studies in the field of science
- Studies carried out abroad

While the classification process was being carried out, information was given firstly on the sample works related to Turkish teaching which constitutes the subject of this thesis study. Computer-based foreign language teaching studies were evaluated as a second topic. In the related literature, as not only the teaching process but also the development process of computerized materials is mentioned, a third title on the preparation process of the CAI materials has been constituted. Studies in fields such as geography, social studies and music studied under the heading of social sciences and studies in fields such as chemistry, mathematics, and physics are studied under the heading of science (Çepni, Ayvaci, Bakirci & Kara, 2014). Finally, this section has been completed by giving information about the studies carried out abroad.

When the use of CAI materials in the process of teaching Turkish analysed from the related literature, it is seen that they are for primary reading-writing, listening, written expression and reading skills, vocabulary teaching, attitude, grammar, and concept errors. So, it can be said that researchers tend to all other skill areas except speaking skills.

Although Yalçın's (2006) research using speech recognition technology is also of a nature that includes speaking skill, it is understood from its aim that it is not a study directly on speaking skill.

When the literature is analysed, it is understood that CAI materials are also used for improving mentally disabled and hearing-impaired students' language skills. Özak (2008) tried to determine the effectiveness of simultaneous clue teaching presented by computer in the teaching of reading skills to mentally disabled students. In the research conducted by Çiftçi (2009), it was tried to solve the effects of the CAI materials on hearing-impaired students' written expression skills such as making sentences and using tenses correctly in sentences. In both studies, it was concluded that the CAI materials were effective in improving basic language skills of disabled students.

When the studies related to the use of CAI materials in the Turkish courses are analysed, it is seen that these researches focus on one or two learning areas (such as primary reading and writing) and there is not any study in which all areas of learning have been taken into account and an example of a holistic course presentation has been taken into consideration. For this reason; this research, which uses interactive computer applications in the same software in all learning areas, is the first.

When the studies on the use of CAI materials in teaching Turkish are evaluated in general, it is understood that these materials increase the students' achievements in primary reading-writing, listening, written expression skills, learning grammar, and positive attitudes towards the lesson; in addition to this they have a reducing influence on concept errors.

When we look at the researches on the use of CAI materials in foreign language teaching, it is seen that they focus on the reinforcement of English and German grammar structures, distance learning and principles to be considered, and success and attitude toward the course.

When we look at the studies conducted for the use of CAI materials in foreign language teaching, the study by Odabaşı (1994) is noteworthy. In this study, although the researcher is based on English as a foreign language and aims to improve grammar structures related to this language, the level of achievement achieved by traditional teaching has not been exceeded. However, a similar research based on German by another researcher achieved a more successful result than traditional teaching. In subsequent researches, it has been found that the CAI method in foreign language teaching has positive influence on both achievement and attitudes towards the course.

When we look at the researches related to the design process of CAI materials, it is seen that these studies are focused on evaluating the cognitive burden, the principles to be followed in preparing an effective multi-learning environment, and multimedia items. These researches are very important in terms of having features that must be found in computer software that is designed to make teaching more effective in different fields.

These studies conducted on how to prepare CAI materials should be carefully analysed by researchers interested in the field before they start to work. Whether the prepared software brings cognitive burden to the student, how display objects are placed, and whether it takes individual characteristics into consideration or not is determining criteria for success or failure (Yeşilyurt & Kara, 2007). For this reason, the results of such studies need to be evaluated thoroughly.

When we look at the studies conducted in the field of social sciences, it is understood that they especially focus on success and attitude and the CAI materials have a positive effect on the success and attitudes of the students.

When we look at the studies carried out for the use of CAI materials in the field of science, it is seen that they focus on issues: misconceptions, interpretation association of the learned, success, attitude, and remembering what is learned.

When the CAI studies carried out in the field of science are evaluated, it is seen that there are failures as well as successful studies. In particular, the CAI materials are ineffective in students' attitudes towards the course in the science classes. It can be considered that the frequent use of laboratories and the facility of learning by watching or experiencing in science courses are effective in this. Therefore, in the social sciences, it can be said that the absence of the laboratory environment and the fact that the CAI materials often fill this gap and help the students to take positive attitudes towards the course.

When we look at the studies about computer-assisted instruction abroad, it is seen that they are related to concept teaching, success, attitude, cognitive burden, and problem solving ability to produce scientific solutions, attention value enhancement, and multi-user educational virtual environments. The summary information about these studies is as follows:

When the studies related to the CAI carried out abroad are evaluated, it is seen that there are studies that give positive results as well as negative results. Considering the studies carried out in Turkey, it is understood that they have similar characteristics with the studies carried out abroad. In studies conducted both at home and abroad, CAI materials in science education did not always give positive results on success or attitude. As mentioned before, it can be said that, in the emergence of these results the use of laboratory facilities in science education have a great influence.

In this study, the abstracts of the master and doctoral dissertations related to the CAI in Turkey between 1989 and 2012 were analysed in terms of methodology, research field, period, and type of thesis then the results of the study were tried to be explained with the help of descriptive statistics methods and cross tables.

The graduate and doctoral thesis studies related to the CAI were reached from the web page of National Dissertation Center of the Higher Education Council. Both Turkish and English key words such as computer aided instruction, multimedia design, computer aided education, educational technology, instructional technology, computer-based learning, computer assisted teaching, and computer-based training were used in order to obtain the related studies through the thesis search page (Bakırcı, Kara & Çepni, 2016). As a result of this screening with these key words, 828 master and doctoral dissertations were reached; 48 of them were excluded from the scope of the review because no information could be found about the study in their summaries.

While the abstracts of 780 master and doctoral dissertations were being analysed from the methodological point of view, the characteristics of scientific report types such as evaluation, theoretical, experimental and case studies in APA Written Guidance (2009) have been taken into consideration. The methodological statistics of the theses are as in Table 3-1.

Table 3-1. Methodological Statistics of Thesis Studies

	Frequency	%
Experimental	502	64,3
Case study	203	26
Evaluation	75	9,6
Theoretical	0	0
Total	780	100

According to Table 3-1, it is understood that most of the master and doctoral thesis studies related to the CAI are experimental studies. When we look at other researches related to the subject, it is understood that most of the studies carried out in the field of educational technologies are experimental researches (Uğur Erdoğmuş & Çağıltay, 2013: p.284, Şimşek et al., 2009: p.947).

It can be considered that these researches made in different areas have helped to spread the CAI projects both in science and social sciences by being an example for each other. A researcher studying in the field of social sciences can take methodology of a study in the field of science as an example and the opposite could be the case. It can be said that the studies carried out in this way contributed to the increase of the number of studies in the field of CAI. Another point which is noteworthy in the methodological analysis is that, case studies are the most used method after experimental studies. Case studies are carried out in order to "consider a problem or to shed light on the issues or theoretical issues related to the research that needs clarification" (APA, 2009: p.32). When the thesis studies conducted in the context of the case study are analysed, it is seen that the opinions of the teachers, students and experts about the computer assisted teaching process are asked. It is understood that the research method that the researchers least interested is the evaluation studies and the theoretical studies are not done in the field of the CAI.

It can be considered that the following characteristics of evaluation studies are influential as there is less interest in such studies than in the experimental and case studies:

- The evaluation studies are voluminous and extensive
- Evaluation studies require more resources, cost and effort
- The researcher needs to possess the relevant literature in the evaluation studies
- Evaluation studies necessitate cooperative and expert assisted research
- There are difficulties in accessing the related documents and resources to be evaluated
- Sorting and analysing the documents obtained requires the effort

Another point that draws attention while analysing the master and doctorate theses related to CAI is that there is no theoretical study in Turkey (Kara, 2009). Theoretical studies are the researches that the researcher concentrates on the relevant literature and put forward a new theory in order to develop a new theory in any field. In theoretical research, the author can analyse an existing theory within its own circumstances and reveal its imperfection to daylight or he/she can put forth its superiority by comparing it with another theory. As can be seen, such studies are long term, detailed, and they require researchers to make careful observations. The lack of theoretical studies on the CAI can be a consequence of researchers' reluctance to detailed studies.

The distribution of thesis studies related to CAI according to social sciences and science is shown in Table 3-2.

Table 3-2. Distribution of Thesis Studies by Social Sciences and Science Fields

	Frequency	%
Science	418	53,6
Social	362	46,4
Total	780	100

A recent literature review on the graduate and doctoral thesis studies in the fields of science and social sciences has been carried out in the study and it has been understood that the graduate studies carried out in these fields have close rates. As seen in Table 3-2, 418 computer-assisted instructional studies were carried out in the field of science and 362 studies were carried out in the field of social sciences.

The distribution of the thesis studies related to CAI according to 5 years periods between 1989-2012 is shown in Table 3.

Table 3-3. Distribution of Thesis Studies Related to CAI by 5-Year Periods

	Frequency	%
Between 1988-1992	29	3,7
Between 1993-1997	98	12,6
Between 1998-2002	167	21,4
Between 2005-2009	189	24,2
Between 2008-2012	297	38,1
Total	780	100

When Table 3-3 is analysed, it is seen that BDI studies have increased from past to present. As the studies revealed the benefits of computerized materials in teaching, it can be considered that the researchers' interest in CAI has increased.

Distribution of thesis studies related to CAI according to the status of being a master's degree or doctorate thesis is shown in Table 3-4.

Table 3-4. Distribution of thesis studies related to CAI according to the status of being a master's degree or doctorate thesis

	Frequency	%
Master's degree	664	85,1
Doctorate	116	14,9
Total	780	100

When Table 3-4 is analysed, by taking into account the fact that some universities did not have doctorate programs in the past periods, it is understood that the studies related to CAI are mostly in master's level.

A crosstab was used to understand how the dissertation studies in the field of natural sciences and social sciences were distributed in terms of methods and the results obtained are shown in Table 3-5.

Table 3-5. Methodological Distributions of Thesis Studies in Institutional Context

		Evaluation	Experimental	Design	Case study	Total
Science	f	33	247	66	72	418
	%	44	58,4	83,5	35,5	53,6
Social	f	42	176	13	131	362
	%	56	41,6	16,5	64,5	46,4
Total	f	75	423	79	203	780
	%	100	100	100	100	100

According to Table 3-5, the studies in the evaluation and case studies were mostly done in social sciences; experimental and design studies were done in the field of science. When Table 5 is analysed, it is seen that the studies related to instructional software design are mostly done in the field of science; whereas the case studies conducted for CAI related studies are mostly done in the field of social sciences.

In order to determine how the dissertation studies in the field of sciences and social sciences are distributed in terms of types, a cross tabulation is used and the results are shown in Table 3-6.

Table 3-6. Distribution of Thesis Studies in Science and Social Sciences in Terms of Types

		Master's degree	Doctorate
Science	*f*	365	53
	%	55	45,7
Social	*f*	299	63
	%	45	54,3
Total	*f*	664	116
	%	100	100

When Table 3-6 is analysed, it is understood that the studies at the master's degree were mostly done in the field of science and the studies at the doctorate degree are done in the field of social sciences.

When we look at the titles of master's and doctoral dissertations in Turkey regarding CAI, it is seen that a total of 1509 different concepts were used in the titles of 780 studies. Among these concepts, those with the highest frequency have been determined as impact, achievement, and computer-assisted instruction. Concepts in the titles of the thesis studies carried out in Turkey on CAI are listed according to frequency and percentages; and the first 24 are given in Table 3-7.

Table 3-7-Frequency and Percentages of Concepts in Thesis Titles

No	Concept	F	%	No	Concept	f	%
1	Effect	283	9,13	13	Permanence	24	0,77
2	Success	168	5,42	14	Preservice Teacher	24	0,71
3	Computer-assisted instruction	159	5,13	15	Research	22	0,65
4	Attitude towards the computer	72	2,33	16	Learning	20	0,45

5	Practice	56	1,81	17	Design	14	0,45
6	Analaysing	49	1,58	18	Traditional teaching method	13	0,42
7	Computer-aided education	48	1,55	19	Perception	11	0,39
8	Evaluation	47	1,52	20	Computing environment	11	0,35
9	Teacher views	28	0,87	21	Computer help	11	0,35
10	Computer assisted teaching method	27	0,87	22	Primary schools	10	0,35
11	Comparison	27	0,87	23	Computer aided teaching material	9	0,32
12	Student views	25	0,77				

When the concepts in Table 3-7 and their frequency values are analysed, it is understood that the results support the results in Table 1, in which methodological statistics of thesis are distributed. It is seen that the concepts with the highest frequencies belong to experimental studies. Other concepts in thesis titles and their frequency values are given in Annex 10.

When the studies in the literature are generally evaluated, it is seen that the use of BDI materials in the field of education is very important and there are principles to be followed while designing such learning environments. They should be prepared by a team of experts otherwise the material may interrupt the teaching process.

It has been determined that the teaching process in which instructional software is used purposefully and carefully is effective in increasing students' achievements, attitudes and interests towards the course. Nevertheless, it is seen that there are studies showing this software are especially not effective in increasing the attitudes, interests and motivations of the students who participate in the learning process especially in the field of science.

Another issue that is noteworthy as a result of the literature review on the studies is whether attention is paid to the cognitive load while preparing the teaching software or not. According to Cognitive Load Theory, the items in the software must be able to facilitate students' information processing procedure. Because when the cognitive burden increases, student's learning is negatively affected. In order to overcome this, multimedia software design principles must be taken into account while preparing teaching software.

References

Akkoyunlu, B. & Tuğrul, B. (2002). Okulöncesi çocuklarının ev yaşantısındaki teknolojik etkileşimlerinin bilgisayar okuryazarlığı becerileri üzerindeki etkisi. *Hacettepe Üniversitesi Eğitim Fakültesi Dergisi, 23,* 12-21.

Aktümen, M. & Kaçar, A. (2003). İlköğretim 8. sınıflarda harfli ifadelerle işlemlerin öğretiminde bilgisayar destekli öğretimin rolü ve bilgisayar destekli öğretim üzerine öğrenci görüşlerinin değerlendirilmesi. *Kastamonu Eğitim Dergisi, 2,* 339-358.

Amerikan Psikoloji Derneği [APA] (2009). İstanbul: Kaknüs Yayıncılık.

Aydın-Yılmaz, Z. & Mahiroğlu, A. (2004). Dilbilgisi öğretiminde yeni geliştirilen öğretim materyallerinin öğrencilerin öğrenme düzeyine etkililiği. *Türk Eğitim Bilimleri Dergisi, 2(1),* 109-123.

Ayvacı H.Ş., Sevim S., Durmuş A., Kara Y. (2016). Analysis of Pre-Service Teachers' Views toward Models and Modeling in Science Education. Turkish Journal of Teacher Education, 5(2), 84-96.

Bakırcı H., Kara Y. & Çepni S. (2016). The Examination of Views of Parents about the Web-Based Performance Evaluation Program in the Science Teaching Process. *Bartın Üniversitesi Eğitim Fakültesi Dergisi,* 5 (3), 893-907.

Çeliköz, N. (1995). Bilgisayar destekli öğretimin gerçeklesme biçimleri. *Eğitim Yönetimi, 4,* 573–579.

Çepni S., Ayvaci H. S., Bakirci H. & Kara Y. (2014). Öğretim Elemanları Gözüyle Velilerin Bilgisayar Okuryazarlık Düzeylerinin Web Tabanlı Performans Değerlendirme Programına Yansımaları. *Journal of Instructional Technologies & Teacher Education,* 3 (1), 1-9.

Çiftçi, E. (2009). *İşitme engelli öğrenciler için hazırlanan bilgisayar destekli yazılı anlatım becerisi geliştirme materyalinin tasarımı, uygulanması ve değerlendirilmesi.* Yayımlanmamış yüksek lisans tezi. Karadeniz Teknik Üniversitesi Fen Bilimleri Enstitüsü, Trabzon.

Demirel, Ö. (2003). *Öğretimde planlama ve değerlendirme: öğretme sanatı,* (Altıncı baskı). Ankara: PegemA Yayıncılık.

Geçer, K. A. & Dağ, F. (2010). Üniversite öğrencilerinin bilgisayar okuryazarlık düzeylerinin belirlenmesi: Kocaeli Üniversitesi örneği. *Yüzüncü Yıl Üniversitesi Eğitim Fakültesi Dergisi, 7 (1),* 20-24.

Kara Y. (2009). Özel Öğretici Yazılımın Kullanıldığı Bilgisayar Destekli Öğretim Yönteminin Öğrenci Başarısına, Kavram Yanılgılarına ve Tutumlarına Etkisi. *Gazi Üniversitesi, Gazi Eğitim Fakültesi Dergisi,* 29 (3), 651-672.

Odabaşı, H. F. (1994). *Yabancı dilde dil bilgisi öğrenmede bilgisayar destekli öğrenme yönteminin öğrenci başarısına etkisi.* Yayımlanmamış doktora tezi. Anadolu Üniversitesi Sosyal Bilimler Enstitüsü, Eskişehir.

Özak, H. (2008). *Zihinsel yetersizliği olan öğrencilere okuma becerilerinin öğretiminde bilgisayar aracılığıyla sunulan eş zamanlı ipucuyla öğretimin etkililiği.* Yayımlanmamış yüksek lisans tezi. Abant İzzet Baysal Üniversitesi Sosyal Bilimler Enstitüsü, Bolu.

Şimşek, A., Özdamar, N., Uysal, Ö., Kobak, K. & Berk, C., (2009). İki binli yıllarda Türkiye'deki eğitim teknolojisi araştırmalarında gözlenen eğilimler. *Kuram ve Uygulamada Eğitim Bilimleri, 9 (2),* 941-966.

Uğur Erdoğmuş, F. & Çağıltay, K. (2013). Türkiye'de eğitim teknolojileri alanında yayımlanan yüksek lisans ve doktora tezlerinde genel eğilimler. Kürşat Çağıltay ve Yüksek Göktaş (Editörler). *Öğretim Teknolojilerinin Temelleri: Teoriler, Araştırmalar, Eğilimler* içinde. Ankara: Pegem Akademi.

Yalçın, N. (2006). *Konuşma tanıma teknolojisi yardımıyla ilköğretim birinci sınıf öğrencilerine ilk okuma yazma öğretimi için bir yazılım geliştirme.* Yayımlanmamış doktora tezi. Gazi Üniversitesi Fen Bilimleri Enstitüsü, Ankara.

Yalın, H. İ. (2003). *Öğretim teknolojileri ve materyal geliştirme.* (8. Baskı). Ankara: Nobel yayın dağıtım.

Yeşilyurt S. & Kara Y. (2007). The effects of tutorial and edutainment software programs on students' achievements, misconceptions and attitudes towards biology on the cell division issue. *Journal of Baltic Science Education,* 6 (2), 5-15.

LANGUAGE TEACHING AND USE OF LEARNING CYCLE MODEL IN LANGUAGE TEACHING

ESENGÜL TAN HATUN

Introduction

Grammar teaching is an integral part of the language teaching process. It is not possible to apply a language teaching model independent of grammar teaching in either native language teaching or foreign language teaching.

"Grammar is defined as information that contains a system of rules concerning the properties of a language such as phonological components (sound), words, syntactic structures (i.e. sentences) and semantic (meaning)" (Karadüz, 2007: p.281). Grammar can be likened to the skeleton of a language. All elements of a language are based on and construed by this skeleton preventing the language from becoming a haphazardly sequenced and meaningless pile of sounds, and putting sounds, syllables, words and sentences in order to transform them into a meaningful whole. Grammar provides mobility for and supports the development of language. Therefore, grammar plays an important role in the teaching process of a language defined as "a multi-faceted and developed system that allows the members of a society to transfer their thoughts and feelings to one another by making use of a set of elements and rules valid in terms of sound and meaning" (Korkmaz et al., 2005: p.2).

With grammar teaching, students learn how to communicate effectively, comprehend and convey transmitted information properly, think systematically and analyse events. The development of four basic language skills can only be achieved by a language teaching process supported by grammar teaching. In other words, grammar teaching has a significant role in the realization of effective language teaching. How and at what level grammar teaching should be carried out within the language teaching process has been an area of interest for scientists for many years. They have addressed learning approaches to analyse how grammar teaching should be and explained these approaches in the light of their views on the realization of learning. Therefore, learning approaches have an important place in grammar teaching. Below are some of the learning approaches and their views on grammar teaching.

Learning Approaches and Their Views on Grammar Teaching

Grammar teaching in the language teaching process has been a matter of debate for many years. Rapid developments in the field of linguistics, especially since the 20th century, have been instrumental in the emergence of many views on the language teaching process. The fact that these complementary or contradictory views have been set forth in a brief period of time since the 20th century has led to a complex accumulation of knowledge, which has called for the systematization of those views on language teaching.

Various studies have been carried out by researchers in order to categorize language teaching approaches and methods in a systematic fashion. Lecomte classified language teaching approaches as "behaviourist, communicative, cognitive, constructivist and exploratory," while Develay classified them as "idealistic, experimental and constructivist" and Germain as "integrated, linguistic and psychological." However, classifications introduced have caused various problems in the field. In order to eliminate these problems, Bailly classified the language teaching approaches into three groups; behaviourist, cognitive and constructive, based on their main views and applications in the field (Güneş, 2011). Grammar teaching is described below based on the classification in question.

1. Behaviorist Approach and Grammar Teaching

Von Glasersfeld (2007) regarded behaviourism as a field of science concerned with observable behaviour and, defined learning as a response to physical stimuli. According to the behaviourist approach, learning occurs as a result of the reaction of an organism to stimuli and the reinforcement of stimuli for the realization of the permanence of the learning. The behaviourist approach explains grammar teaching in the light of behavioural learning principles. The behaviourist approach regards the "organism" as the learner, the "stimulus" as what is taught, the "response" as the reaction to what has been taught and the "reinforcement" as the reward. In other words, in grammar teaching, learning occurs as a result of a response (stimulus) given by a learner (organism) to what is taught (stimulant) and it becomes a behaviour as a result of rewards (reinforcements).

The most important figure of the behaviourist approach in the field of grammar teaching is Skinner, who argues that learners learn languages in a stimulus-response context, and emphasizes the importance of environmental factors, reinforcements and reward-punishment in language learning.

The behaviourist approach envisages a teaching system based on the teaching of grammar rules and rote learning. According to this view, grammar rules should be memorized by students and reinforced by repetition to turn them into behaviour. This approach pushes need-oriented and functional aspect of grammar into the background. It has been criticized for treating communication as of secondary importance, failing to meet students' needs and adopting a teaching approach based on repetition and rote-learning. However, despite all these criticisms, it has been used in grammar teaching.

2. Cognitive Approach and Grammar Teaching

The cognitive approach emphasizes the importance of mental processes and advocates that learning does not have simple stimulus-response associations but that it emerges as a result of mental processes. The cognitive approach has introduced a new dimension to grammar teaching by opposing the behaviourist approach that explained language teaching in the context of stimulus-response associations. In this process, Chomsky, with his views on grammar teaching, has become the most important figure of the cognitive approach.

According to Chomsky, language learning is not a question of habits and conditioning but a creative process that reflects a rational and mental activity rather than external effects (Demirel, 2016). According to generative-transformational grammar theory developed by Chomsky (2009), human beings possess an innate generative grammar, the use of which enables them to construct and comprehend sentences but the properties of which they are unaware. Chomsky (2011) states that the speaker of a language is not in any way aware of the fact that he knows the grammar rules of that language or that he uses them and adds that there is no reason to think that he should be aware of the grammar rules of that language. According to Chomsky, one can gather all kinds of evidence about the phonetic-semantic relation of the language one has acquired by means of intuition.

According to Chomsky's theory, there is a language learning device containing a universal grammar. Once children have a certain level of vocabulary, this device enables them to speak in a grammatically correct fashion (Berk, 2013). According to this theory, language has deep structure and surface structure. Deep structure is universal and abstract while surface structure is concrete and varies from nation to nation. Surface structure is the manifestation of deep structure.

The cognitive approach has opposed the behaviourist approach, which purported that grammar is learned through stimulus-response conditioning, and instead emphasized the importance of rational and intellectual activities. However, the cognitive approach was criticized for falling short in accounting for how grammar teaching should be carried out and therefore, the behaviourist approach was implemented for many years.

3. Constructivist Approach and Grammar Teaching

From a conceptual perspective, constructivism postulates that knowledge generated, in general, by people has a mental record (Aydın, 2007). Constructivism is therefore based on knowledge and learning (Brooks & Brooks, 1999).

The constructivist learning philosophy has a history that goes back to Giambatista Vico's statement, "One who knows something can explain it." Immanuel Kant improved Vico's views and expressed that the individual is not passive in the learning process. Many scientists have also worked on these views. Piaget and John Dewey conducted the first important studies on constructivism (Özden, 2005).

The constructivist learning approach explains how an individual constructs knowledge and accounts for the process in which knowledge is constructed (Fer & Cırık, 2007). According to this approach, in order for learning to occur, individuals need to reconstruct and interpret concepts in their minds using their current knowledge. Individuals compare new knowledge with schematics that they had previously created in their minds through past experiences and find similarities and differences and internalize and make sense of them. In other words, individuals in the learning process construct and interpret the new knowledge by integrating it with the schematics they have generated in their minds through past experiences. Selley (1994) states that the constructivist approach is a student-centred approach in which the teacher participates in the learning process.

According to this approach, teachers encourage students to actively engage in the learning process, guide them through activities and questions, provide them with materials to enable them to construct knowledge and create an interactive classroom environment. In other words, teachers guide students by using all resources of the educational environment to enable them to construct knowledge.

The constructivist approach explains language teaching in the light of its views on the formation of learning. The constructivist language teaching approach has developed around the views of Piaget, Vygotsky and Jerome Bruner. While Piaget addressed language teaching within the boundaries of cognitive developmental theory, Lev Vygotsky and Bruner emphasized the importance of social environment and addressed the issue from an interactionist perspective.

According to the constructivist learning approach, language learning begins in the pre-school period and progresses gradually. The developmental stages, individual characteristics and social environment are of great importance in language learning. In the pre-school period, children first learn a language as a result of their interaction with their immediate surroundings (mother and father). This process is based on verbal expressions as a feature of the child's developmental period. With the beginning of school age, the influence of social environment on language development increases. Written texts also become effective in language learning. According to this approach, grammar teaching as well as language teaching starts in the pre-school period.

In the pre-school period, children learn language as a result of an interaction with the immediate environment. They also learn grammar rules without realizing it in the process. For example, an English-speaking child in the pre-school period says "I go to school." while a Turkish-speaking child expresses the same sentence as "Okula giderim." Although both sentences have the same meaning, they are expressed using different words. The analysis of the sentences in terms of their parts shows that the structure of the sentence in English is subject–verb–object while the structure of the sentence in Turkish is "object-verb," the subject being omitted in colloquial language. The parts of speech are an abstract grammar topic. According to Piaget's theory of cognitive development, a child must be in the formal operational stage in order to be able to learn an abstract expression. However, the pre-school period coincides with the concrete operational stage, which is why it is unlikely that a preschool child can consciously use the parts of speech. However, both children in the pre-school period speak their native languages correctly because they have learned to use them conforming to their grammar rules through their interaction with the social environment without being aware of the process of language learning, which has been realized through intuition and is not based on memorization. In other words, they have learned the languages' grammars spontaneously as they have learned the languages themselves. When children reach school age, they are first taught how to read and write. This time, they use grammar rules, which they have learnt and used in verbal communication so far, in writing without being aware of them. They begin to notice the grammatical features in texts that they read and correct the mistakes that they have been making since the preschool period. Through listening and speaking as well as writing and reading activities, they internalize the languages and begin to use them in accordance with their grammar rules. Since the vast majority of grammar rules are abstract, the rules should begin to be taught in the formal operational stage. Detailed grammar teaching should be performed in high school and, again in this period, the goal should not be rote-learning but should be to teach students how to functionally use those grammar rules. Students should interact with social environments and learn the rules in a conscious way using their current knowledge. What is important here is to use grammar functionally in order to use the language well. Blyth (1997) states grammar teaching is necessary to give meaning to grammatical forms.

According to the constructivist approach, grammar is necessary to understand and describe what is meant to be expressed using the language (Barnier, 2005, Lusignan, 2001, Lasnier 2000; Basque, Rocheleau, and Winer, 1998, Meirieu 1988; in Günes, 2007). For this reason, functional aspects of grammar teaching should be emphasized in order to facilitate children's lives, encourage them to learn the language and enable them to develop the four basic language skills.

The constructivist approach to grammar teaching is a new field for teachers who have been accustomed to teaching grammar topics with traditional methods for many years. Today, many countries are re-planning their curricula according to the constructivist approach. As a consequence, the constructivist approach to language teaching is becoming more and more important. In this process, language teachers have difficulty teaching because they do not have enough knowledge about how to conduct lessons according to the constructivist approach. Although many language teachers know that the constructivist approach to language teaching is a result of individuals reconstructing and making sense of new information in their minds by using prior knowledge, they do not put the theoretical knowledge into practice and are confused when it comes to planning and conducting their lessons. The most important educational component that will help language teachers to recover from complications and to transform their knowledge is education models developed based on the educational principles of constructivism.

Learning Cycle Model and Grammar Education

The learning cycle model is a teaching model allowing the constructivist approach to be implemented in a systematic and planned way in educational environments. Developed by Myton Atkin and Robert Karplus, the first learning cycle model is composed of three phases (exploration, explanation and extension) and referred to as the 3E learning cycle model. Based on the principles of the constructivist approach, this model has been modified by scientists, into the 4E model (exploration, explanation, expansion, evaluation), 5E model (engagement, exploration, explanation, elaboration and evaluation) and 7E model (elicit, engagement, exploration, explanation, elaborate, elaboration and extension). The figures in the model names refer to the number of phases, while the letters "E" represent the initials of each level.

This model enables students to actively engage in the learning process to develop senior skills (practice, analysis, synthesis and evaluation). It contributes to the development of students' positive attitudes towards science and encourages them to be individuals who research, question, think critically and creatively, and produce information (Ayvacı et al., 2016). In this model, teachers guide students to access information and construct knowledge.

Although the learning cycle model is an instructional model developed to be applied in science courses, it can be a useful tool and guide for language teachers to organize contents in grammar teaching and carry out lessons. The analysis of the learning cycle models reveals that the 5E model is the most suitable model for grammar teaching in terms of the content and planning of its phases.

This study addresses the phases of the 5E learning model, discusses the ways in which it can be adapted to grammar teaching and presents examples to guide teachers.

Grammar Teaching with 5E Learning Model

The 5E learning model developed by Bybee consists of five phases (engagement, exploration, explanation, elaboration and evaluation), hence the name. Each phase is designed to complement the previous phase and to provide necessary information infrastructure for the next phase. Köseoğlu & Tümay (2013) states that the 5E model based on the learning cycle model provides a planned instructional index centred on student learning outcomes and objectives, and encourages students to research, construct scientific concepts and relate those concepts to other concepts.

It can be stated that the 5E model's suggestions for planning lessons, detailing contents and maintaining educational conditions are suitable for grammar teaching. This model supports grammar teachers in planning and conducting their lessons in the light of constructive principles. With this model, students can actively engage in the learning process and begin to use grammar rules functionally.

1. Phase: Engagement

"The teacher or a curriculum task helps students become engaged in a new concept through the use of short activities that promote curiosity and elicit prior knowledge. The activity should make connections between past and present learning experiences, expose prior conceptions, and organize students' thinking toward the learning outcomes of current activities" (Bybee, 2014, p.12). In this phase, the teacher draws students' attention to the subject matter with activities such as discussion, asking questions, and presentations that reveal situations that are inconsistent with or support the prior knowledge of students. Both cases allow students to revise their prior knowledge and prepare to learn new information with reference to their prior knowledge.

Many in-field-teachers have problems organizing activities to introduce a new topic. However, language teachers are very fortunate to organize activities related to grammar topics, which are taught sequentially. This means that the ability of students to learn a new subject matter depends on whether they have acquired the prerequisite subject matter knowledge. For example, the subject of nouns is the prerequisite subject matter of adjectives. In this phase, the teacher can benefit from the prerequisite information. Thus, the teacher can help students to remember their prior knowledge and to realize the connections between their prior knowledge and the new information. These activities also provide the teacher with the opportunity to detect and correct students' misconceptions.

Another point that makes it easier for teachers to organize the introduction part of grammar topics is colloquial language. Though students do not know grammar rules, they speak conforming to those rules. In other words, a schema for grammar topics is formed in the minds of students from childhood and even from infancy. However, students are not even aware that they have intuitively acquired this schema. In this phase, activities that will enable them to realize this schema can be performed. Due to the fact that grammar topics are generally abstract, a detailed grammar education is offered to students starting from the formal operational phase. Especially in the first years of grammar teaching in the formal operational stage, activities for recognition and comprehension of the existing schema are important for students to make sense of the rules they have intuitively learned.

In this phase, teachers should organize short activities that engage students in learning and mobilize their prior knowledge to promote their curiosity about the new subject matter. Teachers can ask students various questions and hold short activities. However, teachers should keep in mind that this is only the introduction part of the subject matter and therefore exclude grammatical terminology, rules and detailed educational topics and keep this phase short.

2. Phase: Exploration

"Exploration experiences provide students with a common base of activities within which current concepts (i.e., misconceptions), processes, and skills are identified and conceptual change is facilitated. Learners may complete lab activities that help them use prior knowledge to generate new ideas, explore questions, and design and conduct an investigation" (Bybee, 2014: p.12). "This is the phase in which students use their prior knowledge and collect data on the new knowledge which they will construct; in other words, this is the phase in which they explore new knowledge. Therefore, this phase includes activities that enable students to explore new knowledge" (Tan, 2008: p.29).

In this phase, grammatical concepts should not be taught, but instead, students should be provided with various activities so that they can explore those concepts by themselves. The abstract nature of grammar topics makes it difficult for students to explore concepts. Therefore, teachers should focus more on written activities than oral activities. Working papers are also important materials that teachers can use in this phase.

Students are enabled to explore the characteristics of the grammar topic addressed; however, definitions are not included in this phase. For example, in the introductory part of the lesson covering the subject of adjectives, teachers can mobilize student's prior knowledge on nouns and point out the presence of some words used to distinguish a noun from others. They can get students to engage in activities that will enable them to comprehend that those words used to distinguish a noun from others are a type of word and encourage them to explore their characteristics. Thus, students can discover the properties of an adjective even though they do not know the definition of "adjectives." These activities should be based on the colloquial language with which students are familiar in order to enable them to discover the function of adjectives as a result of their own experiences. A working paper prepared in this way can also allow students to use grammar functionally.

In this phase, teachers should coach students to ensure that they are actively involved in the learning process. Language teachers should guide students with questions and activities and provide them with cues to enable them to discover new concepts. Grammar topics can take time to discover and therefore teachers should give them time and guide them to ensure proper use of time and support them when they are confused by concepts. According to the constructivist approach, language teaching can only be possible in educational settings where communication among students is strong. In this phase characterized by a high level of student activity, teachers can resort to collaborative learning.

3. Phase: Explanation

"The explanation phase focuses students' attention on a particular aspect of their engagement and exploration experiences and provides opportunities to demonstrate their conceptual comprehension, processing skills, or behaviours. In this phase, the teacher directly introduces a concept, process, or skill (Kara, 2018). An explanation from the teacher or other resources may guide learners toward a deeper understanding, which is a critical part of this phase" (Bybee, 2014: p.12). This is the phase where a "definition" is made.

In this phase, the language teacher should support students to reach the definition of the new concept on the basis of the data they have obtained in the phases of introduction and exploration. Based on the information they have discovered, students should first define the concept themselves. Then the teacher should present the definition of the concept in order to avoid inadequate learning and misconceptions. For example, the teacher can explain to students, who have discovered the attributes of adjectives during the phase of exploration, that those types of words are referred to as "adjectives" and ask them to make the definition of adjectives in groups. The teacher can initiate a small class discussion about definitions provided by the groups. In this way, the teacher can identify missing points in the definitions and help students to reach the correct definition. The teacher can move on to the next phase by pointing out the correct definition one last time to prevent wrong or incomplete learning.

In this phase, the language teacher should constantly guide students in order to prevent inadequate learning and misconceptions. The teacher can initiate an activity that enables students to reach a common definition by writing down their definitions of a concept on the board. This helps students to experience grammatical concepts in a concrete fashion and make sense of them in their minds. In this phase, the teacher should provide students with short, simple and understandable definitions of concepts.

4. Phase: Elaboration

"Teachers challenge and extend students' conceptual understanding and skills. Through new experiences, the students develop deeper and broader understanding, more information, and adequate skills. Students apply their understanding of the concept and abilities by conducting additional activities" (Bybee, 2014: p.12). "Students who have gained experience with the concept and constructed the relevant explanations in this phase apply the concepts which they have developed to new situations" (Köseoğlu & Tümay, 2013: p.91).

This is the phase in which grammar topics are learned in more detail and functionally used by associating them with daily life. To this end, language teachers should offer activities that will help students to apply the new knowledge they have already learned to new situations and to obtain more detailed information. When designing activities, the subject matter should be detailed depending on the age level of students to avoid overwhelming students with unnecessary detail. It should be kept in mind that grammar should be functional and rote learning should be avoided. For example, the teacher can conduct activities that will enable students, who have constructed the definition of adjectives at the phase of exploration, to understand that a word can be an "adjective" or a different type of word depending on the way it is used in a sentence. The subject can be elaborated by using working papers prepared to construct the knowledge on the types of adjectives. The teacher can show videos related to daily life to provide the functional use of adjectives. All these activities allow students to adapt the information they are learning to different situations without memorizing it.

The language teacher should, in this phase, challenge students mentally through various activities, which however should not be too difficult for them to reach a solution. The language teacher should enrich the content of activities using different methods, techniques and materials. The language teacher, in this phase, can benefit from a small group or class discussion method. The discussion method is an important method that supports students to exchange their knowledge with one another and adapt it to new situations.

Again, language teachers can utilize materials to present functional grammar in order to enhance students' knowledge. Videos, online educational tools and working papers containing good examples of language use are some of the materials that they can easily access and use in this phase.

5. Phase: Evaluation

The evaluation phase encourages students to assess their understanding and abilities and allows teachers to evaluate student progress towards achieving the learning outcomes (Bybee, 2014: p.12). This is the phase in which students evaluate at what level they have made sense of and constructed the information they have obtained through activities in the previous phases of the learning cycle.

In this phase, language teachers should conduct activities in which students can assess the level of knowledge construction. They should choose a measuring instrument depending on the information they want to measure. For example, they can utilize true-false tests or puzzles to assess the level of construction of "adjectives." They can ask students to write a story using adjectives in order to evaluate to what extent they can relate the information that they have learned about adjectives to daily life. They can also ask students to prepare a puzzle about the characteristics of adjectives in order to assess the level at which they have constructed the properties of adjectives.

Evaluation activities in this phase should be prepared by teachers in general. However, students can also be asked to prepare an activity in order to make them active and get them to evaluate themselves and their friends. In this phase, it would be useful to make use of scales to make an objective assessment and provide feedback to students.

Conclusion

Grammar teaching is an important part of the language teaching process. Scholars have put forward various views on how grammar teaching should be and described their views in the context of learning approaches. Grammar teaching has been conducted for many years in the light of the principles of the behaviourist or cognitive approaches. However, both advancements in technology and changes in expectations of individuals in society have brought up individual-centred education models, in which students actively engage in the learning process, and led to the reformulation of curricula based on the constructivist approach, which has also been the beginning of a new era in language teaching and grammar teaching. Kaufman (2004) states that the constructivist approach is mostly used in science and mathematics fields and that it has been used very little in the field of language pedagogy until now. He also emphasizes that this approach will be increasingly adopted in the field of language learning and that it will provide teachers with a new perspective.

Now the goal is to develop and implement a functional grammar teaching model that avoids rote-learning and support the development of basic language skills. Teachers have become guides to help students construct, interpret and use grammatical concepts in a functional way by applying them to new situations. In this process, teachers who used teacher-centred grammar teaching models based on rote-learning for many years have difficulty conducting grammar lessons according to the constructivist approach. The learning cycle model is an instructional model that helps teachers break the habits they have built up over the years and supports them to practice teaching with a new understanding. It can be stated that especially the 5E model, which is one of the learning cycle models, has a suitable content for grammar teaching and that language teachers can teach in a systematic way based on the 5E model in the light of the constructivist learning principles.

References

Aydın, H. (2007). *Felsefi temeller ışığında yapılandırmacılık*. (1. Edition). Ankara: Nobel Yayın Dağıtım.

Ayvacı H.Ş., Sevim S., Durmuş A., Kara Y. (2016). Analysis of Pre-Service Teachers' Views toward Models and Modeling in Science Education. *Turkish Journal of Teacher Education*, 5(2), 84-96.

Blyth, C. (1997). A constructivist approach to grammar: teaching teachers to teach aspect. *The Modern Language Journal*, 81(1), 50-66. Retrieved from http://lrc.cornell.edu/events/blyth2

Brooks, J. G. & Brooks M.G. (1999). *In search of understanding the case of constructivist classrooms*. Virginia: Association for Supervision and Curricum Development Press.

Bybee, R. W. (2014). The BSCS 5E instructional model: personal reflections and contemporary implications. *Science and Children*, 51(8), 10-13. Retrieved from http://static.nsta.org/files/sc1408_10.pdf

Chomsky, N. (2009). *Selected readings on transformational theory*. J.P.B. Allen & P. Van Buren (Eds.), Newyork: Dover Publications.

Chomsky, N. (2011). *Dil ve zihin*. A. Kocaman (Trans.). (1. Edition). Ankara: Bilgesu Yayıncılık.

Demirel, Ö. (2016). *Yabancı dil öğretimi.* (9. Edition). Ankara: Pegem A Yayıncılık.

Fer, S. & Cırık, İ. (2007). *Yapılandırmacı öğrenme: Kuramdan uygulamaya.* İstanbul: Morpa Kültür Yayınları.

Güneş, F. (2007). *Türkçe öğretimi ve zihinsel yapılandırma.* (1. Edition). Ankara: Nobel Yayın Dağıtım.

Güneş, F. (2011). Dil Öğretim yaklaşımları ve Türkçe öğretimindeki uygulamalar. [language teaching approaches and their applications in teaching Turkish]. *Mustafa Kemal Üniversitesi Sosyal Bilimler Enstitüsü Dergisi,* 15(8), 123–148. Retrieved from http://sbed.mku.edu.tr/article/view/1038000654.

Kara, Y. (2018). *Science Process Skills: Learning through Scientific Method.* Editor Firdevs GÜNEŞ & Yusuf SÖYLEMEZ, Skill Approach in Education: From Theory in Practices, p.305-321. Cambridge Scholar Publishing, London.

Karadüz, A. (2007). Dil bilgisi öğretimi. H. A. Kırkkılıç & H. Akyol (Eds.), in *İlköğretimde Türkçe öğretimi* (pp. 281-308). (1. Edition). Ankara: Pegem A Yayıncılık.

Kaufman, D. (2004). 14. Constructivist issues in language learning and teaching. *Annual review of applied linguistics,* 24, 303-319. doi:10.1017/S0267190504000121

Korkmaz, Z. (2005). *Türk dili ve kompozisyon,* Ankara: Ekin Kitabevi.

Köseoğlu, F. & Tümay, H. (2013). *Bilim eğitiminde yapılandırıcı paradigma teoriden öğretim uygulamalarına.* (1. Edition). Ankara: Pegem A Yayıncılık.

Özden, Y. (2005). *Öğrenme ve öğretme.* (7. Edition). Ankara: Pegem A Yayıncılık.

Selley, N. (1999). *The art of constructivist teaching in the primary school: A Guide for students and teachers.* London: David Fulton Publishers.

Tan, E. (2008*). İlköğretim 7. sınıf dil bilgisi öğretiminde zarflar konusuyla ilgili yapılandırmacı yaklaşıma göre hazırlanmış çalışma yapraklarının öğrenci başarısına etkisi.* [Unpublished master's thesis], Atatürk Üniversitesi Sosyal Bilimler Enstitüsü, Erzurum.

Von Glasersfeld, E. (2007). Giriş: Oluşturmacılığın yansımaları. C. T. Fosnot (Eds.), S. Durmuş (Trans. Eds.), in *Oluşturmacılık: teori, perspektifler ve uygulama* (pp. 3-8). (2. Edition). Ankara: Nobel Yayın Evi.

READING AND A METHOD OF READING: THE SOCRATIC SEMINAR TECHNIQUE

YASEMİN KURTLU

Introduction

Learning is a process that begins with birth and continues, sometimes formally and sometimes informally, until death. The learning process begins with the baby in the womb hearing its mother's voice and developing verbally in early childhood. In later periods, ways of learning become diversified through reading and experiencing. Learning experiences of individuals are based on native language, and linguistic competence builds the framework for the universe of learning. Within the parameters of comprehension and narration, language shapes the learning adventure. The dimension of comprehension is associated with listening and reading while the dimension of narration is associated with speaking and writing. Understanding and making sense of environments or learning objects begin with hearing. Even though listening as a skill is assumed to be innate, it transforms into a conscious skill through formal education. Listening is followed by reading.

Reading is one of the most important ways of obtaining information. Individuals who acquire reading skills and develop the habit of reading are able to develop a variety of mental skills such as recognizing the environment, learning possible roles in the future, achieving a state of mental rest, analysis, synthesis, evaluation and prediction. Individuals who engage in reading as a conscious activity in the direction of their goals can also have experience and knowledge to pursue an academic career, and to better understand and play their social roles. Reading skills are also important variables in choosing, accessing and using appropriate information from the masses of information in the modern world. The broadening of horizons and multi-faceted assessment of events are closely related to the acquisition of reading skills. One of the main supporters of affective development is reading ability. Individuals who acquire reading skills can develop, without noticing, such affective skills as awareness, willingness, intrinsic satisfaction and valorisation. Individuals with reading skills can also improve their social skills. The key to effective communication and success in writing, which is one of the narrative skills, is using reading skills effectively.

Reading methods and techniques are considered critically important for the acquisition of reading skills. The increase in the number of reading styles and the need for quick access to information, especially in recent years, have resulted in a diversification of reading strategies such as oral reading, silent reading, Marking a Text and critical reading. Another reading strategy that has been of growing interest over the past few years is the Socratic seminar, which is claimed to be directly related not only to the development of listening, reading, writing and speaking skills but also to the acquisition of high-level thinking skills. Given the potential benefits of the Socratic seminar method, this study evaluated its usability as a reading strategy.

This study explained the nature of reading, the benefits of reading and reading skills, the reading process, reading activities, and the reading methods and techniques. The study also provided information regarding the Socratic seminar, components of the Socratic seminar, responsibilities of the seminar leader and participants in the Socratic seminar and the seminar process. Finally, the study compared the Socratic seminar process with the reading process and discussed the Socratic seminar as a potential reading strategy.

1. Reading

The acquisition of reading skills is one of the first objectives of formal education. Reading does not refer to the pronunciation of words but to the process of making sense of a text that is physically uttered. The verb 'to read' means "*to look at words or symbols forming a text and to utter them or understand the meaning of them; to learn what a written text wants to convey; to utter aloud; to decipher the meaning of something* (TDK, 2005, p.1994)". "Reading is a complicated process involving physiological, mental and spiritual aspects" (Temizkan, 2009: p.8). Reading is a process in which eyes saccade with short stops on a written text to utter vocable patterns and to decipher their meaning (Öz, 2003: p.193). These definitions show that reading skills involve physical and semantic dimensions. Eye, eye muscles, organs of speech, sounds, syllables, words, phrases, paragraphs, visual field, visual angle and reading distance constitute the physical dimension of reading. Comprehension involves the visual cortex, the transmission of visual information to the brain, processes of meaning-making and formation of meaning through mental processes based on physical elements.

There are many definitions of reading that include both its physical and semantic dimensions. According to Akyol (2005: p.1), reading is a meaning-making process carried out in a regular environment where prior knowledge is used in the direction of an appropriate method and purpose based on the presence of an effective communication between author and reader. According to Gündüz and Şimşek (2011: p.13), reading is an activity of seeing, perceiving, comprehending and making meaning of a word, a phrase or a text in its entirety (Gündüz & Şimşek, 2011: p.13). Güneş (2013: p.128) also defines reading as "a process in which prior knowledge and information conveyed by a text are integrated and re-interpreted".

"Meaningful reading is basically an attempt to understand and a regulation mechanism in which any attempt to understand is interpreted" (Baker & Brown, 1984: p.355). Reading is an activity in which a written text is comprehended through meaning-making processes, and a complex skill that requires the coordination of many related information sources (Anderson, Hiebert, Scott & Wilkinson, 1985: p.7). "Reading is a mental activity of meaning-making, comprehending and interpreting printed words perceived through sense organs" (Özdemir, 1976: p.11). Reading is defined by Calp (2007: p.91) as a process of seeing, perceiving and understanding a text, words or sentences together with punctuation marks and other elements. Yılmaz (2014: p.78) defines it as a meaning-making process in which symbols received through sense organs are subjected to mental processes and interpreted accordingly.

Reading is a process of recognizing and making sense of all units of a text (Göğüş, 1978). Reading activity involves many purposes and tasks. Various activities are displayed during text reading and all activities are performed in a specific context. Text reading requires high-level language skills and every reading activity leads to an increase in knowledge (Snow, 2002).

According to Harris and Sipay (1990), reading is a meaningful interpretation of written language while according to Sever (1995), it is an activity involving the sensory perception and interpretation of words. Külekçi, Kırkkılıç and Gündüz (1999) define reading as a complex activity consisting of movements of organs of sight and speech and meaning-making and comprehension processes of the mind. Perfetti (1986: p.14) states that one of the most important components of reading is word identification and comprehension.

"Reading" and "reading skills" have different meanings within the same concept domain. Reading as an action refers to the act of reading, text analysis or vocalization, while reading skills, also involving the act of reading, refer to the act of reading transformed into a deliberate, conscious and purposeful activity. Reading skills also refer to a competence defined by a cognitive, affective and mental framework that individuals possess. Reading is generally defined on the basis of reading skills. In this context, the definitions of reading and reading skills indicate that reading involves processes of text identification and meaning construction, which are affected by readiness to read and the nature of a text.

Reading involves communicating with, decoding and making meaning of a text through physical and mental processes, and associating the constructed meaning with textual and paratextual readings. The ability to read is a process involving high-level cognitive activities that begin with the correct utterance of the text and progress towards decoding the meaning or meanings acquired by language units within a given context. Gündüz and Şimşek (2011) specify this process as seeing, recognizing, comprehending/perceiving, and memorizing/retaining (p.35). Akyol (2007) states that good reading requires the components of word identification, knowledge of semantics, knowledge of syntax, linguistic processes and comprehension activities during the reading process and argues that the reading process is the association of these components with readers, their competence levels, authors, style and content of their writings, reading environment and information obtained from the reading activity. Güneş (2013), on the other hand, explains reading ability on the basis of constructivism and describes the reading process with domains of reading. Accordingly, reading consists of the dimension of process involving vision, comprehension and mental construction, the dimension of interaction involving physical and mental interaction and the dimension of meaning-making, which is the final and important domain of the reading process. Arıcı (2008) explains the emergence process of reading from physical, mental and social aspects of reading. Reading is an activity initiated by physical organs and sustained by mental processes.

In the reading process, the reader sees, perceives, vocalizes, comprehends and interprets the text with which he/she interacts. The reading activity must include certain features. The reader should not only utter the text but also attempt to research the meaning it conveys. The reader should recognize the purpose of the author of the text, and identify the type of the text, its narrative forms, its narrator, its main idea and auxiliary ideas. The reader should be able to detect the style of the text, the language units and the semantic relations between them, as well as the semantic properties they acquire within the given context. The reader should also demonstrate the skills of interpreting the meaning of the text with prior knowledge and bring that knowledge to his/her next reading experience. Epçaçan (2008) emphasizes that after the reading process, students should acquire the skills of developing vocabulary, making meaning of and evaluating the text, developing a critical approach to the text, adapting the reading activity to life, and identifying social problems and finding solutions to them with knowledge gained. Güneş (2013) states reading require mental processing skills. According to him, searching for the meaning of the text, connecting prior knowledge with new information and mentally constructing it, reaching new meaning, asking questions about the text and engaging in reading activities to learn are some of the properties of reading.

The ability to read requires different skills including recognition, analysis, comprehension and interpretation of the stylistic units of the text. Individuals with reading skills are expected to perform various activities before reading, during reading and after reading. The reader should determine the purpose of reading before beginning to read. For example, an individual can read for purely aesthetic pleasure as well as for acquiring knowledge and conducting research on a specific subject matter. Choosing a text or book to communicate with according to the purpose is also a pre-reading requirement that should be fulfilled by the reader. The reader approaches the text of choice with a suitable reading method. Predicting text content on the basis of prior knowledge about the text to be read and generating text-related questions according to the purpose of reading before reading make the reading process more meaningful.

What is expected of the reader during reading is focusing on the text, identifying new meanings of stylistic units in the context, constructing answers to questions determined before reading, testing predictions regarding the text, ascertaining formal and content features of the text and retaining the new information.

After the reading experience, readers critically evaluate the new knowledge and meanings gained from reading. They check whether reading goals have been achieved and synthesize their prior knowledge with the new information and transfer it to the next reading experiences. Güneş (2013) categorizes the tasks that should be fulfilled for the development of reading skills during reading under the headings of pre-reading, reading and post-reading. Pre-reading involves prior knowledge activation, prediction, determination of the purpose of reading, text identification, method selection and text review. Reading involves applying word identification and phrase or sentence association techniques, establishing links between paragraphs, using text reading techniques, comprehending the text, and constructing and organizing acquired knowledge. Checking whether reading goals have been achieved and questioning the information in the text are other activities that readers are expected to fulfil after reading. Calp (2007) compares good and poor readers and concludes that good readers activate prior knowledge before reading, determine appropriate reading strategies, concentrate during reading, make predictions about the next part of the text, and make use of the context to understand new concepts, combine new information with prior knowledge, think about the text after reading and summarize the information deemed important. Studies on skills demonstrated by individuals with reading skills make similar explanations and yield similar results (Arıcı, 2008; Akyol, 2007; Yılmaz, 2014).

The reading process is also explained by bottom-up (text-driven), top-down (concept-driven) and interactive reading models. Proceeding from part to whole, the bottom-up model is a meaning-making and interpretation process that starts from sound and arrives at an understanding of the author's message. This model is mostly associated with oral reading. In this model, readers are passive in the reading process and vocabulary is an important factor in being a good reader. This model was introduced in the "one second of reading theory" developed by Gough (1972). Another reading approach is the top-down model, in which readers try to understand and interpret text based on their prior knowledge. Meaning is derived from the whole text. In this model, readers actively engage in reading and read selectively and try hard to make meaning depending on their purpose of reading. This model was developed by Goodman in 1967. In this model, readers do not depend on phonemic code in a text. They assign tentative hypotheses regarding the overall meaning of the text (Dechant, 1991; Alderson, 2000; Akyol, 2009, Alvermann, Unrau & Ruddell, 2013, Güneş, 2013). Smith (2004), another proponent of the model, argues that readiness to read and expectations guide readers in the meaning-making process.

The interactive model is another reading approach which combines the physical and mental processes predicted in bottom-up and top-down models. Developed by Rumelhart (1977) and revised in 1984, this model refers to reading skills as the interaction between reader and text. Reading entails an interaction between the reader's mind and the author's text. It provides the synthesis of lower level information with top level information. In this model, meaning emerges as a result of the interaction between the reader's mind and the author's text. The process involves seeing stylistic units of the text, sending them to the visual memory and from there to the data processing centre, evaluating the new information together with prior knowledge in the long-term memory, testing predictions and analysing the meaning of words and phrases to reach meaning layers (Macaro, 2003; Shahnazari & Dabahhi, 2014). Explanatory model, model of teaching techniques and exemplary model are also used to define the reading process. The explanatory model requires teachers to make explanations about language skills and to enable students to structure their prior knowledge. Explained by "What?", "Why?", "How?" and "When?" questions, this model puts an emphasis on teachers' guiding task. The model of teaching techniques entails the teaching and implementation of reading techniques mobilized during the reading process. The exemplary model is a model in which techniques are exemplified and explained (Güneş, 2013). In all reading models, the aim is to achieve reading skills in the best way possible. For this, each model, depending on its own structure, offers examples of activities.

In the reading process, the common point of the activities expected from readers can be coded by purpose, method, interaction, new knowledge and interpretation of new information in words and phrases. Readers with these reading skills develop and use their mental skills at a high level during the reading process. Çiftçi (2007) states that readers carry out the processes of identification, selection and interpretation of words and symbols, sorting, classification, interrogation and association of selected information, and analysis, synthesis, problem solving and evaluation. Bamberger (1990) emphasizes that the development of reading skills depends on the development of learning as a whole.

Readers use such skills as supra-cognitive thinking, reflective thinking, thoughtful thinking, analytical thinking, critical thinking, systematic thinking, abstraction, decision making, problem solving, analysis and synthesis in pre-reading, reading and post-reading processes. They choose reading methods and techniques depending on their use of these skills. Reading strategies, methods and techniques are selected by readers using the supra-cognitive thinking skill depending on their purpose of reading and on the text.

The reading strategies that can be applied prior to reading are *4L1S* (*Title, look, look, look, look, sequence*); *3W* (*What do I know, what do I want to learn, what have I learned?*), which activates students' prior knowledge on text topic and enables them to construct a contextual goal and evaluate what they have learned. *Visual arrangement* involves the creation of a network of ideas for students to explore what they know about the text. *Information circles* strategies enable students carry their prior knowledge into the text reading process. *Inquiry* involves the analysis of the purpose of the author and the forms he/she uses to describe his/her purpose during reading. Thinking aloud about the content of the text is another reading strategy. *Puzzle* involves reading activities that are performed and evaluated by different groups during reading applicable to group teaching. Readers' recess strategies are based on taking brief breaks to discuss and analyse difficult-to-understand texts. Readers summarize the text with their own words after reading. *Text-reader, text-world, text-text associations*, IQ2RU (examining, question designing, reading, recalling, understanding) and questioning strategies are recommended for all reading processes (Ülper, 2010; Kanmaz, 2012).

Based on the information above, Figure 3-1 presents the reading skills prior to reading, during reading and post- reading (Epçaçan, 2008; in Akyol, 2006).

Other than reading strategies, readers can also employ reading methods and techniques in the text reading process. Reading methods, techniques and types are explained in similar ways in different sources. Full reading, silent reading, oral reading, skimming, selective-flexible reading, extensive reading, Marking-a-Text, note-taking, predictive reading, inquisitive reading, choral reading, theatrical cold reading, memorizing, associative reading, argumentative reading, critical reading and detective type reading can be used depending on text and reading type (Gün, 2011; Gündüz & Şimşek, 2011). Some other types of reading are visual reading involving reading different types of texts from any written material, and interpreting graphics and pictures (Ünalan, 2006), screen reading involving the interpretation of texts, images and figures on screens of electronic devices (Foltz, 1996), quick reading for quick access to information (Ruşen, 2016), independent reading, shared reading (Güneş, 2013) and creative reading (Moorman, Ram, 1996).

Due to the seamless flow of information with rapid advancements in technology, readers use various types of reading to obtain the most accurate information that serves their purposes. Some of these are quick reading for quick access to information, screen reading for access to information in digital media and e-books, and critical reading for evaluating and generating new information. Particularly critical reading is a method of reading which good readers should use. Critical reading is a reading method that requires readers to make inquiries about the text, to answer questions during the reading process and to reflect on the text. Critical reading is associated with critical thinking skills. According to Söylemez (2015), critical reading also aims to give students the habit of asking questions about what they read and to think about the subject matter, and to find out their own truths by evaluating the subject matter with its positive and negative aspects from an unbiased point of view.

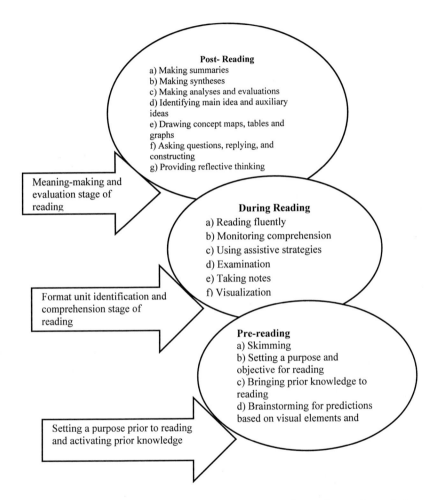

Figure 3-1. Activities expected from readers throughout the whole reading process

Critical reading is the skill of evaluating and making inferences from the text, distinguishing events and ideas, and understanding the author's purpose and perspective. Critical reading suggests that each text has an ideology and reflects its author's thoughts and perspective (Hoody 2008). Critical readers carefully follow the meanings of words and phrases in the text, which enables them to think carefully and approach the text from different perspectives. Critical readers acquire the ability to examine the information they receive and keep it active (Odabaş, Odabaş & Polat, 2008). Critical reading is the key to the development and application of critical thinking skills. The effectiveness of critical reading in understanding and interpreting texts has also brought up different methods and techniques.

Reading skills can also be applied using the argumentative reading method, which is a technique that allows readers to share relevant information, feelings and thoughts regarding subject matter, to benefit from others' knowledge, thoughts and opinions, and to gain a different perspective. Argumentative reading can be applied to the whole text or to its sections. Argumentative reading can be applied in large or small groups. Common thoughts that emerge during discussions are noted down to come to a conclusion and all students are allowed to express their thoughts in a respectful way (Gündüz & Şimşek, 2011). The Socratic seminar, which is also a discussion method, can also be used as a reading method. However, the number of studies on the use of the Socratic seminar as a reading method is very limited. The general structure and application steps of the Socratic seminar suggest that it can be used as a reading method. In this context, it is useful to address the Socratic seminar as a potentially useful method of reading.

2. The Socratic seminar

One of the discussion methods, the Socratic seminar can be defined as a teaching technique based on Socratic argumentation style which allows the discussion of a hard-to-understand text as a group and develops critical thinking and provides an approach to truth-finding. The Socratic seminar is considered a teaching technique in the literature. The application of teaching methods and techniques in different disciplines depend the competences of instructors. For example, a philosophy teacher can apply the Socratic seminar according to the set goal of the course. A native language teacher can use the Socratic seminar together with critical reading, argumentative reading or group reading in order to enable students to acquire reading skills. The Socratic seminar is already defined in the literature as a teaching technique. However, the number of studies on the use of the Socratic seminar for native language teaching is very few. In this context, this study addresses the Socratic seminar as a method of reading.

The Socratic seminar is based on the Socratic Method, which was developed by Leonard Nelson in 1920. Leonard theorized the method on the basis of Socratic dialogues in Plato's writings, the aim of which was to help people discover the way to real wisdom that they already have (Yücesoy, 2006). At the Conference of the Pedagogical Society of Göttingen in 1922, Nelson (2006) stated that the Socratic Method was not philosophy but a way of teaching philosophy. He further stated that the Socratic Method was not the art of teaching philosophy, but the art of making students philosophers.

In his own definition of the method, Socrates used the verbs to examine, investigate, inquire and question. He served the purpose of asking some questions to help people discover inconsistencies in their views and attain the truth (Cevizci, 2009). In the Socratic Method, teachers help students to doubt about their knowledge and reveal the knowledge that they already possess. The Socratic Method aims to develop critical thinking and discussion skills through ironic and maieutic processes. The Socratic Method, which is based on teaching by means of discovery, aims to reach the truth by induction. The Socratic seminar is a technique which has the Socratic Method in its basic philosophy. The Socratic seminar is different from the Socratic Method in the sense that the former focuses on examining a high-level and difficult text. Polite and Adams (1996) state the Socratic seminar became a current issue after the method of inquiry of Socrates.

The Socratic seminar started to be implemented with reference to the Paideia Proposal developed by Mortimer Adler in the 1980s and since then applied in major schools for the development of critical thinking skills (Tredway, 1995). Adler (1982) argues that ideas and values can be understood by questioning important texts. Adler's view has been influential in the embodiment of the Socratic seminar.

The definitions of the Socratic seminar are similar in the literature. According to Kwit (2013), the Socratic seminar is a structured dialogue among learners about important ideas, values or moral issues in a text or texts. The Socratic seminar not only activates critical thinking but also provides the opportunity to acquire the skill of reviewing a subject from different perspectives, to meet the need to prove the truth of claims, to ask questions and answer them, and to construct new information through association with prior knowledge. What distinguishes the Socratic seminar from other class discussions is that when students actively engage in a discussion, the teacher withdraws completely and assumes the role of an observer. The aim of the Socratic seminar is not generating discussion, but quite the contrary, is providing an environment for dialogue for participants to construct the meaning of the thought presented in a text.

The National Paideia Center has identified The Socratic seminar as a collaborative work that allows intellectual conversations facilitated with open-ended questions about a text (Billings and Roberts 2003). In the Socratic seminar centre, the text is an intellectual conversation (Lambright, 1995). It is a questioning to help students improve their ability to understand basic ideas and values in a text they read (Adler, 1984). The Socratic seminar is a formal discussion facilitated by a leader asking open-ended questions. In the context of a discussion, students use their critical thinking skills to listen to others' opinions and reveal their own thoughts and answers to others' thoughts. They learn to interrogate and collaborate in a wise and civilized manner (Israel, 2002). The Socratic seminar is a systematic process for asking and answering questions, and inquiring ideas, which are the fundamental principles of human thought (Copeland, 2005).

According to the explanations, the Socratic seminar is based on a difficult and content-rich text, which requires collaboration to work on. The Socratic seminar is a highly effective dialogue for the development of cognitive and affective skills. Facilitated with reading, listening, speaking and writing language skills, the Socratic seminar provides a profound and new understanding of values and thoughts regarding a text and develops the skills of thinking critically, respecting others' opinions and collaborating with others. In the Socratic seminar, participants are expected to be as active as possible and the teacher to offer instructions and ask open-ended questions from the position of an observer.

The seminar is designed to allow students to explore a text, a problem or an experience. At the seminar, students have the opportunity to ask and think about questions and explore the questions of others. The seminar experience consists of process and content. Students learn not only more about an idea or text, but also learn how to think and discuss the text and gain practicality in important discussions (Kara & Çepni, 2011). What a seminar is not? It is not an interactive lesson or a pre-designed conversation. The seminar is neither a debate nor the direction of a discussion by the teacher. The seminar involves the collective investigation of questions posed or topics addressed by a text or a shared experience. The main goal is to improve everyone's understanding of the topic and also to provide the opportunity for participants to develop their own understanding and shed light on the topic through speaking, listening to, testing and reflecting thoughts (Çepni, Kara & Çil, 2012; Wiggins, 2004).

The aims of the Socratic seminar are explained in a similar fashion. Adler (1984) states that the aim of the Socratic seminar in the Paideia Program is the development of understanding, reading, writing, speaking, listening, and critical, reflective and independent thinking skills. Perkins (1993) states the Socratic seminar aims to provide understanding of ideas and values in a text. According to Polite and Adams (1996) the Socratic seminar concentrates on various subjects including specific reading, scientific demonstrations and arts. The main purpose of the seminar is to develop students' critical thinking and conflict resolution skills and provide them with the opportunity to express and clarify values.

The aims of the Socratic seminar overlap with those of reading education. The main goal of enabling students to acquire reading skills is to improve their ability to comprehend and make sense of what they read and develop high-level thinking skills. In this context, the development of reading skills through the Socratic seminar can facilitate the achievement of the objectives of reading education.

The Socratic seminar enables students to develop critical thinking, creativity, critical reading, and speaking, listening and reflective thinking skills. It also helps students develop teamwork, collaboration and conflict resolution skills (Copeland, 2005).

The Socratic seminar has various components; a very hard and challenging text, seminar questions, a seminar leader and participants.

A text is selected by the seminar leader before a Socratic seminar. A good text chosen as the topic of a Socratic seminar is expected to have the four characteristics described by the National Paideia Center (www.paideia.org, 2008.):

1. Topic for a Socratic seminar should be rich in ideas and values.
2. Texts should be complex, challenging and engaging.
3. Texts should be relevant to seminar participants.
4. Texts should be fundamentally ambiguous. In other words, they should have various layers of meaning.

Films, poems, pictures, sculptures, tables or graphics, maps or diagrams, short stories, oral problems and articles can be used as texts in a Socratic seminar (Alexander, 2011).

Socratic seminar leaders play a dual role as leader and participant. The tasks of seminar leaders are making sure that the discussion does not get out of hand, asking follow-up questions, helping participants in case of confusion, encouraging everyone to participate, limiting dominant participants and presenting mental practices. In addition, leaders, as participants, actively engage in the discussion to help participants to explore the text. In order to be able to do these things effectively, leaders should be able to predict various interpretations, know the text very well and be cognizant of every possibility. Leaders should also help participants to discover original thoughts and unexpected comments and be patient enough to allow the development of participants' understanding (Swanson, 2009).

The roles of Socratic seminar leaders can be listed as follows:

1. They should know the text well before they begin.
2. They should prepare a series of questions regarding the text to help define the discussion and give it direction
3. They should think of themselves as joining a seminar instead of looking for the right answer about the topic.
4. They should be active listeners.
5. They should respect each participant.
6. They should help participants work cooperatively.
7. They should encourage reluctant members to participate and restrain those who dominate the discussion.
8. They should facilitate discussion among participants.
9. They should examine and inquire participants' responses, and make sure that ideas suggested are explained.
10. If necessary, they should give participants the opportunity to repeat their questions and answers for clarity.
11. They should encourage participants to use the text to give responses.
12. They should be patient enough to allow the development of participants' understanding (Filkins, bt.).

Socratic seminar leaders respect participants' perspectives and become a model of critical thinking by showing an interest in their opinions. They establish a stimulating classroom environment and recognize that each student is valuable (Learning and Teaching Development Committee, 2013). They contribute to the success of the seminar with key questions prepared before the seminar.

One of the sine qua non in a Socratic seminar is seminar questions. The seminar leader prepares some questions before the seminar and asks them to participants to initiate the seminar, to draw participants' attention and to lead the discussion.

In a Socratic seminar, questions should be open-ended and reveal the main ideas and values of the text. Questions can be classified as opening questions, development questions and conclusion questions. Opening questions should allow participants to understand the content of the text. Further guiding questions should be raised so that participants can analyse the text and develop understanding. Summary questions should also be asked to ensure that ideas and values can be evaluated by participants. The features of seminar questions can be listed as follows:

1. Questions should be open-ended and trigger many correct responses.
2. Questions should make students think.
3. Questions must be clear and understandable.
4. Participants should be able to understand what is asked.
5. Questions should be able to reveal different perspectives.
6. Questions should encourage participants to evaluate and synthesize their ideas.
7. Questions should be short and clear (Alexander, 2011; National Paideia Center, bt.).

Some examples of questions:

1. What are the keywords of the text?
2. What can be the title of the text?
3. What do you think is the most interesting thing about the text?

There are some things which participants are expected to do in a Socratic seminar. They are expected to actively engage in the seminar and develop an understanding about ideas and values in the text.

In a Socratic seminar, participants and the leader share the responsibilities for the quality of the seminar. For a good seminar, participants should examine the text beforehand, share their ideas and questions during the seminar, provide responses to other participants' questions and use the text to support their ideas (Swanson, 2009). The main task of seminar participants is to engage in the dialogue process. In this process, participants should force themselves to develop their seminar skills. The responsibilities of seminar participants are to think, listen, speak to others, refer to the text and address others respectfully. They are also expected to think about values and ideas emphasized in the dialogue process and to analyse various views from different perspectives. It is the responsibility of seminar participants to look at the person who is talking, take notes of important points, not to talk while others talk, speak loudly enough so that everyone can hear, make eye contact, make specific quotes from the text to support an idea or viewpoint, address other participants by their names, and develop a constructive approach to their ideas or express disagreement in a respectful manner (Pihlgren, 2008). In other words, the main tasks of seminar participants are to think, listen, speak, refer to the text and treat other participants with respect.

The proper execution of a Socratic seminar depends on all components operating correctly. The implementation steps of a Socratic seminar are as follows:

1. On the day before a Socratic seminar, the teacher hands out a short passage of text.
2. At home, students read, analyse and take notes of parts they deem important.
3. The next day, students are divided into two concentric circles; an inner circle and an outer circle.
4. Students in the inner circle read the text aloud and discuss about it for fifteen minutes. Meanwhile, students in the outer circle observe the behaviour and performance of the students in the inner circle.
5. Following the discussion of the text, participants in the outer circle evaluate the performance of those in the inner circle and give feedback to them.
6. Participants in the inner and outer circles exchange their roles and positions.
7. After the exchange of roles and positions, students in the new inner circle engage in a ten-minute discussion and then receive feedback from those in the new outer circle (Copeland, and Goering, bt.).

The Socratic seminar is practiced with a single circle in a small group or classroom while it is carried out in two circles with groups consisting of more than twenty participants. Participants in the inner circle share their questions and ideas as active listeners while those in the outer circle interpret important concepts, ideas, themes or questions raised during the seminar (Kwit, 2013). A Socratic seminar session was illustrated by Ball and Brewer (2000, pp. 23) as follows.

T = Teacher's Seat
* = Students
H = Hot Seats

Figure 3-2. Inner/Outer Circle Diagram

While participants in the inner circle are speaking, those in the outer circle are not involved. Empty chairs in the inner circle referred to as hot seats are strategically placed on three sides to enable participants in the outer circle to engage in the discussion. If students in the outer circle want to participate in the discussion, they quietly leave the outer circle and sit on "hot seats" where they become fully active members of the inner circle. When they are accepted, they leave the hot seats and get back to their seats in the outer circle. In this way, there is room for students who will move from the outer circle to the hot seats (Ball & Brewer, 2000).

Participants in the outer circle perform the seminar-related tasks assigned by the leader. They take notes of and evaluate the behaviour of participants in the inner circle, record the topics and themes discussed during the seminar and share their thoughts and notes with the inner circle at the end of the seminar. The seminar leader makes arrangements to make sure that both groups fulfil their tasks properly throughout the seminar. In this context, tasks that are to be fulfilled before, during and after a seminar are given below.

Before seminar;
1. Selecting an interesting text that is relevant to the purposes of participants and the seminar, and which is difficult enough to discuss
2. Preparing text-related and open-ended questions for textual analysis

3. Providing students with preliminary information about the content to enable readiness
4. Introducing the Socratic seminar and its purposes
5. Making sure students read the text, sharing expectations about the evaluation of the seminar and defining participants' responsibilities
6. Explaining the seminar rules and encouraging participants to set individual goals

During the seminar;
1. Explaining the seminar, seminar rules and seminar objectives
2. Making sure participants sit in the seminar arrangement, assigning students for the inner and outer circles and reminding them that they have to address each other during the seminar
3. Presenting the prepared key question and reminding participants to associate their questions and speeches with the text
4. Asking further questions for clarity. Students can answer questions verbally or in writing. The seminar leader does not give positive or negative feedback on participants' questions or opinions.
5. Drawing participants' attention to the first question in case they digress and asking further questions to direct participants to the main objective
6. Encouraging reluctant participants to engage in the dialogue
7. Encouraging participants to comment before speaking, to contribute to others' statements and to listen to them
8. Taking notes of ideas, values and participants' contributions throughout the seminar
9. Summarizing the ideas and values at a moment of silence or at the end of the seminar
10. Preventing arguments and impositions
11. Raising new questions towards the end of the seminar and associating them with the first question and participants' responses to it
12. Asking a closing question after the thorough examination of the text in order to ensure that participants relate their opinions and values to real life

After the seminar;
1. Taking participants' questions
2. Making self-assessment of participants' personal goals
3. Making evaluations about the seminar's goals

4. Receiving feedback from the outer circle when the inner circle dialogue is completed and sustaining the cycle by exchanging the roles and positions of the inner and outer circles
5. Reporting the seminar process
6. Taking reminder notes for the next seminar (Roberts & Billings, 1999; National Paideia Center, 2008; Chowning, 2009).

Focusing on the analysis of a difficult text, the Socratic seminar can be used as a method of reading, as it not only entails the implementation of reading, speaking, writing and listening skills during the process but also develops them. The Socratic seminar's pre-seminar, seminar and post-seminar stages coincide with pre-reading, reading and assessment stages. This overlap is illustrated in Figure 2.

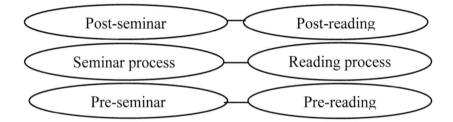

Figure 3-3. Relationship between reading process and Socratic seminar process

The main purpose of implementing the Socratic seminar is to improve participants' language skills, critical, reflective, independent thinking skills and conflict resolution skills. It also positively affects all learning areas of native language. The Socratic seminar also aims to find basic ideas and values in a text and to create new understanding in participants. These goals coincide with the aims of reading.

The Socratic seminar is a method that facilitates textual analysis, group discussion, and dialogue instead of debate. In this respect, the Socratic seminar incorporates the methods of group reading and inquisitive reading. It also includes the methods of textual analysis and textual inquiry, argumentative reading and critical reading, and creative reading for idea generation, and note-taking strategies during the seminar. The Socratic seminar is a synthesis of group reading, inquisitive reading, critical reading, creative reading and argumentative reading, and note-taking methods. Due to its structure and rationale, the Socratic seminar seems like an appropriate method of reading. With pre-seminar, seminar and post-seminar activities coinciding with the stages of the reading process and reading objectives, the Socratic seminar can be considered a method of reading.

The Socratic seminar involves the analysis of a difficult text. The Socratic seminar can be used for the development of reading skills, especially in the analysis of informative texts with layers of meaning.

Conclusion

Reading occurs in two dimensions, physical and mental. In the mental process, students are expected to understand a text they read and construct meaning together with their prior knowledge. In a Socratic seminar, participants are also expected to explore the ideas and values in a text and create a new understanding of them. It can therefore be stated that the Socratic seminar, as a method of reading, directly serves the purposes of reading. Epicachan (2015) studied the effect of reading with the Socratic seminar technique on students 'attitudes towards comprehension skills and reading and concluded that the Socratic seminar technique had a positive effect on students' ability to understand what they read.

There is a positive relationship between the development of reading skills and of thinking skills. The development of reading skills also brings with it the development of many mental skills such as analysis, synthesis, evaluation, critical reflection and empathy. Polite and Adams (1996) state the Socratic seminar has a positive effect on students' conflict resolution and high-level thinking skills. Therefore, the application of the Socratic seminar as a method of reading supports the purposes of reading for the development of thinking skills.

The Socratic seminar activities and reading activities complement each other. Setting an objective and preparing questions before a Socratic seminar correspond to the pre-reading stage of reading which prepares students for the text. Textual analysis and comprehension and meaning construction during the Socratic seminar also play a key role in the reading process. Evaluation and reflection are essential aspects of both the Seminar and reading activities. It does not seem difficult for instructors to address the Socratic seminar process and reading process together and to transform the seminar process into a reading process.

Student-centred education is a key concept in recent years. The Socratic seminar is regarded as a student-centred and highly effective method in the development of cognitive and affective skills. Therefore, the use of the Socratic seminar as a method of reading is likely to positively influence the development of reading skills, especially reading comprehension.

References

Adler, M. (1982). A revolution in education. *American Educator*, 6(4), 20–24.

Adler, M. J. (1984). *The paideia program: An educational syllabus.* New York: Macmillan Publishing Company.

Akyol, H. (2005). *Türkçe ilk okuma yazma öğretimi,* (4th Ed.), Ankara: Pegem A Yayıncılık.

Akyol, H. (2007). Okuma. (Ed. A. Kırkkılıç ve H. Akyol) in *İlköğretimde Türkçe öğretimi* (15-48), (1st Ed.), Ankara: Pegem A Yayıncılık.

Alderson, J. C. (2000). *Assessing reading.* New York: Cambridge University Press.

Alexander, B. (2011). *The paideia Socratic seminar: A strategy for increasing understanding in text, ideas and values, and the self and others.* Online Training 1 Presentation, Pennsylvania Training and Technical Assistance Network. http://www.pattan.net/Videos/Browse/Single/?code_name=socratic_se minar [Accessed 12.08.2017]

Alvermann, D. E., Unrau, N. J. & Ruddell, R. B. Ed. (2013). *Theoretical models and processes of* reading. (6. Edition). Newark, DE: International Reading Association

Anderson, R. C., Hiebert, E. H., Scott, J. A. & Wilkinson, I. A. G. (1985). *Becoming a nation of readers, The Report of the commission on reading.* Washington: The National Institute of Education U.S. Department of Education.

Arıcı, A. F. (2008). *Okuma eğitimi.* (1st Ed.), Ankara: Pegem A Akademi.

Baker, L. & Brown, A. L. (1984). *Metacognitive skills and reading.* P. D. Perason (Prepared for Publication), Handbook of reading redearch in (pp. 353-394), New Jersey: Lawrence Erlbaum Associates Publishers.

Ball, W. H. & Brewer, P. (2000). *Socratic seminars in the block.* Larchmont, NY: Eye on Education.

Bamberger, R. (1990). *Okuma alışkanlığını geliştirme.* (Translated by B. Çapar). Ankara: Kültür Bakanlığı Yayınları.

Billings, L. & Roberts, T. (2003). *The paideia seminar: Active thinking through dialogue.* Chapel Hill, NC: National Paideia Center.

Calp, M. (2007). *Özel öğretim alanı olarak Türkçe öğretimi.* (3rd Ed.), Konya: Eğitim Kitabevi.

Çepni S., Kara Y. & Cil E. (2012). Middle school science and items of high school entrance examination: examining the gap in Turkey. Journal of Testing and Evaluation, 40 (3), 501-511.

Cevizci, A. (2009). *Sokrates*. (2nd Ed.), İstanbul: Say Yayınları.

Chowning, J. T. (2009). *Socratic seminars in science class, Providing a structured format to promote dialogue and understanding. NIH-PA Author Manuscript*, 76(7): 36–41.

Copeland, M. (2005). *Socratic circles, fostering critical and creative thinking in middle and high school*. Portland: Stenhouse Publishers.

Copeland, M. & Goering, C. (bt.). *Empowering Students with Socratic Seminars*, Ad Astra Consulting, https://intc.education.illinois.edu/docs/librariesprovider12/default-document-library/btc_2016/e2.pdf?sfvrsn=2 [Accessed 12. 08.2017]

Çiftçi, Ö. (2007). *İlköğretim 5. sınıf öğrencilerinin Türkçe öğretim programında belirtilen okuduğunu anlamayla ilgili kazanımlara ulaşma düzeyinin belirlenmesi*. Unpublished PhD Thesis. Gazi Üniversitesi, Eğitim Bilimleri Enstitüsü, Ankara.

Dechant, E. V. (1991). *Understanding and teaching reading: An interactive model*. NJ: Lawrence Erlbaum.

Epçaçan, C. (2008). *Okuduğunu anlama stratejilerinin bilişsel ve duyuşsal öğrenme ürünlerine etkisi*. Unpublished PhD Thesis, Hacettepe Üniversitesi Sosyal Bilimler Enstitüsü Eğitim Bilimleri Anabilim Dalı Eğitim Programları ve Öğretim Bilim Dalı, Ankara.

Epçaçan, C. (2015). The Socratic seminar tekniğine dayalı öğretimin öğrencilerin okuduğunu anlama becerisine ve okumaya ilişkin tutuma etkisi. *Uluslararası Akademik Araştırmalar Dergisi*, 15(58), pp. 46-62.

Filkins, S. (bt.). *Socratic Seminars, Strategy Guide*. http://waiakeahigh.k12.hi.us/infodesk/Nov1Handouts/Socratic%20Sem inar/AVID%20Socratic%20Seminar.pdf [Accessed 13.08.2017]

Foltz, P. W. (1996) *Comprehension, Coherence and Strategies in Hpyertext and Linear text*. In Rouet, J.-F., Levonen, J.J., Dillon, A.P. & Spiro, R.J. (Eds.) Hypertext and Cognition. Hillsdale, NJ: Lawrence Erlbaum Associates, http://www-psych.nmsu.edu/~pfoltz/reprints/Ht-Cognition.html, [Accessed 24.08.2017]

Gough, P. B. (1985). *One second of reading*. In H. Singer & R. B. Ruddell (Eds.) Theoretical Models and Processes of Reading (3rd Ed.) Newark, DE: International Reading Association, pp. 687-688.

Göğüş, B. (1978). *Orta dereceli okullarımızda Türkçe ve yazın eğitimi.* Ankara: Gül Yayınevi.

Gün, M. (2011). *Yapılandırmacı eğitim modeliyle ilköğretim ikinci kademe Türkçe dersi okuma becerilerinin kazandırılmasında karşılaşılan sorunların analizi.* Unpublished PhD Thesis, T.C. Selçuk Üniversitesi Eğitim Bilimleri Enstitüsü Türkçe Eğitimi Anabilim Dalı Türkçe Eğitimi Bilim Dalı, Konya.

Gündüz, O. & Şimşek, T. (2011). *Anlama Teknikleri I uygulamalı okuma eğitimi,* (1st Ed.), Ankara: Grafiker Yayınları.

Güneş, F. (2013). *Türkçe öğretimi yaklaşımlar ve modeller,* (1st Ed.), Ankara: Pegem A Akademi.

Harris, A. J. & Sipay, E. R. (1990). *How to increase reading ability: A guide to developmental and remedial methods,* New York: Longman Publishing.

Hoody, M. L. (2008). *Critical literacy in primary education: Policy, praxis and the postmodern.* PhD Thesis. Minnesota: University of Minnesota.

Israel, E. (2002). *Examining multiple perspectives in literature. In inquiry and the literary text: constructing discussions in the English classroom,* (James Holden and John S. Schmit, eds.), Urbana, IL: NCTE.

Kanmaz, A. (2012). *Okuduğunu anlama stratejisi kullanımının, okuduğunu anlama becerisi, bilişsel farkındalık, okumaya yönelik tutum ve kalıcılığa etkisi.* Unpublished PhD Thesis, Adnan Menderes Üniversitesi Sosyal Bilimler Enstitüsü Eğitim Bilimleri Anabilim Dalı, Aydın.

Kara Y. & Cepni S. (2011). Investigation the alignment between school learning and entrance examinations through item analysis. Journal of Baltic Science Education, 10 (2), 73-86.

Külekçi, N. & Kırkkılıç, H. A., Gündüz, O. (1999). *İlk okuma - yazma ve Türkçe öğretimi.* Erzurum: Bakanlar Matbaacılık.

Kwit, H. C. (2013). *Socratic seminars: Making meaningful dialogue. Making the Common Core Come Alive!,* II(IV), http://www.justaskpublications.com/just-ask-resource-center/e-newsletters/msca/mccca-current-issue/, [Accessed 13.08.2017]

Lambright, L. L. (1995). Creating a dialogue: Socratic seminars and educational reform. *Community college journal,* 65(4), 30-34.

Learning and Teaching Development Committee, (2013). *New Faculty Teaching Guide.* https://moodle.stu.ca/pluginfile.php?file=%2F6070%2Fmod_resource %2Fcontent%2F4%2FSTU%20New%20Faculty%20Teaching%20Gui de%202013.pdf, [Accessed 13.08.2017]

Macaro, E. (2003). *Teaching and learning a second language: A guide to recent research and its applications.* London: Continuum.

Moorman, K. & Ram, A. (1996). *The role of ontology in creative understanding*. San DiegoProceedings Of The 18th Annual Cognitive Science Conference.

National Paideia Center (2008). *Planning step 6: Establish the pre- and post-seminar process*. http://www.learnnc.org/lp/editions/paideia/6913, [Accessed 14.08.2017]

Nelson, L. (2006). Sokrat Yöntemi. Yücesoy, S. (Trans.), in *Sokratik konuşma tarih- kuram- uygulama* (37-80), (1st Ed.), İstanbul: İstanbul Bilgi Üniversitesi Yayınları, (2002).

Odabaş, H., Odabaş, Z. Y. & Polat, C. (2008). Üniversite öğrencilerinin okuma alışkanlığı: Ankara Üniversitesi örneği. *Bilgi Dünyası*, 9(2), 431-465.

Öz, F. (2003). *Uygulamalı Türkçe öğretimi* (2nd Ed.), Ankara: Anı Yayıncılık.

Özdemir, E. (1976). *Okuma Sanatı*. İstanbul: İnkılâp Kitabevi.

Perfetti, C. A. (1986). *Continuities in reading acquisition, reading skill, and reading disability*. Remedial and Special Education, 7(1), 11-2.

Pihlgren, A. S. (2008). *Socrates in the classroom. Rationales and effects of philosophizing with children*. D.diss. Stockholm: Pedagogical Institution, Stockholm University.

Polite, V. C. & Adams, A. H. (1996). *Improving Critical thinking through socratic seminars. Spotlight on student success*. Philadelphia: Office of Educational Research and Improvement, https://eric.ed.gov/?id=ED403339, [Accessed 31.07.2017]

Roberts, T. & Billings, L. (1999). *The paideia classroom: Teaching for understanding*. New York: Eye on Education.

Ruşen, M. (2016). *Hızlı okuma*. (29th Ed.), İstanbul: Alfa Yayıncılık

Sever, S. (1995). *Türkçe öğretiminde tam öğrenme*. (1st Ed.), İstanbul: Ya-Pa Yayınları.

Shahnazari, M. T. & Dabaghi, A. (2014). A critical overview of models of reading comprehension with a focus on cognitive aspects. *IJRELT*, 1 (3), pp.7-19.

Smith, F. (2004). *Understanding reading: A psycholinguistic analysis of reading and learning to read*. (6.Edition). New Jersey: Lawrence Erlbaum Associates.

Snow, C. (2002). *Reading for understanding Toward an R&D Program in Reading Comprehension*. Santa Monica: RAND.

Söylemez, Y. (2015). *Ortaokul öğrencilerine yönelik eleştirel temel dil becerileri ölçeklerinin geliştirilmesi*. Unpublished PhD Thesis, Atatürk Üniversitesi Eğitim Bilimleri Enstitüsü Türkçe Eğitimi Ana Bilim Dalı Türkçe Eğitimi Bilim Dalı. Erzurum.

Swanson, J. (2009). *TIE Introduction to socratic seminars, challenging students to think for themselves.* South Dakota: Memorial Middle School, http://jswanson.tie.wikispaces.net/file/view/Socratic+Seminars+-+Sioux+Falls+Packet.pdf [Accessed 13.08.2017]

Temizkan, M. (2009). *Metin türlerine göre okuma eğitimi.* (1st Ed.), Ankara: Nobel Yayınları.

Tredway, L. (1995). Socratic seminars: Engaging students in intellectual discourse. *Educational Leadership*, pp. 26-29.

Türk Dil Kurumu (2005). *Türkçe sözlük.* (10th Ed.), Ankara: Türk Dil Kurumu Yayınları.

Ülper, H. (2010). Okuma süreci: Bilişsel işlemlemeler, kavrama ve okuma stratejileri, *Cito Eğitim: Kuram ve Uygulama*, 8, 32-44.

Ünalan, Ş. (2006). *Türkçe öğretimi.* (3rd Ed.), Ankara: Nobel Yayıncılık.

Wiggins, G. (2004). Socratic seminars: Guidelines. *Authentic Education*, pp. 1-7.

Yılmaz, M. (2014). Okuma eğitimi. M. Yılmaz (Prepared for Publication), in *Yeni gelişmeler ışığında Türkçe öğretimi* (pp.78-108), (1st Ed.), Ankara: Pegem A akademi.

Yücesoy, S. (drl.), (2006). *Sokratik konuşma tarih- kuram- uygulama.* (1st Ed.), İstanbul: İstanbul Bilgi Üniversitesi Yayınları.

CHAPTER FOUR

HISTORY AND GEOGRAPHY

AN EVALUATION OF SULTAN BAYBARS IN TERMS OF EMPEROR AND COMMANDER CHARACTERISTICS WITHIN THE SCOPE OF KUTADGU BILIG

MERYEM DOYGUN

Introduction

Turkish eras of the 10th and 11th centuries, which comprise a significant period of Turkish-Islamic history, apart from being a remarkable growth period in the political sense, entail significant developments that have been engraved in memories from the aspect of cultural history also. The great Turkish scholar Mahmud from Kashgar's words "God has raised the country's sun upon the house of the Turks" display that the Turks were without doubt that only dominant power. The essential phenomenon which gave life to this Turkish-Islamic period was the migrant Turkish culture meeting and merging with Islamic civilization and thus creating Turkish-Islamic culture. In consequence of Turkish-Islamic structure enriching cultural values, literary works have been started to write in Turkish-Islamic states in different languages. Yet Kutadgu Bilig that evolved from the great Turkish scholar Yusuf Has Hacib's pen in the XI Century only comprises one of these works. In this work, which presents the characteristics that are appropriate to the Turkish soul, it is possible to observe the values upon which the idea of Turkish state is founded. The author identified the traditional moral and legal considerations of the Turkish community and provided information about issues like social ethics and state governance. This work still maintains its existence as a cultural treasure today. The Turks, by dominating various fields throughout history, have established many states. As a natural consequence of Turkish domination extending so large, geographical regions have enlarged. However, the fields of Egypt and Syria, which comprise the areas that Sultan Baybars had dominated, are of concern of this research. These fields formed the important movement areas in which the Turkish Middle Ages had evolved. As the method of field research, it is the examination of the profiles of emperor and commander of the Turkish States in the areas mentioned in the paper. The chaotic environment in the field of Egypt and Syria in the XII and XIII Century had greatly been determinative in shaping the emperor and commander characteristics of Sultan Baybars. This leader, who had drawn attention throughout the period he remained on the throne whether with his military and political activities or with his superior ethical traits, have been examined in the scope of Kutadgu Bilig's conceptual framework. By feeding from Kutadgu Bilig's conceptual framework, Baybars's emperor and commander characteristics can be envisioned and things from the reflections of that cultural world can be collected. In this manner, by weighing it on a scale of historical experience, it can be seen that Kutadgu Bilig and therefore Turkish culture is a living entity and ideas concerning the future can be developed from it.

Baybars as an Emperor

In history, most appropriate basis for conceptual analysis of a period of an emperor or for making abstractions at events, most appropriate source for generation of scientific rational knowledge, the source of knowledge for the sake of findings and abstractions at laboratory level, main pillar on which we can monitor phenomena and events of that period and generate idea is the consequence of the emperor being reflected on the sources.

Sultan Baybars had been the real founder of the Mamluk State (Kopraman, 1987). Years of his ruling are an indication for his political success while his ability to govern is an indication for being a good ruler. In Kutadgu Bilig, ruler (beg) is a character on which the author delicately dwelled on. Such that Kutadgu Bilig which became a guide to Turkish cultural history beginning with the XI Century contains many valuable records on state administration. With the current work it is possible to have a grasp of political structure and later developments at Turkish states in Islamic era.

Author of the work Yusuf Has Hacib had also made some points on the characteristics of ruler and commander which constitute the main subject of our work. According to the author, all state dignitaries, particularly the ruler, must bear the qualifications mentioned here and must act in accordance with them. Otherwise, downfall of the state becomes inevitable.

Author of Kutadgu Bilig emphasises the necessity of coming from a noble ancestry for the person who becomes the ruler first. To be a beg person must come from noble ancestry at the first place. Since, for him, if the father is a beg son is born as beg. Thus he becomes beg as his father. Again, for him, as beg is born, he is born with begdom; he knows which is better by seeing and learning. If a person's lineage is fine he is born as a fine person and he moves on to the seat of honour since he is fine. He, who is clean, always asks for cleanliness (Yusuf Has Hacib, 1974, beyit. 1932, 1949, 1950, 1985)".

As can be understood from Yusuf Has Hacib's words, only the ruler coming from a blessed lineage can have a grasp of begdom and fulfil the obligations. In Turkish sovereignty consideration or Turkish state philosophy, ruler's coming from a clean lineage is a natural result of his undertaking state administration and this situation is considerably important.

In ancient Turkish states sovereignty was of divine origin. Person who was granted "kut" had to possess certain qualifications. For this reason, throughout the work, in the conversations between ruler Kun-Togdi and vizier Ögdulmis, qualifications of a beg worthy of begdom had been laid out. When ruler Kün-Toğdı asked his vizier "how beg should be to lead them, perform his work and his reputation and fame spread to World" (Yusuf Has Hacib, beyit. 1924), vizier Öğdülmiş listed the necessary qualifications to be present at a ruler dominating the world.

As evident in the verses, ruler from a noble house rather than from an ordinary person is accepted. But when looking into past we face with the fact that Sultan Baybars came from slavery. Despite of coming from slavery, he took his position in history as a great ruler due to his faith and his struggle for his state. His nobility lays not in his family tree but in his faith and determination resorting to all measures for the continuation of Turkish- Islamic world.

Intelligence and wisdom

The most important qualification of a ruler is intelligence and wisdom (Yusuf Has Hacib, beyit 1951, 1952). While making suggestions to ruler and statesmen in the work, author particularly emphasizes intelligence and wisdom. Just like Plato and Farabi, he places wit, knowledge and wisdom at the basis of state (Arslan, 1986).

As can be seen in the records of the author, ruler leads the people with his knowledge, arranges work of state and people with his mind and knowledge. Author had seen ruler and knowledge so interconnected that, for him word beg is related with knowledge. This issue is noted as such in the work: "Beg as word is related to the word bilig, if [letter] lam is taken out from bilig, word beg is left (Yusuf Has Hacib, beyit. 1953).

"Ruler being knowledgeable alone is not enough on its own, ruler must be intelligent as well. Ruler must know the value of mind. Since all kinds of goodness comes from mind (Yusuf Has Hacib, beyit. 1841)".

"Intelligent person is great and intelligence is the leader of a thousand merits for a human (Yusuf Has Hacib, beyit. 1830). Mind illuminates human like a torch who is dark as night" (Yusuf Has Hacib, beyit. 1840). "Beg handles state business and laws with knowledge and conducts with intelligence" (Yusuf Has Hacib, beyit. 2713). According to the author "Man really gets its man name with intelligence and begs put state in order with knowledge" (Genç, 2002).

Farabi, in his famous work, also drew attention to 12 qualifications that an ideal ruler had to possess and knowledge and intelligence was one of these. According to him, "Ideal ruler must possess by nature the ability to understand and to comprehend things well that is told him. Must be very smart and on seeing a slight indication, he must be able to comprehend what this indication leads to. Moreover, ruler must love acquiring knowledge and learning and must be devoted to these. Must overcome the difficulties of learning, bear the suffering and must not regard this as tiring and troublesome" (Fârâbî, 2012, s. 104-105).

Intelligence and knowledge are aspects which a Middle Ages author Ibn Haldun mentioned with care as well. According to him what differentiated humans from other creatures was the ability to comprehend which God only granted them. According to the author "Mind is the beginning point of humanity's perfection and last border of its superiority and honour over other creatures (Ibn Haldun, 2012).

Other than these, Nizamülmülk is another scholar dealing with mind and knowledge in his Siyasetname. In his work, he made reference to this issue as such: "Science helps sultan have divine majesty and lands and this is happiness in both worlds. Because he cannot do anything without science and cannot consent to illiteracy" (Nizamülmülk, 1999). He also noted "he must be smart enough not to suffer and not to be annoyed by those looking for great evil" (Nizamülmülk, 1999, s. 51).

There are many indications that Sultan Baybars had an intelligent and wise nature. This had also been reflected in the poems. In a poem quoted from a work, Sultan Baybars was mentioned as:

"He is such a sovereign having affinity for science and scholars.

He built madrasa for science. Iraq and Syria gazed him with longing.

Never mention Nizamiye Madrasa. This institution cannot be compared to any other.

When he built this madrasa all other churches shaked (Koçak, 1991, s. 1108).

Courage and valour

According to Yusuf Has Hacib another qualification that should be present at a ruler is courage and valour. "Ruler must be brave (alp), valiant, strong and hard-hearted. Since ruler can only stand against his enemies with boldness and courage (Yusuf Has Hacib, beyit. 1961)".

Courage and valour were also considered by one of the Western thinkers, Plato and in his work, he emphasized that person who would be the guardian of the state had to have sharp senses to feel enemy, agility to go after as soon as he felt it and strength to struggle once he captured it (Platon, 2009).

Farabi also told about necessity for a ruler to undertake the action he had to take without fear and weakness and in a bold manner (Fârâbî, 2012).

Courage and valour is perhaps the most striking qualification in the nature of Sultan Baybars. Ending years long of Mongol and Crusader cruelty with his courage and valour, he stopped the tears of Turkish Islamic world. After Nureddin Zengi and Salahaddin Ayyubi, he had his name written in gold letters in the history as the greatest sultan struggling against Crusader state established in the East. In every battle, he made reputation for being fearless and swift. Among all other Islamic states, Egypt's is preserved from the destructive effects of Mongol invasion had been due to his personal merit (Brockelmann, 1992). Throughout his 17 years in power, there were many operations, military campaigns and sieges. Besides having extraordinary energy, he had physical endurance sustained by doing most extreme sports. Even the toughest weather conditions could not keep him from working. There were times where he covered long distances in snow or in extremely hot temperatures (Clot, 1996).

Sultan Baybars' courage and valour had been crowned with military successes. During his 17-year reign period Sultan Baybars squeezed Crusaders to the few cities; Acre, Tyre and Tripoli castles along the coastline (Ebu'l Ferec, 1999).

In the work of Runciman, successes of Sultan Baybars whose courage and valour were not denied by Western authors either were noted as: "He could not see entire elimination of Franks but he maintained this to become inevitable" (Demirkent, 1997; Runciman, 2008, s. 296).

Virtuousness

Another qualification Yusuf Has Hacib would like to see in a ruler is being virtuous. Virtue is a general name for qualifications like goodness in moral aspect, humbleness, bravery, righteousness, generosity. Turks used the word virtue in the meaning of merit (Genç, 2002).

In the author's work, the necessity for a ruler to have virtue was recorded as such:

"To administer cities and provinces, to maintain peace and calmness ruler must have good nature and thousands of virtues. He must be gracious, complimenting and mild-mannered and all of his actions must be symmetrical to these. He must achieve all sorts of virtues fully and must refrain from acts which are inappropriate and unacceptable. Thousands of virtues are needed for the master of the world; master of the world dominate world with these virtues" (Yusuf Has Hacib, beyit. 1981, 2072, 2073, 2074). As can be understood from the verses, ruler must have virtue to be as useful as the sun. Virtue is one of the most important qualifications differentiating human from other living things and giving humane qualities. It is compulsory for every ruler having the goal of controlling primarily his country and subsequently the world to be virtuous to establish control and perform reign. Ruler being virtuous is a traditionally seen aspect in Turkish state understanding throughout Turkish history. A ruler having these characteristics is also loved by his people and his reign sustains.

Generosity is one of the primary virtues Turks would like to see in their rulers. According to the author "if begs are generous their names spread to the world, with their reputations and fames as long as the world is preserved. If begs are generous many soldiers gather around them so that they form an army. Be generous; donate, let them eat and drink, if your possession decreases clash again and obtain and meet your needs" (Yusuf Has Hacib, beyit. 2050, 2051, 2053). As it can be seen here generosity is not only needed for reputation but also needed for becoming militarily strong. Author's points on generosity are the expression of the most important duty which Turkish government understanding bestow upon the ruler that is feeding the people and those around him (Genç, 2002).

There are many records showing Sultan Baybars had the qualification of generosity. Almost in every source it is mentioned that he was generous toward meliks, amirs and soldiers subject to him with the aim of gaining their loyalty. One of the best examples of his generosity can be seen in the work of Ibn Seddad. Author noted that when Sultan Baybars came to

Damascus for the first time, he granted money to his commanders beginning from five hundred to five thousand dinars and gave fur in every winter and precious goods to lower rank officers and in the beginning of every year he gave adorned swords and golden sashes, golden inlaid headgear, golden inlaid shawls and horses to each and every one of them. Moreover, the author noted that if Baybars came to learn about a debt of one of his commanders, he relieved him from the debt and paid the debts of Amir Sayfaddin Kalavun al- Elfi several times (Ibn Şeddad, 2000).

Every year before winter came Sultan Baybars had distributed winter clothes, horse and sword to amirs and soldiers. A soldier whose horse was lost was given a horse immediately. Fifty dinars were given to the soldier whose horse was dead and 40 dinars were given to soldier whose mule was dead (Ibn Şeddad, 2000; Şeşen, 2009).

Records of expenditures made from Sultan's private divan (from divan el-hassa) are also clear expressions of Baybars' generosity. Annually 170.000 dinars were spent for the salaries, for the servants at the palace and for the poor. Sultan gave food to 5000 people in Ramadan every day. He donated 600 people with clothes every year secretly. There were no limits to the number of people whom he gave clothes and bread openly (Şeşen, 2009).

Another virtue related to generosity and that must be present at a ruler is being contented. Author's "beg must be contented, greedy person cannot be satisfied with anything, entire worldly possessions would not be enough for a greedy one. Being greedy is a disease without cure and medicine and entire oracles of the world cannot cure it even if they come alltogether. Possessions cannot satisfy the greedy man" (Yusuf Has Hacib, beyit. 2000, 2001, 2002, 2003, 2004) points reflect Turkish understanding very well.

Sultan Baybars was a statesman who did not covet worldly possessions and who was not offended by sufficing with less. Arabs, Turkmens, Mongols running from Hulagu's rule took shelter under Sultan Baybars. In August 1264, news about a group of Tatars (Mongols) wanting to take shelter came from Damascus. Since Sultan were suspicious about the sincerity of some of these, he gathered his amirs and discussed the matter with them. Subsequently, Sultan's saying to his amirs "a horse is enough for me, all I gathered is for you, those who want can take the horse or camel they want. If the newcomers are sincere I will give the same things to them as well" (Şeşen, 2002, s. 175) was a sign of a ruler who was not interested in collecting possessions and who was contented.

Another virtue Turkish state understanding wants to see in a ruler is having good nature and being honest. A Western author summarises the reason behind Sultan Baybars' being a good ruler very well.

For him, Sultan Baybars rose up quickly and placed himself on the top of hierarchy since he did not have any moral misgivings and had his own personal skills (Maalouf, 2010).

İbn Haldun also argued someone with good nature had the right to rule others. For him "Good traits witness that person struggling to favour his subjects is accompanied by possessions. Persons having the sense of working in favour of their subjects, who dominated over many people and regions race with each other in terms of doing favour and favourable traits such as bravery, forgiveness, hospitality, care for desperate ones, being patient in the face of difficulties, respecting sharia, respecting elders, being modest to miserables, avoidance of cruelty, deceit, treachery" (Ibn Haldun, 2012, p.356).

Among the qualifications Turks regard as virtue and thereby wish to see in a ruler, there are qualifications such as being mild-tempered, modest, and merciful and forgiving (Yusuf Has Hacib, beyit. 2049, 2072, 2073, 2115, 2116, and 2121).

In his work, Farabi also mentioned the necessity "for an ideal ruler loving rightness and right people due to his nature and hate from lies and liars" (Fârâbî, 2012, s. 104-105). Almost every author noting the qualifications that had to be present at a head of state highlighted the same points.

Many examples recorded about Sultan Baybars showed that he was a merciful ruler. People of Egypt who suffered from the cruelty of Bahri Mamluks worried that same would be repeated during the reign of Sultan Baybars, but in short period of time Sultan Baybars proved their worries were in vain and showed he was a statesman worthy of his seat. He pardoned prisoners and released soldiers under custody when he came to throne and won their hearts (Ibn Tagrıberdi, 2013). He did not show negligence in hosting elders and youngsters of the Ayyubid Dynasty. He showed respect and assured protection to each and every member of the Ayyubids and protected their slaves and odalisques (Ibn Şeddad, 2000).

According to one rumour the number of people Abaga Khan killed amid Erzurum and Kayseri when he entered Anatolia had been somewhere between 200.000 – 500.000 due to Seljuqs' inclination toward the Sultan of Egypt Baybars. In Bayburt while captured Anatolian Turks were being taken, an old man asking for pardon wanted audience with the Khan and he told him "Your enemy (Baybars) entered your lands but did not touch your subjects. While you aim for the enemy you murdered, plundered and ruined their lands" (Turan, 2009, s. 488).

Fighting against Crusaders during his reign, after conquering Safed Castle, Sultan Baybars told his amirs "I apologise if I had been harsh on some of you. I only wanted to motivate you to this great victory. Now, let's mutually forgive each other's rights on ourselves" (Şeşen, 2009, s. 115) proving he was a virtuous ruler.

Once Sultan Baybars reached Kayseri he himself not only touched no one from the population and prevented his soldiers from plundering but also made soldiers pay for everything they bought. Sultan Baybars told "I did not come to this land to destruct. I came to save its Sultan from the Tatars (Ebu'l-Ferec, 1999, s. 599)".

Once gained the authority to rule, Sultan Baybars wrote letters for allegiance and sent them to regents and begs. But regent at Dimask Sencer el-Halebi showed attitudes contrary to this allegiance and declared himself as sultan. Sultan Baybars sent his army from Cairo to Dımask and won victory over Sencer. Alemeddin Sencer el-Halebî was caught and sent to Cairo and in Cairo he was pardoned by Sultan Baybars (Şeşen, 2009).

According to Yusuf Has Hacib among the important qualifications Turkish government understanding wants to see at a ruler are being patient and calm and eventually being cautious. He put forward this aspect with these words: "Beg must be very cautious and very vigilant, bond and lock of the country is made up of two elements, one is caution and the other is law. Beg who is cautious maintains his country, caution expands the beg's lands, negligence on the other hand shakes the foundation of the begdom openly" (Yusuf Has Hacib, beyit. 2014, 2015, 2016, 2021). Thus, being incautious in state affairs would bring the end of sovereignty and begdom.

Nizamülmülk also said haste was the style of weak but not the strong ones. For him "when ruler heard something or suspected of something he must be slow on this matter until he understood the truth, separate lie from truth" (Nizamülmülk, 1999, s. 93).

Gathering many traits in his personality, Sultan Baybars never tolerated negligence and never left caution aside in his dealings. Even in most daring acts he always acted with caution and calculated the consequences and never neglected taking the slightest measures. In state administration he kept all sorts of issues under tight control and he even kept men who gained his confidence most under control (Köprülü, 1961).

He set up a very powerful intelligence organisation against Ilkhanates whom he regarded as his most dangerous enemy. He continuously obtained intelligence about his enemies by sending off spies among Armenians and Franks in Anatolia under Hulagu's control (Şeşen, 2009).

To prevent abuse of these people on this duty Sultan Baybars set up a second spy organisation with the aim of controlling these. By this way he managed to keep all his subjects under control from senior level to a shepherd in the most distant area (Özbek, 1988).

He went on to trips by giving information only to his closest handful of men and no one knew where he was. He spread the news that he would be making long meetings in Cairo but in order not to get attention he went on to Palestine or Syria with a small group of people (Clot, 1996). Just like Harun Rashid did in Baghdad, Sultan Baybars also went on to streets of Cairo at nights under disguise and listened to the complaints of people.

According to Yusuf Has Hacib traits a good ruler must have were not limited to these. Along with these "good ruler must not consume alcohol and must not involve in sedition. Since as a result of these, prosperity vanishes. If worlds beg get addicted to the taste of wine, suffering of the country and its people from this would be severe. If the one mastering the world spent his time gambling he would ruin his country" (Yusuf Has Hacib, beyit. 2091, 2092, and 2093). This issue is also mentioned in the work of Farabi as: "ideal ruler having the qualifications of not running after eating, drinking and sexual pleasures and not having desire for these, avoiding from gambling, worldly items like silver, gold and other similar items have no value in his view" (Fârâbî, 2012, s. 105).

In his entire lifetime, Sultan Baybars never drunk wine and he got signature from those above the slaves stating that they would never let their slaves to drink alcohol of any sort (Ibn Şeddad, 2000). Although it had great contribution to state treasury, as a devoted Muslim Sultan Baybars prohibited the sale of alcoholic drinks (Özbek, 1988). Sultan Baybars were not fond of entertainments since he did not like to live in state of pleasure. Once during his campaign into Anatolia, Seljug dignitaries brought in musicians and dancers to entertain Sultan Baybars who came to Kayseri to claim the Seljuq throne. Sultan Baybars angered with this act told them "I am not here to be entertained. This is not a place for entertainment. Go and entertain someone else" and sent them off from his presence (Özbek, 1988, s. 132).

He was a ruler far from ambitions of entertainment and luxury, so that in his entire life let aside being entertained he did not feel the necessity for resting and in his spare time he dealt with hunting activities and cevghan game [a sort of polo] which were actually equestrian and swordsmanship exercises (Köprülü, 1961; Özbek, 1988).

Another qualification Yusuf Has Hacib sought at a ruler is beeing pious (Yusuf Has Hacib, 1985). Author's records on this matter are as follows: "Beg must be pious and clean, and he who is clean always ask for cleanliness. Pious one act always meticulously not to fall into mistake and begs acting meticoulously do the right things. If beg is not pious and clean he can never act cleanly and correctly (Yusuf Has Hacib, beyit. 1985-1987)".

Sultan Baybars was a devoted Muslim praying five times a day and fulfilling his duties even in battles. He even made his slaves and his servants fulfil their prayers and he appointed teachers to teach Quran and imams to conduct prayers and he also put observers to prevent them from doing anything inappropriate (Ibn Şeddad, 2000). Also, he was known as a sultan trying act in accordance with Islamic principles in his position as head of state or in his personal life.

Being fair

Other than these, one of the most important qualifications that must be present at a ruler is being fair and in relation to this enacting fair law to rule people with justice. According to Yusuf Has Hacib one of the primary duties of the ruler was to rule his people. In the work, ruler Kün- Toğdı told vizier Ay-Toldı that beg was obliged to deliver law with these words: "I cut the works just like cutting with a knife and I do not prolong the business of one seeking for his rights. Whether it may be my son, my close one or kin, whether it may be traveller, by-passer, whether it may be guest, all these are one for me before law and when I give my verdict none would see me differently" (Yusuf Has Hacib, beyit. 811, 817-818). "Main instrument for ruling over this begdom and people is law. Only aim in ruling people with law must be to be just. Bond and lock of a country are made of two elements, one of these is law (the other is being cautious). If beg ruled his country with law it meant he managed to arrange his country and enlightened its day. Cruelty is a burning fire; burn those who comes close, law are like water, if it flows blessing comes to help. The way to rule long goes from the right laws. With law country expands and world gets under order, with cruelty country diminishes and world is disrupted. If begs implement laws begdom prevails and stand for a long time" (Yusuf Has Hacib, beyit. 2017, 2032, 2033, 2034, 2036). "Beg obeying the laws is truly happiness (Yusuf Has Hacib, beyit. 3461)".

Fârâbî as well emphasised that: "Ideal ruler must love justice and just people in accordance with his nature, once he was invited to be just and implement justice he should not be reluctant and persistent in realisation of it" (Fârâbî, 2012, s. 105). Nizamülmülk, on the other hand told about justice aspect of the ruler with these words: "When Sultan is conscientious and just people's work is always peaceful" (Nizamülmülk, 1999, s. 33).

"Sultan must be fair and vigilant, search for the matters, investigate and question the justice and traditions of the past ones" (Nizamülmülk, 1999, s. 113).

Sultan Baybars gave great importance to things being done with justice participated at kadı [religious court] hearings and he gave particular attention to everyone old or young being treated equally before the court (Köprülü, 1961). During his time great commanders could not commit offenses to anyone insignificant or even to Jews or Christians. If any member from the Jewish or Christian communities, even the most insignificant one had a case against someone from the government, their reasoning was examined and justice was preserved. Every New Year's Day and Muslim religious days (Recep, Ramadan and Zilhacce) he asked for the records of prisoners and pardoned some of these (Ibn Şeddad, 2000). On this issue, there is a nice record by Aksarayi. Sultan Baybars "after Mongol army came to Kayseri sat on the throne (1277). He stayed here for 10 days with his army of countless men. In those days since roads were closed prices of wheat soared so that a 'mud'* of wheat could not be purchased for the price of 40 thousand dirhams. Since wheat was not available a 'men'** of dried raisins were purchased for 10 dirhams and used for the forage need of fourlegged animals. In that case Baybars ordered them not to open wheat storages, confiscate of any beasts, people's food or animal food" (Aksarayi, 2000, s. 88). There are many examples as such that made him a symbol of a responsible and fair statesman.

On 23rd day of month Zilhicce on Monday Sultan Baybars came to Darü'l-Adl at Taht el-Kala at Cairo to bring justice to those whose rights were violated and notes were written to claim rights for

*Unit of volume which shows differences from region to region. In general it is between 72,5 and 135 litres.
**Unit of weight equaling 833 grams.

Those whose rights were violated and these notes were read at the pulpits of mosques. In the streets these were announced loudly and in the presence of Sultan Baybars many cases were examined (Ibn Şeddad, 2000).

Once while army was on campaign he had three Mamluk soldiers' noses cut who damaged the cropped field of Muslims (Özbek, 1988). With this, Sultan Baybars tried to tell his subjects that even his soldiers' act of damage against the subjects he promised to protect was unforgivable.

At the same time, with the aim of inspection he went on hunting from time to time and talked to people discreetly and listened to their complaints. One day he went on hunting with this purpose. Garbiye province complained about governor Ibn el-Humam. They told he and his tax officer a Copt named Ibn Mahluf was tormenting people. Sultan examined the issue on this complaint. He executed Ibn Mahluf who was guilty and who also used bad words about the Prophet Muhammad and released the governor from his duties (Şeşen, 2009). He ordered the display of an officer named Ibn el- Buri who embezzled money. On November 4, 1263 he stayed at Cairo. He opened the year with hearings at Daru'l-Adl. Meanwhile, a person named Nasireddin bin Nasir claimed that a garden under his possession had been taken by the fief owners during the time of Aybek and he showed the document proving his ownership. Sultan ordered the garden to be given back to the complainant (Şeşen, 2009).

Just like many other powerful Turkish rulers, Sultan Baybars showed respect to sheiks. He accepted Sheik Hizir bin Ebi Bkr bin Musa el-Adevi el- Mihrani who was in Cairo as his sheik and took him to some campaigns with him and gave share from booties. But sheik and his followers began to be spoilt and they plundered Kıyame Church in Jerusalem and strangled its priest. In the end they began to insult sultan and his Mamluks. Therefore, Sultan examined the acts of these and once he understood the complaints were not baseless he prisoned sheikh Hizir and his followers (Şeşen, 2009).

In a quote from el-Makrizi (1364-1442) who was an Arab historian focusing on the history of Egypt, Sultan Baybars was shown as a fair ruler (Koçak, 1991).

These examples given for the justice of Sultan Baybars is a good reply to the statement of Montesquieu who noted: "In Turkey no one cares about the wealth, life and honour of the subjects. Disagreements are quickly settled. Pasha listens to complainants and then lay them down for falanga and concludes the case by beating them well". This statement telling about continuation of culture shows Sultan Baybars was a ruler shaped with his state and civilisation process.

Baybars as a commander

Turks continued their army-nation qualification throughout their entire history. For this reason, main characteristic of ancient Turkish institutions had been militaristic (Genç, 2002). As it is known for almost all Turks conduct of the army had been named as "beginning to sü" and word 'Sübaşı' meaning commander is related to this (Genç, 2002). Yusuf Has

Hacib takes into consideration two elements for the state; one is the position of vizier and the other is the position of army commander. "While vizier holds the pen commander carries sword" (Yusuf Has Hacib, beyit. 2418). We find the written expression of Ottoman's seyfiye [sword bearers] and kalemiye [pen holders] classes within Turks at Yusuf Has Hacib (Sarıca, 2008).

Ibn Haldun regarded sword and pen as two tools which would be used by the head of state to maintain his reign. According to him members of a dynasty needed sword more than a pen in the process of establishing and maintaining their reign (Ibn Haldun, 2012). As can be understood from here ruler is not only responsible for administrative issues but also responsible for military issues. Depending on the type of the military action he himself performs the function of army commander.

In Kutadgu Bilig, a profile of Turkish commander emerges from the answer of Öğdülmiş to ruler Kün-Toğdı's question to Öğdülmiş where he asked how the army commander should be. Without doubt, author's views on this reflected the dominant understanding of Turkish states.

According to Yusuf Has Hacib "commanding the army and defeating the enemy is a great task. Therefore, the person to be in this position must be distinguished and very agile, tough and experienced" (Yusuf Has Hacib, beyit. 2271, 2272, 2273).

Sultan Baybars was a great commander who organised a powerful and regular army not only for maintaining domestic order but also for protecting the borders and empire's defense (Köprülü, 1961). He was a typical example of a career soldier who determined his own faith with a sword in his hand (Clot, 1996). His heroic deeds became legendary folk tale subjects showing that he was a widely accepted and distinguished commander (Roux, 2000; Koçak, 1991).

Secondly, a good commander must be brave. "Must be brave and strong, the one who fears becomes sick and fells to bed at the sight of enemy (Yusuf Has Hacib, beyit. 2274, 2326). Any missing aspect of the commander would be reflected to ones under his command in an irreparable manner. Even if those under his command are coward, a brave and daring commander would affect them in a better way. Hesitation, cowardice of the commander would result in irreversable outcomes in the field of battle.

There were many instances that proved the courage of Sultan Baybars who at the same time was an extraordinary warrior. The Castle of Kaysariyye had been strengthened by iron columns by St. Louis. This place was famous as the Castle Blue. It was strong and was surrounded by sea. Iron columns prevented opening of mines. There was no option but to conquer it by assault. Sultan participated in person to the assault and threw an arrow over the cathedral. Controlling the assault from top of the cathedral he helped pulling of war machines and checked the breaches that were opened. One day, he fought in person with a shield in his hand. When he returned there were arrows on his shield (Şeşen, 2009). During the siege of Safed, he fought on the first line of battle as well and Sultan's shield had been pierced with many arrows (Özbek, 1988). Once a part of the enemy castle was breached and a hole was opened without fear and without losing any time he personally entered through the hole and achieved a development. He did not refrain from risking his life many times to encourage those under his command. Once, Mamluk army had to cross the Euphrates River urgently when the news of Mongols attacking over Bire had reached. Sultan Baybars first ordered the construction of bridge to cross Euphrates but when he realised this would take time and result in missing the Mongols, he ordered soldiers to cross Euphrates by swimming. He was first to do so with Amir Sayfaddin Kalavun on his side. After seeing their Sultan crossing the Euphrates by swimming, Mamluk soldiers were encouraged and they all crossed to the other side quickly and they defeated the Mongols (Özbek, 1988).

After the conquest of Hısn el-Ekrad it was the time for conquering Castle Akkar which was located on a steep mountain top. Many emperors could not do anything to this castle. Once Sultan reached in front of Akkar (1271) he ordered for roads to be made for the wagons to pass. He ordered transfer of mangonels with wagons near the castle. Once the attack began Franks asked for mercy. Sultan sent a letter to the Count of Tripoli Bohemond V in which he noted: "After Hısn el-Ekrad we laid siege to Castle Akkar. We carried mangonels to mountains where birds were barely making nests. We had great deal of difficulty, bear the rains, while moving these mangonels. We moved these mangonels to so steep locations where even the ants slipped. Our letter gladly informs you that call to prayer had replaced the sound of bells. We released your men who managed to survive...We sent them to carry the news to you and to warn the people of Tripoli to see what is waiting them..." (Şeşen, 2009, s. 132).

In another source Sultan Baybars was mentioned as: "The most important qualifications of Baybars were courage, fighting in the front line at battles and making good plans with his genius" (Koçak, 1991, s. 1104).

Another qualification to be found at a good commander is being generous. "To gather the most distinguished people around him, the head of the army must be very generous. He must distribute all his possessions to the soldiers. A horse, clothes and weapons are enough for him. He must not accumulate items for his children or wife or must not pile silver thinking to acquire garden and land. He must feed and donate his men at arms and allocate many horses, slaves and odalisques to them. To be successful in his undertaking and go on the right direction he must be generous and give gifts" (Yusuf Has Hacib, beyit. 2274, 2275, 2276, 2277, 2278, 2280, 2325).

In his work author recommended that generosity must be observed both in the ruler and the army commander. Since donating gifts by both of those to those in their company would help in increasing belief to themselves. Feeding, donating and making better off the ones around is an essential aspect of Turkish understanding of ruling and therefore sticking to the "hit, take, distribute" philosophy by the rulers and Sübasıs is a main qualification sought for in them (Genç, 2002).

Sultan Baybars who was generous by nature did not like to accumulate possessions and feed ambition for worldly goods just like Sultan Salahaddin Ayyubi. Sultan Baybars was a statesman who distributed the gains to the ones around him without hesitation. As a ruler, he knew too well the necessity to keep his soldiers well off and satisfied as he continuously expected activity and sacrifice from them and he distributed all booties without claiming anything for himself, giving more to those contributions were important. He showed great effort to keep families of fallen soldiers from poverty (Köprülü, 1961).

In addition to these, a good ruler must be modest as well. This way he would be successful in making his people love himself. "A modest person can warm the hearts of people toward himself, person with bad language and temper will alienate people from himself. If the commander of the army is haughty he will be beaten by the enemy. Haughty man neglects and a man who neglects will be harmed or die before his time" (Yusuf Has Hacib, beyit. 2274, 2294, 2295, 2296, 2297). This missing aspect of a commander who is haughty by nature will take him to a disaster. Commander considering him superior will not consult to the views and experiences of those in his command. With this flaw he drifts himself and those around him to the edge of a cliff.

Sultan Baybars having significant qualifications both as a ruler and a commander did not become haughty even after his unique successes and he maintained his modesty in every situation. With these qualifications he maintained his place in the memories and became a subject for folk tales.

After the conquest of Safed, Sultan Baybars ordered the repair and strengthening of walls and by carrying stone personally he motivated the workers and he played a great role in finishing the construction in a very short period of time (Özbek, 1998).

While stones were being hurled from enemy castles he pulled the ropes of mangonels located around this castle and he selected and placed stones to be used by these (Ibn Şeddad, 2000).

As can be seen in these examples Sultan Baybars never differentiated himself from those under his command neither as a ruler nor as a commander and he proved his sincerity by mixing with them. Both in Turkish states before Islam and in the Turkish- Islamic states it was necessary for the ruler to have these qualifications to be accepted by the people. A ruler performing on the contrary will be refrained from the "kut" blessed by the God and as a result of this his rule would be ended.

"Commander of the army must know politics as army affairs were tied to politics. If politics was implemented army would not remain headless. Greatness and politics against evil and always respect is needed for the good ones" (Yusuf Has Hacib, beyit. 2300, 2301, 2303).

Sultan Baybars was statesman who had short temper against mistakes being done and against the enemies. His psychology could be better understood when the conditions he was in is examined. There were Mongols, Crusaders, Armenians and Ismailis waiting at ambush versus Sultan Baybars who stood against these. His responsibilities were heavy and the chances of being unsuccessful were unbearable for him. In the shortest time the country must be saved from bottleneck via diplomacy and through war. Throughout his reign he fought through this end and he fell on his enemies like a nightmare.

Most of the time, he was tough against his enemies. When he entered Damascus he avenged upon Christians who collaborated with Mongols and did cruelties. In return for destructed mosques and buildings he destructed their churches and houses; plundered possessions of Jews. As a punishment he imposed 150.000 dirham tax on Damascus Christians (Turan, 2004).

Upon becoming superior over Mongols and Crusaders, Sultan Baybars mobilised his army and conquered cities of Kaysariyye, Yafa, Asruf, Safed, and Resule. He sent an army under command of Kalavun over Cilician Armenians who collaborated with Mongols and defeated Armenians and their allies (Sevim ve Merçil, 1995).

As can be seen in these examples Sultan Baybars did not forgive treachery of his enemies and keep himself away from punishing them.

"Many Frank (European) and Tatar envoys waited for mercy and forgiveness at his door. His way going to their country had been flat entirely due to stepping on. However, their way coming to his country had not been stepped on at all (Koçak, 1991, s. 1109)".

Sultan Baybars had been a patient and a determined commander at the same time. It was not possible for him to return from his decisions. He took Egypt from el-Melik Mansur who then had one-thousand strong cavalry with a force of 600 cavalry and only this is enough to prove his gallantry and patience and strength in battle (Ibn Şeddad, 2000).

Although he had difficulty in the assault on Mongols in winter of 1264 he did not refrain from not helping with his army. In the army which was mobilised without prior preparations discontent emerged and many of the animals were lost. When Sultan Baybars saw actions contrary to his orders he said "I am not having animals for transport, my only thinking is the defence of Islam". Moving hastily thinking he could not be at Bire on time, despite falling twice from his horse and getting injuries, Sultan Baybars sustained the campaign without any interruptions (Özbek, 1988).

Again, in the year 1268 he did not change his decision he gave about the peace offer of Ilkhanate ruler Abaka. In this peace offer Abaka complimented him but at the same time threatened Sultan Baybars reminding him that he was a Mamluk sent to Sivas (Ibn Tagrıberdi, 2013; Kopraman, 1987). Not being shaken in this war of nerves, Sultan Baybars told the envoy that he was not in favour of peace and would fight against Ilkhanates to the end (Kopraman, 1987).

Yusuf Has Hacib noted "a commander campaigning against the enemy with his army must be trickster as a fox. The commander must know the ways of deceit and cunning" (Yusuf Has Hacib, beyit. 2312, 2327).

Having a sharp intelligence in diplomacy as well as in the battlefields, Sultan Baybars always managed to reach a solution to save him even under very desperate conditions. He was a genius strategist and a cunning administrator. He was quite successful in getting to an advantageous position from a disadvantageous position. One of the measures Sultan Baybars took against potential Mongol assault was to establish friendship and alliance with the ruler of Golden Horde Berke. Through this alliance he provoked Berke against Hulagu and fanned the animosity between two Mongolian dynasties turning into an open war. This way he kept Hulagu away from Egypt and Syria and prevented him from attacking Mamluk lands with a powerful army. Fighting between Hulagu and Berke over Azerbaijan served Sultan Baybars more than anyone else. Using this war to his benefit he had opportunity to prepare his army and strengthen his castles (Özbek, 1988).

Other than these "a good commander must be cautious and vigilant. He must keep himself more cautious than a magpie. Whoever acts more cautious in battle would be successful. Whoever acts cautious and vigilant in battle would bring disaster to the enemy" (Yusuf Has Hacib, beyit. 2313, 2353, 2358).

On the field of battle Sultan Baybars never acted arbitrarily and never left prudence aside. He thought the next step meticulously and reach a conclusion with precise calculations. Although he achieved victory over his greatest enemy Mongols at Ayn-ı Calut, Mongols were always on the ambush. His second most dangerous enemy was Franks who invaded the coastline of Syria during the Crusades. For this reason, Sultan Baybars acted with great caution and with his fine policy he refrained from getting into war with these two adversaries as long as possible (Özbek, 1988).

Sultan Baybars drew their attention to other side by prolonging the peace talks with them and he attacked in year of 1265 before launching a full-scale attack on the Crusaders (Kopraman, 1987).

He also gave importance to equip his army with the best weapons and to prepare his soldiers with constant trainings. Best siege and war machines of the time had been built in the workshops of the Sultan and training of the special soldiers who would use them was the main preoccupation of Sultan Baybars (Köprülü, 1961).

While stating qualifications to be found in a commander Yusuf Has Hacib made some striking analogies:

"When fighting his heart must be like the heart of a lion in battle and his wrist must be like the claw of a tiger.

He must be as stubborn as a boar, as strong as a wolf, as fierce as a bear and as vengeful as a buffalo.

At the same time, he must be as tricky as a red fox; must have vengeance like a male camel.

He must keep himself more cautious than a magpie and turn his eyes ahead like a rock raven.

Like a lion, must keep his rule high and must be without sleep at night like an owl." (Yusuf Has Hacib, beyit. 2310, 2311, 3212, 2313, 2314).

To conclude, during his reign Sultan Baybars defended his state which was in dire situation against internal and external enemies with great effort with his successful policy and his spirit for struggle. He participated in the majority of the battles made during his reign and he commanded his army personally. With his determination stronger than steel and importance he gave to military affairs he achieved many successes. He gave maximum effort for the development of military activities and he did not forgive any mistakes on this matter.

Conclusion

As a classic of history of Turkish thought and politics, Kutadgu Bilig is one of the deepest and greatest masterpieces created by human intelligence. The invisible hand outreaching from past to present and its meticulous embroidering the mind are signs of its being a significant work. In the work, Kutadgu Bilig's living theory had been presented by practices in the examples of Egypt-Syria.

With this work, Yusuf Has Hacib carefully completed the unfinished work of Prometus. Author presents us the burning source of knowledge, the Kutadgu Bilig. The work is connected to an ongoing process between past and present tied with an invisible bond. What make it live are the author's thoughts and faith that create storms. Our work made us understand that his writings were not illustrating imaginary situations but showing actual ones.

This work is the memory; thus, it is the Turkish nation by own. This book, touching upon the gaps, darkness and tunnels of human envisions, was built on wisdom and justice. With this form, the work does not only provide answers to the problems of the period it was written in but also offers help for today's problems and questions generously with its various aspects.

Kutadgu Bilig contains the values on which Turkish state understanding was built upon. The author helped us greatly in forming a profile of a Turkish ruler and a commander which is the main topic of this work with the statements he made on the qualifications of a ruler and a commander. Reality of a historical statesman and commander typology has been achieved in the personality of Sultan Baybars.

In ancient Turkish states, as well as in Turkish-Islamic states the ruler had responsibilities coming from the position of being the leader of the state organisation. To fulfil these very heavy responsibilities, he needed to have some high qualifications. As it can be seen in Kutadgu Bilig main qualifications were the traits like intelligence and wisdom, courage, virtuousness and being just. Ruler in particular and all other state dignitaries must be distinct with such moral traits.

From these, wisdom plays an important role both in social and political morality as well as in personal morality. Only ruler and commanders having this qualification have the ability to turn knowledge into action blended with intelligence. Through this they keep away from indecent actions and reach happiness.

Courage is one of the most important qualifications desired to be present in a ruler and a commander. They can break the courage of those violating the rights of people only if they have this qualification. The courage of a ruler and commander is like the ink of the pen determining the destiny of a country and nation. If the ink of the pen goes dry, the security of the state will be in great danger. This analysis at the Mamluk State reveals this aspect of rulers clearly.

Virtue is a concept getting its source from the mind and is fed on mind. Reaching a higher life form is only possible for human beings by being virtuous. Even in times when personal interests run in the forefront rulers and commanders are obliged to be virtuous and maintain it with their lives. Hence, with this virtue they attract masses and maintain their trust.

Being just in a chaotic world is more important than anything else for a ruler and a commander. Therefore, according to Turkish understanding of government justice had always been a treasure being sought and a target to be reached. In places where there is justice it emits light to thousand leagues away like the sun. When there is cruelty it will take everywhere under darkness within thousand leagues.

The examination made about the ruler and commander in Egypt-Syria had been realised beyond the abstract romanticism and presented the state philosophy of Mamluk State as appeared in Kutadgu Bilig in the personality of Sultan Baybars. This study presented that Turkish state and statesman typology was not a utopia but a reality that can be achieved on different basis.

With its power it derived from idea, history is a laboratuary of movements of idea. Within the scope of Kutadgu Bilig, the typology of a ruler and commander for Turkish state philosophy and thought has been presented in a reasonable way with this study.

Sultan Baybars is a historical personality opening a door to immortality where his ruler and commander qualifications found deep meaning as laid out in the work of Yusuf Has Hacib which first developed in his mind and continued with his writings. These leaders knew fully that they had responsibilities to people around themselves and with this sensitivity they demonstrated to the public that they were the servants of these superior morals and reality by living accordingly. It was obvious that their actions and attitudes were fed by moral values, faith, and consciousness during the years they were reigning. Sultan Baybars quickly realised the targeted outcomes could be achieved through these qualifications and he acted in accordance with those. If this leader lacked these qualifications or showed negligence on these qualifications without doubt there will be outcomes contrary to expectations and he would be deemed to be forgotten.

It was understood that Turkish history and culture was a living and a period-based reality with the examination of a ruler and commander typology from XI to XII centuries. It was also understood that Turkish history is a history of culture and civilisation with the help of the information provided by Kutadgu Bilig. Sultan Baybars presented a model of ruler and commander as a sample of this living nature and thought which went into action. With this aspect, while research proved the reasonability of examining Turkish history according to field classification, it is understood that Kutadgu Bilig is a theory of a living culture as well.

References

Arslan, M. (1986). Kutadgu-Bilig'deki Ahlak ve Siyaset Felsefesi. İstanbul Üniversitesi İktisat Fakültesi Metodolojisi ve Sosyoloji Araştırmaları Merkezi, No:21, İstanbul.

Brockelmann, C. (1992). İslam Ulusları Ve Devletleri Tarihi. (Translated by Neşet Çağatay), Ankara: Turkish History Institution.

Clot, A. (1996). Kölelerin İmparatorluğu Memluklerin Mısır'ı (1250-1517). (Translated by Turhan Ilgaz), Ankara: Epsilon Publishing.

Demirkent, I. (1997). Haçlı Seferleri. İstanbul: Dünya Publishing.

Ebu'l Ferec (1999). Ebu'l Ferec Tarihi. (Translated by Ömer Riza Doğrul), Ankara: Turkish History Institution.

Fârâbî (2012). El-Medinetü'l-Fazıla. (Translated by Ahmet Arslan), İstanbul: Divan Publishing.

Genç, R. (2002). Karahanlı Devlet Teşkilatı, Ankara: Turkish History Institution.

Ibn Haldun (2012). Mukaddime. (Prepared by Süleyman Uludağ), (Vol. II,). İstanbul: Dergâh Publishing.

Ibn Şeddad (2000). Baypars Tarihi. (Translated by M. Şerefüddün Yaltkaya), Ankara: Turkish History Institution.

Ibn Tagriberdi (2013). En-Nücumu'z-Zahire (Parlayan Yıldızlar). (Translated by Ahsen Batur), İstanbul: Slenge Publishing.

Aksarayi, K. (2000). Müsameretü'l-Ahbar. (Translated by Mürsel Öztürk), Ankara: Turkish History Institution.

Koçak, İ. (1991). Arap Kaynaklarında Türk Memluk Sultanı Baybars. X. Türk Tarih Kongresi, (Vol. III,). Ankara.

Kopraman, K.Y. (1987). Mısır Memlûkleri. Doğuştan Günümüze Büyük İslam Ansiklopedisi, (Vol. VI,). İstanbul: Çağ Publishing.

Köprülü, M. F. (1961). Baybars I, İslam Ansiklopedisi. (Vol. II,). İstanbul: Milli Eğitim Bakanlığı Publishing.

Maalouf, A. (2010). Arapların Gözünden Haçlı Seferleri. (Translated by Ali Berktay), İstanbul: Yapı Kredi Publishing.

Nizamülmülk (1999). Siyasetname. (Prepared by Mehmet Altay Köymen), Ankara: Turkish History Institution.

Özbek, S. (1988). el- Melikü'z- Zahir Rükne'd- Din Baybars el-Bundukdari (? -1277) Hayatı ve Faaliyetleri, (Unpublished Postgraduate Dissertation), Ankara University Social Sciences Institute.

Platon. (2009). Devlet. (Translated by Sabahattin Eyüboğlu-M. Ali Cimcoz), İstanbul: İş Bankası Kültür Publishing.

Roux, J. P. (2000). Türklerin Tarihi. (Translated by Aykut Kazancıgil-Lale Arslan Özcan), İstanbul: Kabalcı Publishing.

Runciman, S. (2008). Haçlı Seferleri Tarihi. (Translated by Fikret Işıltan), (Vol.III,). Ankara: Turkish History Institution.

Sarıca, B. (2008). Kutadgu-Bilig'deki Komutan ve Ordunun Nitelikleri, Atatürk Üniversitesi Türkiyat Araştırmaları Enstitüsü Dergisi, No.37, Erzurum.

Sevim, A. & Merçil, E. (1995). Selçuklu Devletleri Tarihi, Ankara: Turkish History Institution.

Şeşen, R. (2009). Sultan Baybars ve Devri (1260-1277), İstanbul: İsar Foundation.

Turan. O. (2004). Doğu Anadolu Türk Devletleri Tarihi, İstanbul: Ötüken Publishing.

Turan, O. (2009). Selçuklular Tarihi ve Türk-İslam Medeniyeti, İstanbul: Ötüken Publishing.

Has Hacib, Y. (1974). Kutadgu Bilig, (translated by Reşit Rahmeti Arat), Ankara: Turkish History Institution.

HISTORY EDUCATION/HISTORICAL CONSCIOUSNESS AND DYSTOPIA

SEFA YILDIRIM

Introduction

"One of the most classical 'messages' given by the dystopic fiction is that access to past records is vitally important for the mental health of the society. Heroes that live in the nightmarish world of mythical thought with such a mental illness that cannot distinguish between now and then, cause and effect, lie and truth, give in to living by hanging on to the real records of the past that the totalitarian regime tries to damage or deny completely" (Gottlieb, 2012: p.31).

To have an idea about history education/historical awareness and dystopia, first we need to take a look at dystopia, utopia and some of the important works on dystopia. In addition, handling the concept of general history based on philosophy and education would provide important advantages regarding the explanation of historical consciousness.

Dystopia

Although many terms that correspond to the term dystopia *(such as nasty utopia, inverse utopia, anti-utopia, and negative utopia)* had been invented by literary, scientific and arts circles, we observe that mostly, the word dystopia is preferred.

In general, the word dystopia, which is regarded as the synonym of the word cacotopia, was first invented by John Stuart Mill, with the negator prefix *"dus" – " "* (dys) from ancient Greek. The word, which is used for "negative place", "bad place" and "abnormal" in a parliamentary speech on 12 March 1868, is mostly used to describe "societies with poor living conditions", "negative society", "pressure", and "violence", totalitarian and tyrannic systems by many scientific and arts circles today (Booker, 1994: p.22; Claeys, 2010: p.107; Celgin, 2011: p.182-343; Mill, 1868: p.349;

Mill, 1909: p.168; Mill, 1958: p.xxvii, 249; Millward, 2006: p.7; Silverman, 1997: p.326; Vieira, 2010: p.16; Yildirim, 2017, p.129- 150).

Nowadays, dystopic works are subjected to various classifications based on time, concept, content and region (Somay, 2010: pp. 53-70). Considering the philosophical, literary, political, socio-political, socio-cultural, psychological and socio-psychological analyses and arguments from the experts on the subject, it can be seen that there are significant differences between the dystopic works written in the Western's, Eastern's and Central European's Cultures. The major reason behind these differences is, of course, the intellectual changes that emerge with the political, economic and social development at the time. This situation is explained in the following way by Gottlieb *"The works considered as classical dystopic fiction by the Western readers are based on the observation that the authors fear that their societies will become a totalitarian dictatorship in the future. In contrast, dystopic works from Eastern and Central Europe give us the nightmarish world of Zamyatin's totalitarian dictatorship as a real reflection of "the worst of all possible worlds" experienced as a historical fact rather than a vision in the future made up of imaginary scenes"* (Gottlieb, 2012: p.25).

In addition, some literati, historians, authors and artists who analysed the dystopic works in terms of philosophy, literature and religion claim that there are reciprocations between the medieval literature and art which frequently deal with subjects such as *the Divine Comedy/Divina Commedia of Dante*, anthropotheism, God-like humans, devil, messiah, and medieval inquisition. Moreover, as a result of the political, economic and technological developments within the last century, we observe that there are some important kinetic and evolutionary changes in the dystopic works. For instance, while the speculative-futuristic dystopia was initially frequently used in the western and eastern literature, we see that it was interrupted for a long time since it was prohibited in the Stalin-era Eastern Europe. However, some experts argue that, at the time, eastern literati had focused on the mistakes of the day and the past and thus produced works far from fantasy. This is probably why some of the important emotional elements in dystopic fiction such as female figure, feminism, love, romanticism, and sexuality are frequently found in the western literature whereas these are found after the late 20th century (1970s) and only partially in the works written in Eastern and Central Europe. In this context, we can say that the Eastern dystopia is generally fictionalized based on political discourse and male hegemony is dominant as the main character (Gottlieb, 2012: p.25-34).

From a descriptive and fictional point of view, although there is a great correlation between dystopic works and science-fiction works, they are separate since the dystopic works mainly deal with social and political developments and criticisms (Booker, 2012: p.35-46). However, with advances in trade, industry, technology and the emergence of space age or age of knowledge with today's nomenclature, increase in different points of view and diversity are observed in dystopic works (Gottlieb, 2001: p.95-112; Somay, 2010: p.91-142).

In this context, to list a few of the dystopic works that are still under the spotlight for many experts, authors and readers today; "H. G. Wells ' *The Time Machine (1895)* and *When the Sleeper Awakes* (1899) , Jack London's *The Iron Heel* (1908), Yevgeny Zamiatin's *"We"* (1924), Franz Kafka's *Der Proceß* (1925), Aldous Huxley's *Brave New World* (1932), George Orwell's *Nineteen Eighty-Four (1984)* (1949*)*, Anthony Burgess's *A Clockwork Orange* (1962), Doris Lessing's *The Memoirs of a Survivor* (1974), Alan Moore & David Lloyd's *V For Vendetta (1982/1983)*, Margaret Atwood's *The Handmaid's Tale* (1985)*,* Ray Bradbury's *Fahrenheit 451* (1951, 1953), Lois Lowry's *The Giver* (1993), Kazuo Ishiguro's *Never Let Me Go* (20 05) and David Mitchell's *The Bone Clocks* (2014) (Atwood, 2017; Booker, 1994: p.16; Booker, 2012: p.35-46; Bradbury, 2013; Burgess, 2017; Gottlieb, 2012: p.25-34; Ishiguro, 2017; Kafka, 2016; Lessing, 2017; London, 2016; Lowry, 2014; Mitchell, 2016; Moore & Lloyd, 2005; Orwell, 2014; Somay, 2010: p.91-142; Wells, 2013; Wells, 2016; Zamyatin, 2016).

Nowadays there exists a strong correlation between public opinion on the discrepancies between utopia and dystopia and the prevalence of these concepts in science, art, and literature. Meanwhile, to briefly introduce the subject of Utopia, we can say that the word utopia which came to the fore with the novel *"Utopia"* written by Thomas More in 1516, is believed to be derived from the Greek " ov " ov (no) and $τόπος$ (place) "ou-topos", which means "no place". Utopia is the homophone of Eutopia (*eutopos*), which is again a Greek word derived from $ευ$ "good or well", $τόπος$ (place) = "good place". Another view on the word Utopia is that it derives from "eugenics" (Atwood, 2012: p.47-51). In short, when we consider the word Utopia from a semantic and conceptual point of view, we can imagine it as a perfect, happy society which solved all its problems and exists in a perfect geographical location. In line with these explanations, considering Utopia spatially and in terms of the quality of life, we can see it as some kind of perception of heaven which mankind wants to build on earth; whereas dystopia is a kind of fear or envisioning of hell (Atwood, 2012: p.47; Babaee et al., 2015: p.64-76; Bentham, 1818: p.5-73; Gotllieb 2012:

p. 25-34; Kumar, 2005: p.17-31; Kumar, 2010: p.554; More, 2013; Somay, 2010: p.33-52).

An Overview of the Concept of History

According to Powicke (1955),

> *"The craving for an interpretation of history is so deep-methods that, unless clearly stated otherwise we have a constructive outlook over the past, we are drawn either to mysticism or to cynicism"* (as cited in Carr, 2008: p.123)

The word History which is *histori- historia in Latin, meaning* "history, inquiry, investigation; story", is derived from the Greek word ἱστορία *"istoria"*, meaning *"*investigation, examination, story, discovery, knowledge". In addition, it is found that Ionians have used the word in question as to acquire knowledge by receiving information or to report, whereas in Attica dialect it is used as to learn by witnessing and more generally as natural history. Its use in today's Western languages is: *history in English, historie in German and histoire in French.* Also, it should be kept in mind that another word for history in German *is Geschichte.* The word *Geschichte* is different from the word story in English as it also carries the meaning *"done, past, and happening"* (Celgin, 2011: p.335; Demirel, 2009: p.1; Howatson, 2013: p.387-402; Iplikcioglu, 1994: p.11-13; Kabaağaç & Alova, 1995: p.270; Lewis, 1918: p.367; Ortayli, 2003: p. 1-22; Ozlem, 2004: p.21; Steuerwald, 1995: p.252, 297; Tekeli, 2014: p.22; Yildirim, 2017).

The first thing that comes to our minds when we talk about *History* is Herodotus, who is called the *"Father of History"* by Cicero. He called his work *histories apodeksis* (Howatson, 2013: p.387-937) or *istorias apodeisis* (Özlem, 2004: p.21; Arendt, 2014: p.69; Warrington, 2014: p.282), which *is "the exposition of the things witnessed and heard of"* or *"presenting the investigation".* Herodotus did not limit the meaning of the word *Istoria* to the natural history and used it for the first time as the information obtained through the record *of human* experiences. Another important *historia*n after Herodotus, Thucydides, expanded the meaning of the word Istoria to connotate interpreting, investigating, evaluating and addressing the social events, in addition to the connotations of recorded and told experiences.

Until the mid-18t*h century*, the word Istoria had double meaning. Moreover, we observe that the concept of Historiosophy is included in the terminology of Social Sciences for the first time by another great philosopher of the same period, François Marie Arouet de Voltaire (Bicak 2004c: p.21-122; Collingwood, 2010: p.35; Ozlem, 2004: p.61).

It is seen that different opinions on the development of Historiosophy and on the concept and contents of History have been stated by many historians and intellectuals such as Giambattista Vico, Oswald Spengler, J.G. Herder, G.W.F. Hegel, Wilhelm Dilthey, E.H. Carr, R.G. Collingwood, Fernand Braudel, March Bloch, Leopold Von Ranke, Arnold J. Toynbee, W.H. Walsh, Hayden White, Eric Hobsbawm, Lucien Febvre, Benedetto Croce, Natalie Zemon Davis, Thomas Babington Macaulay, Thomas Samuel Kuhn, Friedrich Nietzsche, Friedrick Jackson Turner, Edward Gibbon, Carl Gustav Hempel, Immanuel Kant and Michel Foucault (Freund, 1997: p.15-49; Warrington, 2014: p.5-7).

For instance, according to Walsh, "*History begins to deal with the past starting from the first moment mankind appears. History's main occupation is human experience and activities.*" (Walsh, 2006: p.34), or according to Collingwood, "*So, the value of history is to teach us what man is doing, thus, what man is.*" (Collingwood, 2010: p.46). Again, according to Vico, another important philosopher of time, "*With the axiom 'sciences should begin where their actual subjects begin' (314), it begins from the time when humans started to think in a humanistic way (338); not when the philosophers begin to think about humanistic ideas*" (Vico, 2007: p.140). Bıçak briefly summarizes Vico's idea of history as follows: "*According to Vico, history is a kind of knowledge in which the questions about ideas and questions about events are not separated from each other*" (Bıçak 2004c: p.118). Finally, the bond Ibn Khaldun establishes between the notion of past and future is "*The past resembles the future more than one drop of water resembles another.*" (Ibn Khaldun, 2015 V.I: p.62).

As we have tried to address above, the answer to the question of "What is History?", which is comprehensive and hard to explain philosophically, can be generally summarized as the investigation of the events that happened in the past in light of documents and remains in the context of place and time. It is the past of mankind. It is the memory of mankind. It is the scientific, technologic, economic, socio-cultural, socio-psychological, sociological, psychological, traditional, religious and notable activities of mankind in the past (Southgate, 2012: p.41-53; Toynbee, 1956: p.1-50).

History as a science is the attempt or art of exploring the past with a moral objective in light of the knowledge attained as a result of thousands of years of intellectual and cultural evolution of mankind. The task of the historian is to perform this divine task or art fastidiously with a systemic plan.

The Importance of Historical Consciousness
and History Education

"Our Human consciousness, after its self-generating- or reality's generating- articulative act, goes on to dissect reality further into the conscious and the subconscious, soul and body, mind and matter, life and environment, freedom and necessity, creator and creatures, god and devil, good and bad, right and wrong, love and power, old and new, cause and effect. Such binary structures are indispensable categories of thought; they are our means of apprehending reality, as far as this is within our power. At the same time, they are so many boundary-marks indicating the limits of human understanding since they misrepresent reality by breaking up its unity in our apprehension of it. They are as baffling as they are enlightening. We cannot do without them yet cannot do with them either. We cannot afford either to discount them completely or to take them at their full face-value (Toynbee, 1988: p.485)".

Many theologians and historians accept that, throughout the process of thousands of years of evolution from the beginning of mankind until today, mankind has historical consciousness since the period of myth-based culture. On this subject, we should immediately mention the sayings such as *"Myth is a sacred history, that is, it tells a primal event that occurred ab initio, at the beginning of Time."* (Eliade, 1991: p. 74) or *"the progress of mankind since its inception is so obvious and clear that every attempt to discuss them will eventually arrive at a rhetorical work."* And *"the diversity of cultures is behind us, around us, in front of us. The only thing we can demand on this subject is that this diversity occurs in a way that each kind will most generously contribute to the other."* By Claude Lévi-Straus (Lévi-Strauss, 2010: p.35-63). We begin to realize that the historical consciousness that began with the ability of mankind to speak, has taken a great leap with the discovery of writing which has great importance in terms of human history, albeit with a delay of thousands of years (Poe, 2015: p.51-101).

To summarize this period briefly; with the development of art and writing that started with cave engravings which give the impression of childlike drawings today *(such as the incomparable works at Lascaux, Niaux, Trois Fréres, Les Eyzies "Dordogne", Peche Merle, Castillo and Altamira)*, and petroglyph, pictography, hieroglyph, hieratic, demotic, graffiti, ideography *(ideogram)*, acrophone, phonetism, cuneiform, and finally with the use of the Phoenician alphabet, which is the basis of many of today's writing systems, human beings have made great economic, political and socio-cultural progress (Bauer, 2013: p.66: 348; Gombrich,

2015: p.76-92; Hauser, 2005: p.XXII-XXVI: 5-10; Jean, 2006: p.11-57; Lewin, 2008: p.176-207; Turani, 2007: p.23-37; Yildiz, 2014: p.1-40).

In light of this, it would probably not be inappropriate to say that literary texts (especially novels, stories, tales and poems) have played a big role in the development of our humanistic consciousness. In this context, we can claim that, with the writing revolution started by Sumerians approximately five thousand years ago, humanity in a way has reached to the level of becoming civilized as the inevitable ending to its background of thousands of years (Akman, 2016; Akman, 2017; Bergsträsser, 2006: p.22-27; Bicak 2004c, p.135; Childe, 2007: p.147: Collingwood, 2010: p.51; Corballis, 2003: p.96: 214-231; Friedrich, 2000: p.46-63; Karabag, 2014; Kramer, 2002: p.13-61; Kula, 2012: p.256-263; Payzin, 1992: p.1-10; Renfrew & Bahn, 2013: p.62-65: 149: 234-264; Schiller, 1943: p.48: 66: 77: 81: 125: 134: 153: 167).

It is an undeniable fact that historical consciousness plays an important role in the thousand-year struggle for human existence in a positive way. It is known that many historical concepts such as theological, positivist, Marxist, nationalist and romantic concepts shape the history education of the societies depending on the political and economic conjuncture. In addition, when looking at the history of education studies of the modern societies in general, it can be easily seen that the main objective is to raise virtuous citizens who love their country, are respectful of the past, honest, conscious and equipped with general moral codes. In light of this view, we can hypothesize that historical consciousness and history of education can provide the individual and society with the ability to touch and feel the past without any prejudice and the ability to focus on the past with a democratic approach. In this context, it would not be inappropriate to state that historical consciousness and history education are closely related to the socialization of the society and individual (Atkinson, 1978; Bicak, 2004a; Bicak, 2004b, Bicak, 2004c; Bloch, 2015; Thorp, 2014; Touraine 2004: p.43: 200-22; Yildirim, 2017). This phenomenon can be briefly explained by the definition of historical consciousness provided by Tekeli:

"Historical consciousness is the awareness of the change setup that gives meaning to the past, perceives today, and moves forward with the expectations from the future" mentions the relationship between the past, today and the future, how this relationship will be established is not described. In one of his later articles, Bodo von Borries states that this relationship can be established in four different ways. The first of these emerges in the form of collective loyalty of a social group to a tradition. The second one is to show the success or failure of a general rule or regulation in the past and to make deductions from the outcomes of

implementing it on that day or in the future. The third is the relationship established in the form of requesting to change traditions based on the outcomes of implementing them in the past. The fourth regards the past, today and the future as the necessary stages to go through within a developmental process (or grand narrative). It can easily be seen that the second one complies with the concept of history in the pre-modern era, whereas the fourth complies with the concept of history in the modern era.... One of the most important features of the human mind is the capacity of symbolization. Humans who can symbolize can form the language, develop writing, and can transfer the experiments to each other and to the future generations by this way. Which means, he can establish history based on legends or writing. The second feature of the humans is to constantly reflect on what he has done (reflection). The two features of humans described above enable them to develop a historical consciousness as described above. It can be said that these features of humans enable them to see themselves within the constant flow of a temporal dimension" (Tekeli, 2014: p.33-34).

Again, according to Tekeli, the socialization process of the individual includes the following stages:

"It is stated that, throughout the process of socialization, the individual is equipped with the formation on three subjects that are significant in terms of historical consciousness. These subjects can be grouped under three headings, which are: 1) knowledge, 2) values, ideological orientations and 3) responsibilities and standing at attention. While the process of socialization equips the individual in those aspects, it is required to accept that this will not be uniform, there will be significant differences among the individuals and these differences should be allowed" (Tekeli, 2014: 28).

To briefly address the socio-psychological and educational role of history in the society and the individual, during the decline or collapse periods of societies, society and history intelligentsia tried to strengthen the historical consciousness to the utmost extent. Therefore; using a modern narrative, bright periods and achievements of the society in the past are introduced to the masses, especially to the ruling class, with great devotion. In the bright periods of the societies, the intelligentsia in question tries to provide a socio-psychological support by placing the society they live into the center of the world in order to sustain economic and socio-cultural dynamism (Bicak, 2004a; Bicak, 2004b; Bicak, 2004c).

As a result, historians have great responsibilities and duties in either case. It should be noted that, at the basis of every social problem or achievement lies the accumulation of past events and incidents. Historians have to present the required materials to investigate these events in detail and for the realization of social goals.

Finally, I think it would be appropriate to conclude this subject with the words of Leibniz.

"Et comme tout présent état d'une substance simple est naturellement une suite de son état précédent, tellement que le présent y est gros de l'avenir. The present state of a simple ore is the continuation of its previous self; such that the present is big with the future" (Leibniz, 2011: p.22).

What are the possible contributions of dystopic works to historical consciousness and history education?

In the final analysis, the most important contribution of dystopian thought may be to provide opposing voices that challenge utopian ideals, thus keeping those ideals fresh and viable and preventing them from degenerating into dogma. By taking dystopian fiction seriously and by using the dystopian impulse as a focal point for polyphonic confrontations among literature, popular culture, and social criticism we as readers can contribute to this challenge, which is ultimately a positive one. Indeed, it may be that dystopian warnings of impending nightmares are ultimately necessary to preserve any possible dream of a better future (Booker, 1994: p.177).

Today, we realize that dystopic works, which are spreading rapidly especially in literature and visual arts, are frequently used in different educational levels of developed countries. It is seen that dystopic works are used as ancillary elements primarily in the support/development of democratic consciousness, in citizenship and social sciences education, language and literature education, historical consciousness, the development of critical reading and thinking skills, reinforcement of creative thinking, number, colour, perception and metaphor education, explanation and analysis of utopic and dystopic subjects included in some of the philosophical and political subjects (Alsup, 2014; Basbas, 2012; Booker, 1994; Booker, 2012; Bucher & Manning, 2007; Burnett & Rollin, 2000; Bushman & McNerny, 2004; Boyd & Bailey, 2009; Celik, 2015; Curwood et al., 2013; Elzakker, 2014; Ford, 2007; Gardner, 2004: p.430-470; Gardner, 2007: p.83-107; Gordon, 2012; Gottlieb, 2012; Papastephanou, 2008; Parr & Campbell, 2012; Soylemez, 2015; p.6-119; Wilhelm, 2016; Wilhelm & Smith, 2016).

In this context, it would not be inappropriate to state that dystopic works by intellectual authors and educators can make important contributions to many subjects such as psycho-, socio-, socio-cultural and political consciousness of the society and individual. Moreover, we should keep in mind that the ingenious authors of these works, which are written with great sacrifice and intellectual infrastructure, also carry great responsibility. Therefore, dystopic works should be studied in great detail and it is important to offer them to the benefit of humanity.

What kind of contributions can dystopic works make to the development of society and the individual?

- Dystopic works can make important contributions to the development and spread of a sense of social justice (Booker, 1994; Booker, 2012; Celik, 2015; Gottlieb, 2001: p.267-285; Gottlieb, 2012).
- By bringing humanistic feelings (respect, love, and mercy, and compassion) to the fore, they can play a key role in building a democratic, virtuous society. Moreover, when transferring these feelings, dystopic works can take advantage of the movements such as dadaism, surrealism, expressionism, impressionism, neo-impressionism, naturalism, neoclassicism, romanticism and futurism, creating unforgettable images-symbols and pictures in one's mind. This can probably contribute greatly to the sociocultural and social consciousness and intellectual development of mankind (Fischer, 2016: p.21-29; Gombrich, 2016: p.435; Tunali, 2011: p.140; Tunali, 2013: p.234-245; Tunali, 2014: p.50; Turani, 2015: p.73-85; Yetkin, 2007a: p.166-172; Yetkin, 2007b: p.110).
- If carefully examined, dystopic works, with their fiction and content, strikingly present the fact that realities of life carry shades of grey besides black and white to society and individual. In that sense, considering dystopic works in general, we can say that they have a more entropic approach than other literary genres. This can be an important guide for mankind with its portraiture, fiction and content when looking for a solution to prevent social and individual chaos, ensure social and universal peace, prevent the damage caused by mankind to nature and environment and prevent earthly disasters (Moran, 2017: p.229, 232, 288, 306; Rifkin & Howard, 1992: p.21-24, 71-77, 284).
- It is known that, until now, Dystopic works have been greatly influenced by the political, sociological and philosophical movements established by many valuable scientists. In addition, it should be noted that dystopia, which made great progress in the recent years as a literary genre, will make significant contribution to the development of social sciences and humanities (Gottlieb, 2001; Scott, 2010).

- In addition, it should be kept in mind that these works make important contributions to the critical, constructive and creative tendency/education of the society and individual.
- Considering the dystopic works in general, it is clearly seen that basic moral values are the main philosophy. Therefore, in dystopic works, the necessity that the ruler and intellectual class should frequently and uncompromisingly hold on to the basic moral values for the construction of the modern society is fictionally and descriptively expressed in the most striking way. In light of this, we can say that the society and individual should have a strong intellectual perspective and historical consciousness in order to have a more consistent, self-confident, constructive, creative and conscious stand against positive or negative events and incidents throughout their lives. In order to do that, the system/education of basic moral values and history of education/historical consciousness should be built with a modern mentality, the intelligentsia of the developing societies in a way that would include all sections of the society (Carrol, 2016: p.90, 264, 282).
- It is widely known that works that give pleasure or joy evoke a zest for life. But, again, it should be kept in mind that, as seen in many art movements such as impressionism and expressionism, descriptions that give pain or sorrow create an aesthetic pain in the mental world of the individual. In a way, this strengthens the survival resistance of mankind. Considering the dystopic works in this aspect, we can accept them as literary masterpieces that strengthen the sense of struggle against the negativities that society and the individual can face throughout the course of their lives (Carr, 2016: p.45-61; Ricceur, 2012: p.220: 274; Zima, 2015: p.85, 193, 215, 260).
- The most important subconscious association evoked by the dystopic works can be the fact that universal tolerance, love and respect are present in the nature of mankind. It's well known that, these are the feelings that are at the top of the list of virtues that make a human. In order to uncover these emotions and certain moral virtues, the individual has to travel through his inner world with a critical and empathetic perspective. Sometimes this travel can become traumatic. In that case, mankind will turn to itself and find reality and truth in the most perfect way. In addition, it should be noted that, a conscience cannot be expected from an individual or society [intelligentsia] that does not perform self-criticism. Surely, a conscience is a sort of moral identity for the individual in society. Conscience is maybe one of the most important compasses that determine the acceptance or rejection of the individual by the society. Besides, I suppose that, the desire and

defence of virtuous and wise people for love, respect, compassion, freedom, justice and social justice for all humanity and their great efforts in this direction is a result of their empathetic and conscientious self-criticism. In addition, we can say that empathy culture is critically important for the development of freedom of thought and the sense of social justice, which are the basis of democracy. In light of this, it would not be inappropriate to say that empathy culture is among the basic elements that constitute the main profile of the democratic individual and society (Assmann, 2015; Ayer, 2010: p.97-109; Schiller, 1943: p14-170; Yazici, 2014: p.183-191).

I would like to conclude my words with the meaningful expression below, which is found in Huxley's novel Brave New World, in order to emphasize the importance of dystopic works in History education and historical consciousness.

"You all remember," said the Controller, in his strong deep voice, "you all remember, I suppose, that beautiful and inspired saying of Our Ford's: History is bunk. History," he repeated slowly, "is bunk."

He waved his hand; and it was as though, with an invisible feather whisk, he had brushed away a little dust, and the dust was Harappa, was Ur of the Chaldees; some spider-webs, and they were Thebes and Babylon and Cnossos and Mycenae. Whisk. Whisk–and where was Odysseus, where was Job? Where were Jupiter and Gotama and Jesus? Whisk–and those specks of antique dirt called Athens and Rome, Jerusalem and the Middle Kingdom–all were gone. Whisk–the place where Italy had been—was empty whisk, the cathedrals; whisk, whisk, King Lear and the Thoughts of Pascal. Whisk, Passion; whisk, Requiem; whisk, Symphony; whisk" (Huxley, 2017: p.59).

Conclusion

Dystopic works, which contribute greatly to the cultural evolution of mankind, can strengthen the sense of social justice among the individuals and in the society while significantly contributing to democratic consciousness taking root. In this context, we can say that the works in question have both literary and philosophical content. Furthermore, as will be noticed, Dystopic works are mainly taken into consideration in terms of literary, philosophical and political awareness around the world and studies are performed on this subject. In addition to these studies, dystopic works on the development of history education and historical awareness to be written by intellectual authors and experts on the subject can also provide important contributions to the development of critical and creative minds, especially in terms of socio-cultural development. Moreover, if dystopic works are regarded in terms of the development of history education and historical awareness and can be used efficiently and correctly in the education systems worldwide, as seen in the Johari window, important contributions can be made to the open area of the individual (Shenton, 2007: p.487-496; Tandon, 2013). Thus, it can strengthen social communication and sharing. At the same time, while strengthening socialization and respect in the society and among the individuals, it can establish a universal democratic common sense.

References

Akman, O. (2016). The Importance of Using Archive in Social Studies Education. *Research Highlights in Education and Science 2016, pp. 28-33 [Ed.Wenxia Wu,Selahattin Alan &Mustafa Tevfik Hebebci] Isres Publishing.*

Akman, O. (2017). Şiirlerle sosyal bilgiler öğretimi. *Alternatif Yaklaşımlarla Sosyal Bilgiler Eğitimi.* [Ed.Ramazan Sever, Mesut Aydin &Erol Kocoglu] Pegem Akademi. 2nd pp. 402-417.

Alsup, J. (2014). More than a 'Time of Storm and Stress' The Complex Depiction of Adolescent Identity in Contemporary Young Adult Novels", *The Critical Merits of Young Adult Literature: Coming of Age,* [Ed. Crag Hill], p.27.

Arendt, H. (2014). *Geçmişle Gelecek Arasında,* [Between Past and Future], (Bahadır Sina Şener & Onur Eylül Kara.Trans) İstanbul: İletişim

Assmann, J. (2015). *Kültürel Bellek, Eski Yüksek Kültürlerde Yazı, Hatırlama ve Politik Kimlik* [Original title: Das Kulturelle Gedächtnis-Schrift, Erinnerung und Politische Identität in frühen Hockhkulturen] (Ayşe Tekin, Trans.). İstanbul: Ayrıntı.

Atkinson, R. F. (1978). *Knowledge and Explanation in History. An Introduction to the Philosophy of History. Modern Introductions to Philosophy* (D. J. O'Connor, Ed.). https://doi.org/10.1007/978-1-349-15965-9

Atwood, M. (2012). Artık Herkes Mutlu. *Notos Öykü,* 36, pp.47-51.

Atwood, M. (2017). *Damızlık Kızın Öyküsü* [Original title:*The Handmaid's Tale*] (Sevinç Altınçekiç & Özcan Kabakçıoğlu, Trans.). İstanbul.Doğan Kitap

Ayer, J. A. (2010). *Dil, Doğruluk ve Mantık.* [Original title: *Language, Truth and Logic*] (Vehbi Hacıkadiroğlu.Trans.). İstanbul.Metis

Babaee, R., Singh, H. & Zhicheng, Z. & Haiqing, Z. (2015). Critical Review on the Idea of Dystopia" *Review of European Studies;* pp.64-76; V. 7, No. 11; ISSN 1918-7173 E-ISSN 1918-7181 Published by Canadian Center of Science and Education, DOI: http://dx.doi.org/10.5539/res.v7n11p64

Basbas, A. (2012). Collins "On Fire": Teaching Cultural Literacy Through The Hunger Games. *Rivier Academic Journal, 8*(2), 1-6.

Bauer, S.W. (2013) *Antik Dünya –İlk Kayitlardan Roma'nin Dağilmasina Kadar-* [Original title: The History of the Ancient World- From Earliest Accounts to the Fall of Rome], (Mehmet Morali.Trans.) 2[nd.] Istanbul. Alfa.

Bentham, J. (1818). *Plan of Parliamentary Reform, in The Form of a Catechism, with Reasons for Each Article. With and Introduction, Shewing. The Necessity of Radical, and The Inaduquacy of Moderate, Reform* (p. 73). London.

Bergsträsser, G. (2006), *Sâmî Dilleri Tarihi,* [Original title: Elsine-i Sâmîyye Tarihi.] (Hulusi KILIÇ & Dr.Eyyüp Tanrıverdi.Trans.) , İstanbul: Anka.

Bicak, A. (2004a). *Tarih Düşüncesi I, Tarih Düşüncesinin Oluşumu.* İstanbul: Dergah.

Bicak, A. (2004b). *Tarih Düşüncesi II, Felsefe ve Tarih.* İstanbul:Dergâh.

Bicak, A. (2004c). *Tarih Düşüncesi III, Tarih Felsefesinin Oluşumu.* İstanbul:Dergâh.

Bloch, M. (2015). *Tarih Savunusu veya Tarihçilik Mesleği* [Original title: Apologie pour I' histoire ou Métier d'historien] (Ali Berktay, Trans.). İstanbul: İletişim.

Booker, M. K. (1994). The Dystopian Impulse in Modern Literature: Fiction as Social Criticism. In *Contributions to the Study of Science Fiction and Fantasy* (No. 58). London: Greenwood Press.

Booker, M. K. (2012). Ütopya, Distopya, Toplumsal Eleştiri. *Notos Öykü, 36,* 35-46.

Boyd, F. B., & Bailey, N. M. (2009). Censorship in Three Metaphors. *Journal of Adolescent & Adult Literacy, 52*(8), 653-661. https://doi.org/10.1598/JAAL.52.8.1

Bradbury, R. (2013). *"Fahrenheit 451"* (Zerrin Kayalıoğlu&Korkut Kayalıoğlu.trans).Istanbul.Ithaki Y.

Bucher, T. K. & Manning, M. L. (2007). Intellectual Freedom for Young Adolescents. *Childhood Education, 84*(1), 8-14. https://doi.org/10.1080/00094056.2007.10522961

Burgess, A. (2017). *"Otomatik Portakal"* [Original title: A Clockwork Orange] (Dost Körpe, Trans.). İstanbul.Türkiye İş Bankası Yayınları.

Burnett, G. W. & Rollin, L. (2000). Anti-leisure in dystopian fiction: The literature of leisure in the worst of all possible worlds. *Leisure Studies*, *19*(2), 77-90. https://doi.org/10.1080/026143600374761

Bushman, J. H. & McNerny, S. (2004). Moral Choices: Building a Bridge between YA Literature and Life. *The Alan Review*, *32*(1), 61-67. Retrieved October 13, 2016, from https://scholar.lib.vt.edu/ejournals/ALAN/v32n1/v32n1.pdf#page=61

Carr, E. H. (2008). *Tarih Nedir?* [Original title: What is History?] (Misket Gizem Gürtürk, Trans.). İstanbul: İletişim. (Powicke , *1955, p. 174* ; F.Powicke, *Modern Historians and the Study of History*)

Carr, W. H. (2016). *Benedetto Croce Felsefesi-Sanat ve Tarih Sorunu*. (Nesrin Atasoy Ertürk. Trans).Istanbul. Değişim Y.

Carrol, N. (2016). *Sanat Felsefesi-Çağdaş Bir Giriş*. (Güliz Korkmaz Tirkeş, Trans).Istanbul.Utopya Y.

Celgin, G. (2011). *Eski Yunanca-Türkçe Sözlük*. İstanbul: Kabalcı.

Celik, E. (2015). Distopik Romanlarda Toplumsal Kurgu. *Journal of Sociological Research*, *18*(1), 57-79.

Childe, V. G. (2007). *Tarihte Neler Oldu?* [Original title: What Happened in History] (Alâedddin Şenel-Mete Tunçay) Istanbul: Kırmızı.

Claeys, G. (2010). The origins of dystopia: Wells, Huxley and Orwell. In G. Claeys (Ed.), *Utopian Literature* (pp. 107-131). London: Cambridge University Press. https://doi.org/10.1017/ccol9780521886659.005

Collingwood, R. G. (2010). *Tarih Tasarımı* [Original title: The Idea of History] (Kurtuluş Dinçer, Trans). İstanbul: Doğu Batı.

Corballis, M. C. (2003), *İşaretten Konuşmaya Dilin Kökeni ve Gelişimi*, [Original title: From Hand to Mouth] [Aybek Görey.trans] İstanbul: Kitap

Curwood, S. J., Magnifico, M. A., & Lammers, C. J. (2013). Writing in the Wild Writers Motivation in Fan-Based Affinity Spaces. *Journal of Adolescent & Adult Literacy*, *56*(8), 677-685. https://doi.org/10.1002/JAAL.192

Demirel, M. (2009). Tarih Biliminin Gelişimi. In M. Demirel, & İ. Turan (Eds.), *Tarih Öğretim Yöntemleri* (pp. 1-5). İstanbul: Nobel.

Eliade, M. (1991), *Kutsal ve Din Dışı*, [Original title:Le Sacré et Le Profane] (Mehmet Ali Kılıçbay.Trans) Ankara: Gece.pp.74

Elzakker, van F. G. (2014). *Dystopian Fiction in the English Language Classroom*. MA Education & Communication, English Utrecht University.

Fischer, E. (2016). *Sanatın Gerekliliği.* [Original title:The Necessity of Art], (Cevat Çapan),Istanbul.Sozcukler Y.

Ford, L. C. (2007). *Constructing the Novel: Teacher Education* (Norway International Master Degree Programme Master Thesis). Rudolf Steiner University College.

Freund, J. (1997). *Beşerî Bilim Teorileri*, [Bahaeddin Yediyıldız.trans], Ankara: TTK.

Friedrich, J. (2000). *Kayıp Yazılar ve Diller*, [original title: Entzifferung verschollener Schriften und Sprachen] [Recai Tekoğlu.trans.], İstanbul: Arkeoloji ve Sanat.

Gardner, H. (2004). *Zihin Çerçeveleri Çoklu Zekâ Kuramı* [Original title: Frames of Mind-The Theory of Multiple Intelligences.] (Ebru Kılıç.trans). Istanbul.Alfa.

Gardner, H. (2007). *Geleceği İnşa edecek Beş Zihin* (Filiz Şar&Asiye Hekimoğlu Gül, Trans.). İstanbul: Optimist

Gombrich, H. E. (2015). *Sanat ve Yanilsama-Resim Yoluyla Betimlemenin Psikolojisi*, [Ahmet Cemal.trans.], İstanbul: Remzi.

Gombrich, H. E. (2016). *Sanatın Öyküsü.* [Original title:The Story of Art.] (Erol Erduran & Ömer Erduran.trans.) İstanbul: Remzi.

Gordon, M. (2012). *Reel Recognition: Examining Why Film and Images Should Be Used More in English and History Classrooms* (Masters Thesis). Pennsylvania State University.

Gottlieb, E. (2001). *"Dystopian Fiction East and West A Universe of Terror and Trial"* McGill-Queen's University Press. Montreal & Kingston. London. Ithaca

Gottlieb, E. (2012). Distopya Batı, Distopya Doğu. *Notos Öykü*, *36*, pp.25-34

Hauser, A. (2005), *The Social History of Art with An Introduction by Jonathan Harris - Volume I from Prehistoric Times to The Middle Ages.* Newyork: Taylor&Francis.

Howatson, M. C. (2013). *Oxford Antikçağ Sözlüğü* [Oxford Companion to Classical Literature] (Faruk Ersöz, Trans.). İstanbul: Kitap.

Huxley, A. (2017). *"Cesur Yeni Dünya"* [Original title: Brave New World] (Ümit Tosun, Trans.). İstanbul.İthaki

Ibn Haldun (2015). *"Mukaddime".* *(Dr. Arslan Tekin by prepare).* *İstanbul.İlgi Kültür Sanat Yayıncılık V.I. p.62.*

Iplikçioglu, B. (1994). *Eskiçağ Tarihinin Ana Hatları* (2nd ed.). İstanbul, Bilim Teknik.

Ishiguro,K. (2017). *"Beni Asla Bırakma"* [Original title: Never Let Me Go] (Mine Haydaroğlu, Trans.). İstanbul.YKY.

Jean, G. (2006). *Yazı İnsanlığın Belleği*, [Original title: L'écriture mémoire des homes] (Nami Başer.trans.), İstanbul: YKY.

Kabaagac, S. & Alova, E. (1995). *Latince/Türkçe Sözlük.* İstanbul. Sosyal Yayınlar.

Kafka, F. (2016). *"Dava"* [Original title: Der Proceβ] (Ahmet Cemal, Trans.). İstanbul.Can.

Karabag, Ş. G. (2014). Tarihsel Empati Becerisi: Öğretimi, Ölçülmesi ve Değerlendirilmesi. In M. Safran (Ed.), *Tarih Nasıl Öğretilir? Tarih Öğretmenleri İçin Özel Öğretim Yöntemleri* (pp. 137-143). İstanbul: Yeni İnsan.

Kramer, N, S. (2002). *"Tarih Sümer'de Başlar.:Yazılı Tarihteki Otuzdokuz İlk"* [Original title: "History Begins at Sumer: Thirty-Nine Firsts in Recorded History".] (Hamide Koyukan.Trans.) Kabalci Yayınevi.

Kula, B. O. (2012). *Dil Felsefesi Edebiyat Kuramı- II.*Istanbul.Türkiye İş Bankası Y.

Kumar, K. (2005). Aspects of the Western Utopian Tradition. In J. Rüsen, M. Fehr, & T. W. Rieger (Eds.), *Thinking Utopia: Steps Into Other Worlds (Makings Sense of History)* (pp. 17-31). Berghahn Books.

Kumar, K. (2010). The Ends of Utopia. *New Literary History, 41,* pp.549-569

Leibniz, G.W. (2011). Monadoloji ve İlgili Yazılar, Mektuplar [original title: "1714, La Monadologie"] (Devrim Çetinkasap.Trans.) Pinhan Yayıncılık.p.22

Lessing, D. (2017). *"Hayatta Kalma Güncesi"* [Original title: The Memoirs of a Survivor] (Püren Özgören,trans), Istanbul, Can.

Lévi-Strauss, C. (2010). *Irk, Tarih ve Kültür,* [Original title: Race et Histoire, Unesco broşürü,1959; "Race et Culture",Revue internationale des sciences sociales], İstanbul:Metis. (Haldun Bayrı, Reha Erdem, Arzu Oyacıoğlu, Işık Ergüden. Trans.) v.XXIII, *4, 1971;* Entretienes avec Claude Lévi-Strauss,

Lewin, R. (2008), *Modern İnsanın Kökeni,* [Original title: "The Origin of Modern Humans"]. (Nazım Özüaydın.Trans), Ankara: Tubitak.

Lewis, C. T. (1918). *An Elementary Latin Dictionary.* New York, Cincinnati, Chicago, American Book Company.

London, J. (2016). *"Demir Ökçe"* [Original title: The Iron Heel] (Levent Cinemre.Trans.). Levent Cin Emre. Istanbul Türkiye İş Bankası Y.

Lowry, L. (2014). *"The Giver"*—"Seçilmiş Kişi" (4nd ed.) (Esra Davutoğlu, Trans., Ümit Türkoğlu, Ed.). Arkadaş Yayınevi.

Mill, J. S. (1868). *The Collected Works of John Stuart Mill, Volume XXVIII. The Collected Works of John Stuart Mill, Volume XXVIII-Public and Parliamentary Speeches Part I November 1850-November 1868.* Toronto: University of Toronto Press.

Mill, J. S. (1909). *Autobiography.* Watts and Co. 17 Johnson's Court, Fleet Street, London.

Mill, J. S. (1958). *Considerations on Representative Government—With an Introduction by Howard Penniman* (p. 249). Newyork: Forum Books

Millward, J. (2006). *Dystopian Wor(l)ds: Language Within and Beyond Experience.* The University of Sheffield, School of English, Literature, Language and Linguistics, Sheffield.

Mitchell, D. (2016). *"Kemik Saatler"* [Original title: The Bone Clocks] (Sıla Okur.trans) Istanbul.Doğan Kitap.

Moore, A. & Lloyd, D. (2005). "V for Vendetta" DC Comics 1700 Broodway, New York NY 10019 A Warner Bros. Entertainment Company Printed in the USA Eleventh Printing. ISBN:978-1-4012-0841-7

Moran, B. (2017). *Edebiyat Kuramları ve Eleştiriler.* Istanbul. İletisim Y.

More, T. (2013) *"Utopia"* (Ismail Yerguz.Trans.) Istanbul.Say Y.

Orwell, G. (2014). *Bin Dokuz Yüz Seksen Dört* [Original title: Nineteen Eighty-Four] [Celâl Üster & Can Yayın, Trans.].

Ortayli, I. (2003). Tarih Nedir? In *Türkiye Günlüğü* (pp. 1-22). Ankara.

Ozlem, D. (2004). *Tarih Felsefesi.* İstanbul: İnkılâp Kitabevi.

Papastephanou, M. (2008). Dystopian Reality, Utopian Thought and Educational Practice. *Stud Philos Educ, 27,* 89-102. https://doi.org/10.1007/s11217-007-9092-9

Parr, M. & Campbell, A. T. (2012). Understanding literacy as our WORLD inheritance: Re-visioning literacy discourse and its implications for teaching practice. *Int Rev Educ, 58,* 557-574. https://doi.org/10.1007/s11159-012-9297-1

Payzin, S, H. (1992). *Tarihte Dil,Yazı,Bilim ve Toplum.* Doğruluk M.

Poe, M. (2015), *İletişim Tarihi (Konuşmanın Evriminden İnternete Medya ve Toplum,* [Original title: A History of Communications (Media and Society from the Evolution of Speech to the Internet)]. (Umut Yener Karatrans). Cambridge University Press. Islık Yayınları.Istanbul

Renfrew, C & Bahn,,P. (2013)., *Arkeoloji. Anahtar Kavramlar.* [orginal title: Archaeology. The Key Concepts.] Selda Somuncuoğlu.Trans.) İletişim Yayıncılık A.Ş.

Ricceur, P. (2012). *Zaman ve Anlatı: üç.* [Original title: Temps et Récit II:3. La Configuration du temps dans le récit de fiction, Mehmet Rıfat.Trans, Istanbul, YKY.

Rifkin, J. & Howard,T. (1992). *Entropi Dünyaya Yeni Bir Bakış.* (Hakan Okay.Trans). Istanbul. Ağaç Y.

Schiller, F. (1943). *İnsanın Estetik Terbiyesi Üzerine (1795)*. [Original title: Über die ästhetische Erziehung des Menschen,in einer Reihe von Briefen].[Melâhat Özgü, Trans]. Ankara-Maarif Matbaası.

Shenton, A. K. (2007). Viewing information needs through a Johari Window. Reference Services Review, 35 (3), pp.487-496, https://doi.org/10.1108/00907320710774337

Silverman, H. J. (1997). *Inscriptions After Phenomenology and Structuralism* (p.326). Illinois: Northwestern University.

Somay, B. (2010). *"The View from the Masthead Journey through Dystopia towards an Open-Ended Utopia"*. Istanbul Bilgi University Press.

Southgate, B. (2012). *Tarih : Ne ve Neden. Antik,Modern ve Postmodern Yaklaşımlar*, [Original title:History:What and Why ? Ancient,Modern and Postmodern Perspective.] (Çağdaş Dizdar,Erhan Baltacı,Didem Salihoğlu,Tuba Altın,Berkay Ekrem Ersöz.Trans.), İstanbul:Phoenix

Soylemez, Y. (2015). *Ortaokul Öğrencilerine Yönelik Eleştirel Temel Dil Becerileri Ölçeklerinin Geliştirilmesi* (Developing Scales For Critical Basic Language Skills Intended For Secondary School Students) (Doctora Thesis). Ataturk University Egitim Bilimleri Enstitüsü Türkçe Eğitimi Ana Bilim Dalı Türkçe Eğitimi Bilim Dalı

Steuerwald, K. (1995). *Almanca-Türkçe Sözlük* [Original title: Deutsch-Türkishches Wörterbuch]. İstanbul: ABC.

Tandon, R. (2013). "New Area in Johari Window" *International Journal of Engineering and Innovative Technology (IJEIT)* 3 (2).83-85.

Tekeli, İ. (2014). *Tarih Bilinci ve Gençlik—Karşılaştırmalı Avrupa ve Türkiye Araştırması*. İstanbul: Tarih Vakfı Yurt Yayınları.

Thorp, R. (2014). Historical Consciousness and Historical Media—A History Didactical Approach to Educational Media. *Education Inquiry*, 5(4), 497-516. https://doi.org/10.3402/edui.v5.24282

Touraine, A. (2004). *Demokrasi Nedir?* [Orginal title:Qu'est-Ce Que La Démocratie?], (Olcay Kunal.Trans.) Istanbul.YKY

Toynbee, A. (1956). *"A Study of History"* v.I. Oxford University Press,Amen House,London

Toynbee, A. (1988) *A Study of History*, The One – Volume Edition Illustrated.This edition©1972 Oxford University Press and Thames and Hudson Ltd.First Paperback edition 1988. London. For Turkish edition of the same work see "Tarih Bilinci (A Study of History), the new and shortened issue reviewed by the author and Jane Caplan. 90 coloured, 507 photos, 23 maps and schemas" v.II.1978.Bates Y.p.511.

Tunali, I. (2011*). "Estetik Beğeni"*. Istanbul.Remzi K.

Tunali, I. (2013). *"Estetik"*. Istanbul.Remzi K.

Tunali, I. (2014). *"Sanat Ontolojisi."* Istanbul. Inkılap K.

Turani, A. (2007), *Dünya Sanat Tarihi*, İstanbul.Remzi.

Turani, A. (2015). Çağdaş Sanat Felsefesi.İstanbul.Remzi

Vico, G. (2007), *Yeni Bilim, [Original title:Principi di una scienza nuova intorno alla comune nature delle nazioni,1744/The New Science of Giambattista Vico,1984]*, (Sema Önal.Trans), İstanbul, Doğu Batı.

Vieira, F. (2010). The Concept of Utopia. In G. Claeys (Ed.), *Utopian Literature* (p. 16). London: Cambridge University Press. https://doi.org/10.1017/ccol9780521886659.001

Walsh, H, W. (2006). *"Tarih Felsefesine Giriş"* (Yusuf Ziya Çelikkaya Trans) Ankara, Hece Y.

Warrington, H. M. (2014). *Tarih Bilimine Yön veren Düşünürler- En Önemli 50 Tarihçi*, [İbrahim Kapaklıkaya, Trans], İstanbul: Etkileşim.

Wells, G. H. (2013). *Efendi Uyanıyor* [Original title: The Sleeper Awakes]. (Egemen Yılgür trans.) Maya Kitap.

Wells, G. H. (2016). *Zaman Makinesi* [Original title:The Time Machine]. (Volkan Gürses. trans) İstanbul.İthaki.

Wilhelm, D. J. (2016). Recognising the power of pleasure: What engaged adolescent readers get from their free-choice reading, and how teachers can leverage this for all. *Australian Journal of Language and Literacy, 39*(1), 30-41.

Wilhelm, D. J. & Smith, W. M. (2016). The Power of Pleasure Reading: What We Can Learn from the Secret Reading Lives of Teens. *English Journal, 105*(6), 25-30.

Yazici, S. (2014). *"Karakter Epistemolojisi" Kişi,Kişilik ve Kimlik* (Ed. Sedat Yazıcı & Seyit Coşkun), Ankara, Divan Kitap.

Yildiz, N. (2014). *Eskiçağda Yazı Malzemeleri ve Kitabın Oluşumu*, Ankara: TTK.

Yetkin, K. S. (2007 a). *"Estetik Doktrinler."* Ankara Palme Y.

Yetkin, K, S. (2007 b). *"Büyük Ressamlar"* Ankara Palme Y

Yildirim, S. (2017). "Raising Historical Consciousnes in the Novel "The Giver", a Dystopic Work According to Social Studies Teacher Candidates." *Journal of Education and Learning,* 6 (3), pp.129-150.

Zamyati, Y. (2016). *"Biz"* [Original title:Mıy (We)]. (Füsun Tülek.trans) İstanbul.Ayrıntı.

Zima, V. P. (2015). *"Modern Edebiyat Teorilerinin Felsefesi"* [Original title: The Philosophy of Modern Literary Theory]. (Mustafa Özsarı. trans) Ankara: Hece.

AN ESSAY ON CULTURAL GEOGRAPHY: GASTRONOMY IN TURKISH CULTURE[*]

ALPEREN KAYSERİLİ

Introduction: A General Evaluation of Gastronomic Culture

First of all, it is necessary to define the concepts of food and gastronomic culture to form the conceptual framework of the subject. The concept of food refers to any substance containing essential nutrients for the maintenance of and support for vital functions of living organisms (Kittler & Sucher, 2008: 3) while gastronomic culture includes cooking and serving dishes (Albala, 2011: p.1). The concept of gastronomic culture is the product of common taste constructed by a community (Visentin, 2011: p.1). It is also possible to elicit information on cultural history by focusing on geographical, cultural and conceptual frameworks of gastronomy (Goodman & Redclift, 2003: p.2).

Gastronomic culture is particularly in the field of interest of anthropologists. Anthropologists consider eating habits entirely to be within the limits of cultural anthropology. They argue that culture is the basic indicator of what we eat, that culture is constructed and that eating habits are not easy to change as they are taught through enculturation. Lastly, they maintain that food constitutes one of the most important parts of culture, which therefore has a special place in cultural anthropology (Tezcan, 2000: p.1).

One of the important issues to be addressed about gastronomic culture is finding answers to the question "Do we live to eat or eat to live?" Our ancestors and we today have mostly leaned towards the second option (to eat to live) and therefore have focused on fulfilling the need for food throughout history (Belge, 2010: p.34). Though food has different meanings for everyone, it is a necessity for survival, an addiction, a source

---

[*] In this section "the city of Erzurum Cultural Geography (According to Item Material Culture)" has been derived from doctoral thesis of author.

of pleasure and at the same time a social phenomenon (Avcıkurt et al., 2007: p.4).

In prehistoric times, human beings had two alternatives to obtain food; hunting and gathering. Here is another question that needs to be answered; "Which precedes the other; hunting or gathering?" Of course, the answer is gathering since hunting is a process that requires the development of some techniques and invention of various tools. Gathering, on the other hand, is the process of collecting fruits, vegetables or various plants and plant shells. Therefore, human beings firstly engaged in gathering activities. In this process, primitive humans consumed the food they found and constantly migrated to find food as they did not know how to domesticate animals (Kutluay, 1982: p.42).

However, human beings did not content themselves only with the food they gathered from the wild. They discovered that animals that live on nutrients or other living creatures are also edible. They came to think that an animal which eats another animal (specially an herbivore) must taste good. With this thought, a new system in which animal flesh is eaten as food had to be established. What needed to be done was to catch animals first. Therefore, they needed to hunt them, as a result of which a second food substance, meat, entered our diets. Human beings eat both animals and plants. Therefore, human beings are omnivorous. At this stage, it can be concluded that human beings have changed their food habits (Kittler & Sucher, 2008: p.5), which means that they have changed their eating habits to obtain more chemical energy and nutrients.

From the perspective of today's gastronomic culture, the quests for food resulted in some trials that are deemed unacceptable today. Since human beings had no chance to cook meat before fire was invented, they had two options for meat consumption. The first option was consuming insects. Since insects are rich in nutrients and proteins, we can say that it was not a mistake to include them in diet. The second option was imitating the practice of some animals and rotting and tenderizing meat, in other words, consuming animal carcass (Belge, 2010: p.35). However, given the fact that historical events should be analysed in their proper context, it would be wrong to judge the practice of carcass eating carried out by primitive humans. At this point, we can ask, "Did people at that time only eat animal carcass?" the answer to which is obvious. They did not only eat animal carcass until before the invention of fire, they also pounded on meat for a long time to tenderize it and added various herbs to enhance flavour. It is possible to see the repercussion of this practice even today. For example, *çiğ köfte* (raw meatballs) in Anatolia, sushi in Japan and *carpaccio* in Italy are still important parts of the culinary culture of those countries (Gürsoy, 2004: p.11).

At this stage, another question can be posed; "Did human beings regard any kind of meat they found as food?" The answer to this question reveals the reality of natural life because it was not an easy task to catch carnivores. Besides, it was simply impossible to domesticate carnivores with techniques at hand at the time even if they were caught. Adapting to the environment and natural life, human beings started feeding and domesticating herbivores. In consequence, they learned the skills of feeding and herding animals, which provided them with the opportunity to make use of the meat, bones and skin of animals.

Another noteworthy aspect of the period of hunting and gathering is the division of labour between men and women. According to the cave paintings discovered by archaeologists, men were involved in hunting, which is believed to be due to men's greater physical strength and their ability to run faster than women. Women, on the other hand, were involved in gathering. The next stage of gathering is re-cultivating the collected products, which led to the emergence of agricultural activities initiated by women (Belge, 2010: p.35).

Fruits are the nutrients to which human beings have the easiest access. However, the problem is that fruits are seasonal substances which are rapidly consumed. Embarking on a new quest, human beings probably observed the consumptions habits of animals and grains mostly consumed by birds came to their notice. They also started consuming grains and discovered that they are crops that can be grown on land. This discovery was the beginning of agriculture. Cave paintings indicate that women were involved in nascent agricultural activities while men concentrated on hunting activities. The following period witnessed the discovery of fire. With fire, human beings figured out that they could cook not only meat but also some plants. This milestone in the history of mankind also triggered the development of gastronomic culture. Roasted corn grains, which we call *kavurga* today, unearthed in archaeological excavations carried out in mounds reveal that the practice of roasting corn grains dates back to hundreds of years ago (Gürsoy, 2004: p.12).

The earliest method of baking bread was carried out with crushing grains into flour, mixing it with water and placing the lumps of dough on hot stones around a fire and leaving them to cook. Archeological finds show that bulgur pilaf and soups with lumps of meat have passed down from generation to generation until today. It is even believed that these meals were first made in a Hittite city called *Kussara* located between Erzurum and Erzincan today. It is known that fish dishes and olive oil dishes were mostly discovered by the civilizations located on the seaside. Remains of small metal hooks found in the archaeological excavations carried out in the lower layers of Troy are important evidence of fishing activities in the region.

Human beings began cooking and creating cultural products together during the stages of acculturation and enculturation. Initially concerned with consuming food to survive, human beings started to perform such activities as setting a table and having food substances containing various kinds of nutrients on the table after they adopted a sedentary lifestyle. In fact, the following stages of sedentary lifestyle witnessed the stratification of society into rich and poor segments who started to consume different kinds of food from each other (Mertol, 1998: p.137).

People have always thought about cooking activities and tried to improve them. They have never contented themselves with the taste they had and always searched for new tastes. To this end, they have mixed various foods with each other, applied different cooking techniques and learned to enjoy eating (Arlı, 1981: p.19). In this respect, foods show distinctive characteristics from continent to continent. For example, European people mostly prefer soft foods. People living in the tropical zones of Africa prefer to eat hard foods that need to be chewed while those living in the forestry areas of Africa prefer root and tuber vegetables. The Inuit are known to eat raw meat (Tezcan, 2000: p.12).

Following the brief assessment of ancient ages, it will be useful to address the effect of religions, especially monotheistic religions, on gastronomic culture. This is due to the fact that the effect of human-made religions on gastronomic culture has not been extensively researched, which makes it impossible to provide accurate information. However, orders and prohibitions of monotheistic religions are very clear and it is therefore possible to elicit information on their effect on gastronomic culture.

Among monotheistic religions, Judaism applies the most extensive laws on foods. The Torah, the sacred book of Jews, makes it very clear as to which foods are permitted and which ones are forbidden to be consumed (Beşirli, 2010: p.166). For example, the Torah prohibits the consumption of blood; therefore, Jewish people are not allowed to eat rare cooked meat or meat that contains blood. It also prohibits the consumption of tallow, pork, horse meat, donkey meat, mussel, oyster, bat, stork, fish-eating water-birds, reptiles, insects, carcass, and any products that contain milk and meat together (Şenol, 2007: p.39).

Since Jesus came to the world after Moses and lived under the commandments of Judaism before Christianity was introduced to the world by him, all prohibitions on foods in Judaism should also be in Christianity. Christianity introduced many new laws, yet, the vast majority of laws on eating and drinking activities remained the same as those of the Torah. However, as Christianity spread to Europe, it has undergone many changes, including laws on eating and drinking. As a result, the interpretations of Christian clergymen overshadow the religion itself. These clergymen have interesting interpretations of the laws on eating and drinking. For example, they went as far as to state, "*That which enters into the mouth does not defile the man*" and lifted all prohibitions on eating and drinking (Şenol, 2007: p.55).

Islam, on the other hand, introduced prohibitions that have deeply affected eating and drinking culture. Acting within the framework of these prohibitions, Muslims have also conducted scientific studies and determined that these prohibitions are beneficial for health. For example, it is forbidden to eat carcass, animals that eat its own faces, non-ruminant animals, reptiles, fish-eating water-birds and insects. In addition, it is forbidden to consume intoxicating substances, animals that have not been caught and slaughtered according to the laws of Islam, and blood. It is clear that these substances are banned in the interest of health for Islam commands that Muslims abstain from practices that could lead to health problems.

Another practice of Islam is fasting. Muslims should not eat and drink between Morning Prayer and evening prayer during the month of Ramadan. This form of worship is referred to as fasting, which is not only about restrictions on eating and drinking for a certain period but also many other activities are suggested to be performed after evening prayer during the month of Ramadan. Some researchers, who appear on TV or make a statement to the press, argue that fasting has a positive effect on health. There are also some studies which support this argument (Büyükbaş, 2002: p.23).

It is evident that Islam has given great importance to the dietary practices of Muslims, discouraged them from consuming harmful substances and invited them to be content with good, clean and halal food. Islam has imposed prohibitions on some foods and substances which people should already avoid consuming for their health and advised them to act within the limits of reasonableness and prudence. There are essential things that an individual should perform for a good and healthy life (Yüceler, 2010: p.143).

There is a connection between gastronomic culture and technology. Many different systems were developed in ancient times, such as development of agricultural activities and olive oil production. During the following historical periods, foods were salted and preserved for a long time and this way, they were available even out of season. The canning method was also developed. In the eighteenth century, the French armies were suffering from shortage of food and in 1795, the French leader, Napoleon, offered a big reward to anyone who could develop a method of preserving large quantities of food. Thus, the French discovered canned food techniques (Mertol, 1998: p.139). Another development is the invention of fork and spoon. For a long time, people ate their food with their hands. According to the available evidence, the first fork was used by the Byzantines in the tenth century and then spread to other countries.

Gastronomy in Turkish Culture

One of the cultural values that the Turkish nation has introduced to human history is its own unique dishes. Turkish nomads in Central Asia discovered several types of food which were suitable for that dynamic lifestyle and introduced them to the world. Agricultural activities of Turkish nomads, who systematically migrated from one location to another depending on season, were not highly developed. Agricultural production was based on seasonal harvesting, and cultivation activities were also limited and therefore they concentrated on husbandry. They were involved in livestock farming, which offered them many benefits such as meat, milk and hides or skin.

Shaped by environmental conditions and cultural values, nutrition is one of the basic needs for human survival. Hence, dietary and culinary cultures of Turkish communities that spread over different geographical regions vary, especially in feasts and ceremonies, in which state officials participate (Birol & Akpınar: 2009: p.310).

The livelihoods of Turks in Central Asia or Anatolia were agriculture and animal husbandry, which naturally affected their nourishment. Most of the ingredients used in traditional Turkish dishes are animal products and meat, which give traditional Turkish food its unique taste and texture (Toygar, 1981: p.154). Some basic principles played a role in the development of this dietary and culinary culture. These principles are using mutton and onion in dishes and cooking them in copper pots and on a charcoal fire.

The gastronomic culture of the Turks is based especially on animal products. Dishes with milk, yoghurt, and lumps of meat or dough are important contributions of the Turks to the world's cuisine (Commission, 1997: 1). In addition, the Turks started to use some vegetables in dishes, especially after they migrated to Anatolia. They prepared *dolma* by stuffing these vegetables with a filling consisting of rice and meat or made *sarma* by wrapping cabbage or grape leaves around a filling. *Dolma* and *sarma* are also important contributions of the Turks to the world's gastronomic culture. Dishes with meat and dough such as *mantı* and *Tatar böreği* were invented by the nomadic Turks (Ögel, 1981: p.17). The soup, which is cooked in many regions of Anatolia and referred to as *tutmaç* or *ovmaç*, is one of the dishes that Seljuks introduced to the world's gastronomic culture (Genç, 1981: p.60). A method that the nomadic Turks used to preserve their meat, *pastırma* is another great contribution to the world's cuisine.

Eating habits developed within the Turkish gastronomic culture are also important. The Turkish table culture has a male-dominant structure. If the household is crowded or there are guests in the house, firstly men sit at the table and eat. After they are done, the remaining dishes are served among women. If there is no leftover, food that is prepared quickly is served to women. There is also a habit of setting up two separate tables at the same time. Men eat at the table set up in the guestroom while women eat in the kitchen (Tezcan, 1998: p.159). With the influence of Islam, entertaining guests at dinner became a custom in the Turkish gastronomic culture. Having guests at the table was considered a matter of pride and honor in the Turkish culture. Therefore, the Turks were in the habit of inviting people over for dinner. It was actually a widespread practice for the Turks to go out on the street and invite people over for dinner to breakfast during Ramadan.

Overall, the Turkish gastronomic culture can be summarized as follows, the staple foods of the Turkish cuisine are meat and bread. Pastry is consumed very much. Though there are various kinds of kebabs; stews are also consumed a lot. Meat dishes contain various vegetables, especially onions, peppers and tomatoes, which are fried before meat is added. Boiled vegetables besides meat are never preferred. Herbs that naturally grow such as knotweed, tarragon and thyme are used. Tallow, lard and butterfat are profusely used for flavour. Bulgur is an essential ingredient of the Turkish dishes. Some fruits such as quince, mulberry and apricot are cooked in oil together with meat to obtain different flavours. Yogurt is one of the most important complementary foods. Either plain or with crushed garlic, yogurt is poured over many dishes to add flavour to them and also to balance the high cholesterol content in meat. The Turks did not use spices, except red pepper, before they were involved in an interaction with Greek culture. With the effect of Greek culture, many spices were included in dishes. Spices not only provide flavour and taste but also enhance the aesthetic of dishes (Sever, 1982: p.109). They also balance the aroma. Adopted from Greek culture, spices are used to balance sweet with bitter and sour, and to enhance the flavour of the dish (Dalby, Grainger, 2001, p.2).

The Turkish gastronomic culture in Anatolia varies even between regions that are close to each other. Nomadism and economic structure play a significant role in it. Production and consumption of various kinds of food are caused by the disparity in the social and economic structure of society. Encounters and interaction with various cultures led to the invention of different kinds of food and adoption of table cultures. Religion also played a significant role in this process (Tezcan, 1981: p.115). For example, the Turks who consumed horse meat before they accepted Islam started to abandon this habit after they accepted Islam. However, in some parts of Central Asia today people still consume horse meat.

In particular, the Ottoman State invented different kinds of dishes that have enriched the Turkish gastronomic culture. Besides the variety in dishes, the Ottoman State interacted with other countries and adopted elements of table culture and consumption manners from those countries. The Ottoman State also had important laws which shaped the Turkish gastronomic culture. For example, the Ottoman State enacted and upheld various laws and took various precautions to preserve public health and to enforce Islamic religious orders. According to these laws, it was forbidden to mix the meats of some certain animals, to make pastry with stale yeast, and to use too much salt or to undercook. As a precaution, the Ottoman State made sure about high-quality tableware craftsmanship (Toygar, 1982: p.64).

Today, many cultural values are disappearing and the Turkish gastronomical culture is experiencing its share of this problem. Such factors as interaction with different cultures, changing environment and women's participation in working life cause the Turkish gastronomical culture to change as well. Many traditional flavors are being abandoned and replaced with fast food and quick-frozen foods. Working women who spend a large part of their day at work unfortunately do not have much time to go home and cook and therefore, they also prefer to buy pre-cooked frozen food from supermarkets or food from restaurants. Fast-food is becoming more and more popular among young people causing them to abandon and forget the making of many traditional dishes. As mentioned before in clothing culture, one of the symbolic elements of American imperialism, McDonald's, has penetrated into Turkey as well as many countries of the world. People consume unhealthy foods without knowing what they contain and lose their health.

Various precautions should be taken to protect the Turkish gastronomic culture from adverse conditions and to preserve the traditional Turkish cuisine, for this purpose, young people should be educated about the cultural wealth of the Turks and informed on the importance of traditional values as cultural heritage. They should also be taught that it is necessary to pass down those traditional values from generation to generation for a better future (Dağdeviren & Dağdeviren, 2009: p.65).

Conclusion and Discussion

The gastronomic culture of the Turks is based especially on animal products. Dishes with milk, yogurt, and lumps of meat or dough are important contributions of the Turks to the world's cuisine. Due to climate and topography, the agricultural and cultivation activities of the Turks were limited. As a result, they were mostly involved in animal husbandry and livestock farming, which offered them many benefits such as meat, milk and hides or skin. Husbandry-based economic activities heavily influenced the Turkish gastronomical culture.

Most of the ingredients used in traditional Turkish dishes are animal products and meat, which give them their unique taste and texture (Toygar, 1981: p.154). Some basic principles played a role in the development of this dietary and culinary culture. These principles are using mutton and onion in dishes and cooking them in copper pots and on a charcoal fire.

The Turkish gastronomical culture has experienced a significant transformation with the introduction of different cooking methods and the availability of food items and agricultural products that cannot be produced or grown but can easily be brought from different countries thanks to the development in transportation and communication technology.

Increasing in number every day and imposing an unhealthy lifestyle and poor eating habits all over the world, fast food restaurants and cafeterias not only affect the Turkish gastronomic culture but also traditional gastronomic cultures in various parts of the world.

The Turkish gastronomic culture is facing the risk of disappearing due to globalization and therefore should be promoted all over the world so that it can be practiced and kept alive in different regions.

People should be encouraged to consume natural, healthy and traditional foods. In this respect, they should be informed on adverse effects of fast food products to reduce their consumption.

References

Albala, K. (2011). Food *Cultures of the World Encyclopedia*, Greenwood Publishers, UK.

Arlı, M. (1981). "Türk Mutfağına Genel Bakış", *Türk Mutfağı Sempozyumu Bildirileri*, Kültür ve Turizm Bakanlığı Milli Folklor Araştırma Dairesi Yayınları No:41, Seminer, Kongre Bildirileri Dizisi No:12, Ankara.

Avcıkurt, C., Sarıoğlan, M. & Girgin, G. K. (2007). "Yiyecek-İçecek Olgusuna Sosyolojik Bir Bakış", *I. Ulusal Gastronomi Sempozyumu ve Sanatsal Etkinlikler 4-5 Mayıs 2007*, (pp. 1-7) Antalya.

Belge, M. (2010). *Tarih Boyunca Yemek Kültürü*, İletişim Yayınları, İstanbul.

Beşirli, H. (2010). "Yemek, Kültür ve Kimlik", *Milli Kültür Dergisi*, Issue: 87, 159-169.

Birol, N. & Akpınar, E. (2009). "XIII ve XIV Yüzyıl Seyyahlarına Göre Deşt-i Kıpçak ve Türkistan'da Mutfak Kültürü", *Erzincan Üniversitesi Sosyal Bilimler Enstitüsü Dergisi*, 2(2), 307-318.

Büyükbaş, M. (2002). *Nurettin Topçu'da Dini Yaşayışın Psikolojisi*, (Unpublished Master's Thesis), Süleyman Demirel Üniversitesi Sosyal Bilimler Enstitüsü Din Felsefesi Anabilim Dalı, Isparta.

Dağdeviren, Z. & Dağdeviren, M. (2009). "Yemeğin Milliyeti Olur mu?", *I. Uluslararası Doğu Anadolu Bölgesi Geleneksel Mutfak Kültürü ve Yemekleri Sempozyumu*, Bitlis.

Dalby, A. & Grainger, S. (2001). *Antik Çağ Yemekleri ve Yemek Kültürü*, (Translated by Betül Avunç), Homer Kitabevi, İstanbul.

Genç, R., (1981). "IX. Yüzyılda Türk Mutfağı", *Türk Mutfağı Sempozyumu Bildirileri*, Kültür ve Turizm Bakanlığı Milli Folklor Araştırma Dairesi Yayınları No: 41, Seminer, Kongre Bildirileri Dizisi No: 12, Ankara.

Goodman, D. & Redclift, M. (2003). *Refashioning Nature Food Ecology and Culture*, Routledge Publishing, New York.

Gürsoy, D. (2004). *Tarihin Süzgecinde Mutfak Kültürümüz*, Oğlak Güzel Kitaplar No, 3, İstanbul.

Kittler, P. G. & Sucher, K. P. (2008). *Food and Culture*, Thomson Wadsworth, USA.

Komisyon, (1997). Türk *Mutfağı*, Geçit Kitabevi, İstanbul.

Kutluay, T. (1982). Dünyanın Çeşitli Bölgelerinde Yemek Alışkanlıkları, *Geleneksel Türk Mutfağı Türk Yemekleri ve Beslenme Sempozyumu Bildirileri 10-11 Eylül 1982*, Konya 1982, p. 42.

Mertol, T. K. (1998). "Tarihten Günümüze Toplumlar ve Beslenme Alışkanlıkları", *Türk Mutfak Kültürü Üzerine Araştırmalar*, Türk Halk Kültürünü Araştırma ve Tanıtma Vakfı Yayınları No, 22, Ankara.

Ögel, B. (1981). "Türk Mutfağının Gelişmesi ve Türk Tarihi Gelenekleri", *Türk Mutfağı Sempozyumu Bildirileri*, Kültür ve Turizm Bakanlığı Milli Folklor Araştırma Dairesi Yayınları No: 41, Seminer, Kongre Bildirileri Dizisi No: 12, (pp. 15-33) Ankara.

Şenol, Y. (2007). *Tevrat İncil ve Kur-an'da Eti Haram Kılınan Hayvanlar*, (Unpublished Master's Thesis) İstanbul Üniversitesi Sosyal Bilimler Enstitüsü Temel İslam Bilimleri Anabilim Dalı, İstanbul.

Sever, B. (1982). "Eski Yemeklerin ve Aşçılığın Kayboluş Sebepleriyle Yemeklerimizde Baharatın Önemli Yeri", *Geleneksel Türk Mutfağı Türk Yemekleri ve Beslenme Sempozyumu Bildirileri 10-11 Eylül 1982*, Konya.

Tezcan, M. (1981). Türklerde Yemek Yeme Alışkanlıkları, *Türk Mutfağı Sempozyumu Bildirileri*, Kültür ve Turizm Bakanlığı Milli Folklor Araştırma Dairesi Yayınları No: 41, Seminer, Kongre Bildirileri Dizisi No: 12, Ankara.

Tezcan, M. (1998). Yemek Kültüründe Cinsel Farklılaşma, Türk *Mutfak Kültürü Üzerine Araştırmalar*, Türk Halk Kültürünü Araştırma ve Tanıtma Vakfı Yayınları No: 22, Ankara.

Tezcan, M. (2000). *Türk Yemek Antropolojisi Yazıları*, T.C. Kültür Bakanlığı Yayınları No: 2515, Halk Kültürlerini Araştırma ve Geliştirme Genel Müdürlüğü Yayınları No: 307, Maddi Kültür Dizisi No: 27, Ankara.

Toygar, K. (1981). Değişen Türk Mutfağı, Türk *Mutfağı Sempozyumu Bildirileri*, Kültür ve Turizm Bakanlığı Milli Folklor Araştırma Dairesi Yayınları No: 41, Seminer, Kongre Bildirileri Dizisi No: 12, Ankara.

Toygar, K. (1982). Türk Mutfağının Tarihi Kaynakları Üzerine Bir Deneme, Geleneksel *Türk Mutfağı Türk Yemekleri ve Beslenme Sempozyumu Bildirileri 10-11 Eylül 1982*, Konya.

Visentin, C. (2011). Food, Agri-Culture, and Tourism, *Food, Agri-Culture, and Tourism Linking Local Gastronomy And Rural Tourism: İnterdisciplinary Perspectives*, (Edited by Katia Laura Sidali, Achim Spiller), Birgit Schulze Springer Publishing, NewYork.

Yaman, A. (2010). *İslam İbadet Esasları*, İlahiyat Fakültesi Önlisans Programı, T.C. Anadolu Üniversitesi Yayınları No:2074, Açıköğretim Fakültesi Yayınları No: 1108, Eskişehir.

Yüceler, İ. (2009). Dinde Sofra Kültürü, *I. Uluslararası Doğu Anadolu Bölgesi Geleneksel Mutfak Kültürü ve Yemekleri Sempozyumu*, Bitlis.

CONTRIBUTORS

Esmeray Alacadağlı is an Assistant Professor at the Public Administration Department of Bayburt University Faculty of Economics and Administrative Sciences. She has a PhD in the field of environment and urbanization from Ankara University, Ankara, Turkey. Her main research fields are environment, health, public administration, urbanization, total quality management, migration, industrialization, and reorganization.

Sibel Ismailçebi Başar is a lecturer at Bayburt University, Vocational School of Social Sciences, and Department of Logistics. Her research interests are logistics, civil aviation and logistics management.

Demir Bahar is an associate professor in the Russian Academy of Natural Sciences and she is currently Head of the Department of Russian Language and Literature at Ataturk University, Faculty of Letters.

Ayhan Bulut is Assistant Professor at the Turkish Education Department, The Faculty of Education in Cumhuriyet University. He is working in new or modern Turkish literature, poetry, philosophy and novels. He is specially interested in revealing the relation of literary works with philosophy.

Ömer Çınar is an Assistant Professor at Ağrı İbrahim Çeçen University Faculty of Economics and Administrative Sciences Numerical Methods Department. His research interests are statistics, multivariate statistical methods, structural equation modelling, quantitative decision methods and scientific research methods.

Dinevich I. A., 6, Miklukho-Maklaya, Moscow, Russia, the Russian Language Department#2, People's Friendship University of Russia, Moscow, the Russian Federation (e-mail: dinevich_irina@mail.ru)

Meryem Doygun is currently research assistant at Ağrı İbrahim Çeçen University Department of History. Her research interests are Seljuk History, Mongolian History, Khwarazmshahs History, Middle Age History Persian sources, and Central Asian Turkish Cultural History.

Marianna Andreevna Dudareva, Candidate of Philology, Professor of the Russian Language Department No.2, Faculty of the Russian Language and General Education, PFUR

İsmail Dursunoğlu was born in Bayburt in 1988. He graduated from the Suleyman Demirel University Department of Public Administration. He received his Master's degree at the same university in 2012. His Master's thesis subject was The NGO in Democracy. He is completing his doctorate program at Karadeniz Technical University. He is interested in the subjects of political behaviour, culture, and political science.

Esengül Tan Hatun is currently a PhD candidate at Atatürk University Educational Sciences Institute Turkish Education Department. Her research interests are Turkish teaching, grammar teaching and constructivist approach.

Hakan Irak is a lecturer in the Department of Management and Organization at the Vocational School of Iğdır University. Areas of interest include Marketing Communications, Political Marketing, Political Commercials, Image and Reputation Management, and Social Media.

Alperen Kayserili is the head of the Department of Geography within the Faculty Science and Literature at Ağrı İbrahim Çeçen University. His areas of interest include cultural geography, cultural heritage and tourism, and globalization.

Kübra Karakuş is a lecturer in business at Mus Alparslan University, Vocational School of Social Sciences, Departman of Management and Organization. Her research interests are economic development, regional development, economic growth, foreign trade, ıntra-ındustry trade and competition.

J.V. Karpova, Miklukho-Maklaya, Moscow, Russia, the Russian Language Department#2, People's Friendship University of Russia, Moscow, the Russian Federation.

Neda Hashemi Khosroshahi is a PhD candidate at Ataturk University Social Science Institute, Department of Economics. Her research interests are health economics, externalities and welfare economics.

Yasemin Kurtlu has been working as a Turkish teacher and a university lecturer since 2008 and is still teaching Turkish. She is currently continuing her doctorate program in the Department of Turkish Language

Education of the Institute of Educational Sciences at Atatürk University. Her areas of interest are usability of Classical Turkish Literature Texts in Turkish Education, Turkish Education, Education Science, Linguistics and Folklore.

Myers G.N., 6, Miklukho-Maklaya, Moscow, Russia, the Russian Language Department#2, People's Friendship University of Russia, Moscow, the Russian Federation (e-mail: galinamyers@yandex.ru)

Polyanskaya Ekaterina Nikolaevna is a senior lecturer of the Department of Psychology and Pedagogics, of Peoples' Friendship University of Russia (RUDN University), Russia 6, Miklukho-Maklaya st., Moscow, 117198, polyanskayae@mail.ru

Goeva Nina Pavlovna is a senior lecturer of the Department of Russian Language and General Studies, Faculty of Russian Language and General Educational Disciplines, of Peoples' Friendship University of Russia (RUDN University), Russia 6, Miklukho-Maklaya st., Moscow, 117198, goeva@kulturamoskvi.ru

Fisenko Olga Sergeevna, Assistant Professor Department of Russian Language №2, Faculty of Russian Language and General Educational Disciplines, of Peoples' Friendship University of Russia (RUDN University), Russia, 6, Miklukho-Maklaya st., Moscow, 117198,

Oguzhan Sevim is a associate professor at Atatürk University's Department of Turkish Language Teaching at Kâzım Karabekir Education Faculty. He has received a PhD at Atatürk University Educational Sciences Institute Turkish Education Department.

Smirnova S.V., 6, Miklukho-Maklaya, Moscow, Russia, the Russian Language Department#2, People's Friendship University of Russia Moscow, the Russian Federation, (e-mail: smirnova.smirnova@yandex.ru)

Hayriye Şengün is an associate professor at Bayburt University, Economics and Administrative Sciences Faculty, Public Administration Depertmant. Her research interests are disaster management, urbanization, and environmental problems.

Zeliha Tekin is an Assistant Professor of Business in the Department of Management and Organization, Vocational School of Social Sciences, at Mus Alparslan University, Turkey. She also worked as an academic visiting researcher at The University of Manchester, UK. Her research interests are innovation, knowledge management, entrepreneurship, akhism and ethics.

Fatma Temelli is an Assistant Professor at Ağrı İbrahim Çeçen University Faculty of Economics and Administrative Sciences Accounting and Finance Department. Her research interests are accounting, finance, auditing, auditing of accounting and cost accounting.

Sinan Yazıcı is an assistant professor at Bayburt University, Faculty of Economics and Administrative Sciences, Department of Public Administration. His research interests are migration, management, and administration history.

Sefa Yıldırım is Assistant Professor at the History Department, The Faculty of Art and Science in Agri İbrahim Cecen University. His research fields include ancient history, ancient and general history education, use of literary elements in history education and historiosophy.

Seçil Gül Meydan Yıldız is an assistant professor at Bozok University Faculty of Engineering and Architecture, City and Regional Planning Department. Her research interests are urban rent, development law, disaster management, urban sociology, ecology and urban plannings.